SURVEILLANCE CINEMA

POSTMILLENNIAL POP

General Editors: Karen Tongson and Henry Jenkins

Surveillance Cinema

Catherine Zimmer

NEW YORK UNIVERSITY PRESS
New York and London

NEW YORK UNIVERSITY PRESS
New York and London
www.nyupress.org

© 2015 by New York University
All rights reserved

References to Internet websites (URLs) were accurate at the time of writing. Neither the author nor New York University Press is responsible for URLs that may have expired or changed since the manuscript was prepared.

Library of Congress Cataloging-in-Publication Data
Zimmer, Catherine, 1969-
Surveillance cinema / Catherine Zimmer.
pages cm. -- (Postmillennial pop)
Includes bibliographical references and index.
ISBN 978-1-4798-6437-9 (cl : alk. paper) -- ISBN 978-1-4798-3667-3 (pb : alk. paper)
1. Electronic surveillance in motion pictures. I. Title.
PN1995.9.E38Z56 2015
791.4302'3--dc23
2014040538

New York University Press books are printed on acid-free paper, and their binding materials are chosen for strength and durability. We strive to use environmentally responsible suppliers and materials to the greatest extent possible in publishing our books.

Manufactured in the United States of America

10 9 8 7 6 5 4 3 2 1

Also available as an ebook

For my father, Karl Ernst Zimmer

CONTENTS

ACKNOWLEDGMENTS

I would like to extend enormous thanks to those who have helped me in the writing of this book—a process that exceeds, in so many ways, what I have written.

Many thanks to Sarah Blackwood, Tom Henthorne, Sid Ray, Stephanie Hsu, Erica Johnson, Patricia Pender, Matthew Bolton, Emily Welty, Helane Levine-Keating, and Nancy Reagin for creating a community of support at Pace University. I am tremendously grateful to Ruth Johnston, founding director of Film and Screen Studies at Pace, for her mentoring and support, and to Dean Nira Hermann, Associate Deans Richard Schlesinger and Adelia Williams, and the Scholarly Research Committee for their ongoing sponsorship of my projects. Thanks also to Cathy Dwyer, my co-instructor in a course on surveillance culture, for her insightful perspectives and her commitment to keeping conversations about surveillance politics central to the intellectual community at Pace.

Very special thanks to those who have offered feedback, advice, and assistance with numerous elements of the publication process: Gillian Harkins, Zahid Chaudhary, Matthew Bolton, Tom Henthorne, Homay King, and Aviva Briefel have all been generous with their brilliance and time, and their comments on portions of this book helped me improve them considerably. Mary Peelen, Catherine Mills, Chantal Bruchez-Hall, Meredith Martin, Jasbir Puar, Christina Hanhardt, Eva Hageman, Patricia Shuldiner, Josie Saldaña, David Kazanjian, Rob Miotke, Eric Taylor, and Sara Pursley have each at various moments talked me through ideas, confusion, dismay, etc. Sheila McLaughlin, Jennie Portnof, and Rebecca Coleman have assisted me in more ways than they know, and I am tremendously grateful for their friendship. Barbara Herman and Galadrielle Allman: we have been in this together as long as I can remember. Your talents, insights, and strength inspire me every day.

Eric Zinner, Alicia Nadkarni, and Dorothea Halliday at NYU Press have been and continue to be wonderful to work with, and I want to thank them for their guidance throughout the process. I am, happily, forever indebted to Karen Tongson for shepherding this project through its publication: in no uncertain terms, Karen made this book a reality for me. Many thanks also to her coeditor, Henry Jenkins; I am honored to be included in the Postmillennial Pop series. I am indebted as well to the anonymous reviewers who took such care with the manuscript and whose detailed suggestions have been invaluable. Many thanks also go to Cathy Hannabach, for her excellent work on indexing my book.

In a very different form, this project began in graduate school, and my professors and cohort from UC Berkeley are the gift that keeps on giving. Linda Williams, B. Ruby Rich, and Kaja Silverman: I can't thank them enough for what they taught me about thinking and writing, for their mentoring, and for their continued friendship. Anton Kaes and Marilyn Fabe, and their work in developing a film education at Berkeley, provided the foundation that I am fortunate to stand on, and I am forever grateful for that support. Homay King, Erik Schneider, Barbara Herman, Gillian Harkins, Gayle Salamon, Dale Carrico, James Salazar, David Kazanjian, Rob Miotke, Emma Bianchi, Jill Stauffer, and Amy Zilliax brilliantly disguised the rigors of a graduate education as a group of hilarious, talented, loving, gorgeous weirdoes whom I am now delighted to call family. And my beloved Flippy, who died as I was completing this manuscript, saw me through from graduate school to tenure and beyond, and was the perfect constant throughout. Though he never made the slightest effort to do a damn thing, he has earned a place in print.

Karl Zimmer, Ronelle Alexander, Paul Zimmer, Silvia Valisa, Serafina Valisa, Lucas Zimmer, and my late mother, Suzanne Clements Zimmer: thank you for being my wonderful family. You are all everywhere throughout this book. Finally, I offer immense gratitude and love to Kate Taylor, whose confidence in me and dedication to a world of meaning has been the backbone of this work. It is simply unimaginable to me to have done this without her.

AUTHOR'S NOTE

Portions of the Introduction were published as "Surveillance Cinema: Narrative between Technology and Politics," in *Surveillance and Society* vol. 8 no. 4 (Spring 2011). An earlier version of Chapter One was published as "Caught on Tape? The Politics of Video in the New Torture Film," in *Horror Film after 9/11*, edited by Aviva Briefel and Sam Miller (Austin: University of Texas Press, 2011). A different version of Chapter Five was published as "Surveillance and Social Memory: *Strange Days* Indeed," in *Discourse* vol. 32 no. 3 (Fall 2010). Many thanks to the peer reviewers and editors of these publications for their input on those essays.

Introduction

Surveillance Cinema in Theory and Practice

In Paris, a video camera's unblinking gaze fixes on the exterior of a bourgeois home and eventually leads to the disintegration of two families. An American labor attorney sprints through a Washington, D.C., high-rise hotel as he evades satellite surveillance and NSA assassins seeking to cover up the political murder of a congressman. A webcam in Portland documents the torture and death of kidnap victims, while each visitor to the host website hastens the death of the subject and each site "hit" thus becomes a literal act of violence. A terrorist attack in New Orleans is prevented by an experimental surveillance technology and a heroic federal agent—*after* the attack has already taken place. And in a series of basements, warehouses, hotel rooms, and remote cabins throughout the world, myriad individuals and organizations dedicate themselves to the development and use of complex video surveillance systems for elaborate torture scenarios.

The above film plots represent only a fraction of the narrative focus on surveillance technologies that has become increasingly common since the 1990s in a variety of cinematic arenas, in these examples ranging from European "art" cinema to American action-thrillers and the global reinvestment in horror. Works such as *Enemy of the State, Rising Sun, The End of Violence, Closed Circuit, Vantage Point, The Bourne Ultimatum, Déjà vu, Surveillance, Minority Report, Sliver, Caché, The Wire, Homeland,* and *The Lives of Others* all organize their narratives entirely around surveillance technologies and practices, while others such as the *Saw* series, *District 9, Body of Lies, Lost Highway, Panic Room, Snake Eyes,* and innumerable contemporary action-thrillers utilize surveillance technologies as a frequent narrative or stylistic device. Taking as a starting point the millennial surge in films and television series organized around and by surveillance technologies, in conjunction with the ever-widening role of surveillance in contemporary democratic state power, consumer economies, and daily social interactions, this book examines how technology and narrative have come together in cinematic form to play a functional role in the politics of surveillance.

Far more than just cultural symptoms of what is increasingly called a "surveillance society," films about surveillance do both ideological and practical labor by joining the form and content of surveillance practice in a narrative structure. Surveillance techniques and technologies, from closed-circuit television to global positioning systems, and cinematic techniques and technologies, from continuity editing to camera movement, coalesce as *narrative logic*. What I call "surveillance cinema" is not simply the recurring tropes or iconographies of surveillance as films emerge alongside developments in surveillance politics, technologies, and social history, though that is certainly part of the history of surveillance in cinema. Rather this book addresses the multiple mediations that occur through the cinematic narration of surveillance, through which practices of surveillance become representational and representational practices become surveillant, and ultimately the distinctions between the two begin to fade away. "Cinema"—here broadly defined as the thematic and stylistic elements of individual films and the historical constitution of cinematic genre conventions, as well as the economic and industrial media complex surrounding any given film—is thus considered as a functional element of "surveillance," also broadly defined. Cinematic narratives of surveillance have informed and been informed by multiple aspects of actual surveillance: technological instances range from satellite imaging to consumer video recording, while related political iterations range from contemporary counterterrorism and national security to the trial of LAPD officers for their "caught on tape" assault of Rodney King in 1991. As video surveillance has diversified and multiplied in form and use throughout personal and social worlds, its incorporation into film as trope and technique has become commonplace. Video imagery occupies cinematic space so prevalently that the ambiguous middle ground of a hypermediated, "reflexive" film begins to appear more as a rule than an exception. GPS, satellite imaging, consumer tracking and targeting, and peer-to-peer monitoring also merge with cinematic formations at numerous levels: from editing principles, camera angles, and character development to spectatorship and global marketing. Analyses of the aesthetic and structural elements of surveillance narratives in historical terms demonstrate that the cinematic mediation of surveillance is part of a framework that organizes, in often reversible relations, subjective formations through technological, political formations through cultural, and functional formations through representational.

To say that these elements are organized and structural, however, is not to indicate that they are always seamless, effective, or logical. Thus, even with the ideological and practical labor that cinematic surveillance narratives perform, such narratives, in order to function *as* narratives, also frequently betray premises such as evidentiary truth, verifiable identity, and logical chronology upon which surveillance functions politically and socially. The simplest investigation stories demand miscues and ambiguities, evasions and misinterpretations. While the "truth" frequently emerges as narrative closure in a detective drama, such truths maintain a provisional status in the face of the narrative process that designs suspense—definitionally—to resist such closure. Science fiction tales of fantasy surveillance technologies so powerful that they can monitor and alter both past and future encounter the paradoxes and circular logics of the time travel narrative: thus the fantasies of omniscience, preemption, and prevention that have rationalized much of U.S. surveillance and security practice, while mirrored in cinematic science fiction, are also exposed as fantasies built upon a structure that can do nothing else but fold in on itself. Time emerges as a force that defies the logic of power.

Despite the manner in which such surveillance narratives thus often exceed the terms that they set, the analytical frameworks by which cinema and surveillance have both been understood, particularly in relation to one another, have often been taken for granted. Psychoanalytic conceptions of voyeurism and Foucault's account of panopticism have dominated explanations of a variety of disparate surveillance-themed narratives, even as discussions of surveillance in other arenas have developed profound engagements between these and other theoretical models. In discussions of cinema in particular, the voyeuristic model has been trenchant. A greater attention to the historical specificity of the surveillance/cinema relationship reveals that such accounts must themselves be historicized, and more importantly, that the manner in which surveillance cinema has been narratively (and extranarratively) organized around issues ranging from temporality to online social networking, means that the forms and functions of such narratives exceed the bounds of any single explanatory structure. This book thus provides an account of the most significant trends in recent cinematic surveillance narratives, as well as a theoretical and historical reexamination of the relationship between cinema and surveillance that takes into consideration the formal elements of film narrative, the technological bases of both cinema and surveillance, and recent critical discussions of surveillance, particularly as related to the "war on terror," racial projects, and contemporary digital economies.[1] Through these considerations, *Surveillance Cinema* connects film studies with the growing field of surveillance studies, which, though an extremely compelling model of interdisciplinary work, has at this point surprisingly little crossover with cinema studies arenas.

Cinema History, Surveillance History

Beyond the attention paid to surveillance in recent cinema, and the clear debt cinematic surveillance narratives owe to literary imaginings of surveillance cultures (most obviously represented by Orwell's *1984*), surveillance has been both a theme and practice of cinema from its origins and antecedents. The visual technologies associated with cinema are intimately connected with surveillance practice and the production of knowledge through visibility, even as "cinema" exceeds categorization as a purely visual medium. Alan Sekula and others have shown in their scholarly accounts that visual mediation, particularly photography, was central to the production of modern forms of identity and identification, both normative and deviant.[2] And, following Foucault and Weber, it is this emergence of identification and categorization that Christian Parenti, in his popular account of surveillance history in the United States, traces as the genealogy of contemporary surveillance culture. In combination with fingerprinting and Bertillonage (bodily measurement and typing), photography "extended and enhanced state power, operating at two levels: defining and constructing social types, and identifying individuals."[3] The production of the body as visible, measurable, and categorizable is one of the defining facets of both surveillance practice and modern subjectification. And while it is important not to conflate cinematic practice with that of still photography, as an essential element of cinematic production the historical uses of the photograph weigh on those of moving images.

Most exemplary of the relationship between photography and cinema is the late-nineteenth-century "series photography" of Eadweard Muybdrige and Étienne-Jules Marey, used in their respective studies of motion that are most often cited as the immediate precursors to cinema. As a middle ground between still photographs and motion pictures, these attempts to measure and record the movement of both animal and human bodies are a part of the biometric practices accumulating around the body in multiple discursive fields at that time. The motion studies of Muybridge and Marey have been the topic of many analyses emphasizing the scientific and epistemological origins of cinema, perhaps most famously in *Hard Core*, Linda Williams's seminal account of pornography, in which she declares, "[T]he desire to see and know more of the human body—in this case to answer 'academic questions' of the mechanics of body movement—underlies the very invention of cinema."[4] And as Lisa Cartwright has succinctly argued in her book on medicine and visual culture, "[T]he cinematic apparatus can be considered as a cultural technology for the discipline and management of the human body, and . . . the long history of bodily analysis in medicine and science is critically tied to the history of the development of the cinema as a popular cultural institution and a technological apparatus."[5]

Broader accounts of the cinematic apparatus, most famously those of Jean-Louis Comolli and Jean-Louis Baudry in the early 1970s, also emphasize the ideological underpinnings of the technological or scientific aspects of cinema.[6] Comolli's "Technique and Ideology" and "Machines of the Visible," among other works, argue that the production of the world as visible was and is a part of the appropriative projects of colonialism and capitalism, and that even cinema's most basic technologies are implicated in such projects.[7] The discourse of indexical realism that has surrounded photography and cinema has served as a disavowal of the ideological elements of both the technologies and uses of those technologies. Such realist claims around cinematic representation are inevitably tied to the evidentiary value afforded photographic, filmic, and, more recently video imagery within the realm of surveillance. Viewed alongside the discourse of realism, the biometric aspects of cinema's technological history and their more direct relationships to histories of bodily identification and management are in some ways simply the most obvious instances of much broader ideological and technological relationships between cinema and modern surveillance. Though it is reductive to view cinema as performing any one role (or even referring to any one phenomenon), the accumulation of historical, technological, and discursive coincidences between cinema and surveillance emerges as less than coincidental. The inseparability of technology and ideology in both cinema and surveillance—and the fact that the technologies and ideologies of each have been coextensive from the beginning—demonstrates that the historical emergence of cinema is deeply implicated in the production of a visible world that is increasingly recognized as the emergence of a modern, "global" culture defined by mediation and surveillance.

Surveillance has also been thematically present in film from the beginning, in one way or another, even before narrative came to dominate cinematic production. As film scholar Thomas Levin has pointed out in his influential essay on surveillance in cinema, one of the first films ever made—the Lumière Brothers' *Sortie d'usine* [*Workers Leaving the Factory*] (1895)—was a film of the Lumières' own employees, and thus a form of workplace surveillance.[8] The phenomenon was certainly not limited to this early experiment. In the United States in 1904, the American Mutoscope and Biograph Company produced a series of films showcasing the operations of various factories of the Westinghouse Works.[9] However benign in these early incarnations, the monitoring and control of the workplace has become one of the most predominant forms of surveillance. Even the documentary impulse behind the majority of the Lumière *actualité* productions is on a certain level logically inseparable from the evidentiary claims of the visual surveillance that were to follow. It is thus not surprising that *Workers Leaving the Factory*, a celebration of the Lumière industry both in front of the camera and in the medium itself, would find itself quoted by the video surveillance now ubiquitously positioned at the threshold of the vast majority of businesses, be they corporate, industrial, family-owned, urban or suburban, and so on.

While the early Lumière productions were exemplary of the documentary functions of the new cinematic technology, other early explorations were more spectacular and performance driven, particularly in the United States. And as these performances assumed a narrative form, themes of surveillance soon followed. Early shorts such as *Grandma's Reading Glass* (1900), *As Seen through a Telescope* (1900), and *Photographing a Female Crook* (1904) incorporate visual technologies onscreen and reflexively thematize the act of watching (in the case of *Photographing a Female Crook*, explicitly for the purposes of identification). Beyond these reflexive examples of voyeurism narratives and/or those focusing on visual apparatus as narrative devices (which remain a staple of surveillance cinema), the first ten years of cinema saw the Edison Company regularly churning out "caught in the act" stories, implicitly casting both the construction of cinematic narrative and cinematic technology as a revelatory device around crime and sexuality in particular. Such films as *Interrupted Lovers* (1896), *Tenderloin at Night* (1899), *The Chicken Thieves* (1896), *Grandma and the Bad Boys* (1900), *Why Mrs. Jones Got a Divorce* (1900), *Subub Surprises the Burglar* (1903), *The Kleptomaniac* (1905), *The Burglar's Slide for Life* (1905), and numerous others show a variety of sexually and criminally illicit behaviors as accessible (and at times punishable) by the motion picture camera, in the service of effects ranging from "simple" spectacle to comedy, adventure, and, occasionally, social commentary. Tom Gunning has noted in his essay on photography, detective fiction, and early cinema that "[t]he camera recording the very act of malefaction appears in drama, literature, and early film before it was really an important process of criminal detection."[10] These early films laid the groundwork for cinematic genres to come, but they also mapped formations of both surveillance narrative and surveillance practice that are often considered more contemporary: "While the perfection of video has now made the recording of a crime a pervasive and effective form of surveillance (as well as a form of media entertainment), a fascination with photographic evidence of misdeeds seems to predate considerably its widespread application in reality."[11] Though Gunning is addressing cinematic and literary works that *explicitly* incorporated photography and motion picture cameras into their narratives, I would extend the point to include all those early films presenting an illicit act as their focus, and argue that both the nondiegetic motion picture camera and the drive toward narrative are also structured around the surveillant capacities of cinema.

The technical structure of these films is retroactively familiar in this light: the camera is placed in the scene before the actors appear and the crime takes place; it waits for them and captures the action that unfolds. What were then limitations on camera movement and editing practice appear in retrospect extremely similar to the look of a stationary surveillance video camera positioned to wait for something to occur in front of it. Even with the elaborate forms of editing and camerawork that have developed in narrative cinema since these "crude" early examples, it is still basic continuity practice to place the camera in a location and begin the shot so that it precedes and anticipates (if only by a second) the entry of characters or occurrence of action in that space. This is just one of numerous formal elements that tie cinematic representation to surveillant. As Dietmar Kammerer points out in "Video Surveillance in Hollywood Films": "The techniques of editing and montage in cinema rely on the same principles that can be found in any surveillance system. Therefore, even if cinema and TV have in the last years started to incorporate CCTV into their formats, plots, storylines, the relation between these 'texts' of popular cultures and this technology of surveillance is not a simple one."[12] In many ways, the "caught on tape" forms of both surveillance practice and entertainment characteristic of later-twentieth- and early-twenty-first-century televisual media, based on the increasing ubiquity of video, are forms that preceded video surveillance by over half a century.

The prescience of cinematic narrative formations around surveillance continued in ever more specific forms, perhaps culminating in the silent era with Fritz Lang's representation of what appears to be closed-circuit television in *Metropolis* (1927), an image and narrative usage that precedes the emergence of the television apparatus by ten years (and of course it was even longer until televisual technologies would be deployed in such an explicitly surveillant capacity).[13] Following Gunning, I would argue that the "caught on tape" phenomenon, a form that has had not just cultural but political and legal effects, is suggested by cinema history to be a *narrative conceit* of film, as well as a basic function of continuity practice, long before it was an operational mode of surveillance technology. However, it is also true that, as Kammerer states, "there is no simple cause-and-effect relation between these two [surveillance and cultural texts]," and thus even in reevaluating chronological history we should not assume that one is merely reflecting the other.[14]

From the simplest narratives of early cinema to the most complex psychological, aesthetic, philosophical, and political explorations of contemporary film, narration and surveillance continued to intersect in dynamic and structurally significant ways. For instance, a number of these early crime films were also chase films, such as *Stop Thief* (1901), *A Desperate Poaching Affray* (1903), *Daring Daylight Burglary* (1903), and most famously *The Great Train Robbery* (1903). Theorists and historians of early cinema such as Noël Burch have discussed how integral the chase film was to the development of the basic techniques of narrative cinema, with Burch going so far as to claim that "institutional continuity was born with the chase, or rather the latter came into being and proliferated so that continuity could be established."[15] Within this argument, the continuity editing that became definitional of narrative cinema as it allowed smooth and motivated transitions between spaces does not serve merely to promote the surveillant capacities of cinema; cinematic continuity—and thus narrative—is predicated on visualizable crime and discipline. These early films anticipate the way more recent action-thrillers like *Enemy of the State* (1998) and *The Bourne Ultimatum* (2007) would incorporate surveillance into their continuity devices as a narrative technology in a manner that has now become standardized. What in the early unedited films is simply the capture (and production) of a crime and chase on film becomes in more recent examples the narrative inclusion of satellites, global positioning systems, and closed-circuit television in order to motivate, advance, and legitimize fast-paced crosscutting that establishes complex narrative connectivity, as will be addressed in greater detail in Chapter Three. Once again, the technologies of surveillance seem primarily to serve the devices of narrative as cinematically defined: the ability to visually track individuals over space and time was presented as the domain of cinematic narrative long before such a possibility would be offered by satellite and GPS, and such tracking would in turn be reincorporated into cinema as narrative style.

Despite their part in the development of lasting continuity systems, these early films simultaneously reveal that even as the camera might stage, expose, chase, and capture an illicit act or figure, the visual production of these moments and subjects hardly functions as a structure of seamless disciplinary efficiency—in fact it is rife with contradictions and slippages, and these slippages are often produced by the same mechanisms that function as surveillant. The ambiguities that come to define even some of the simplest early surveillance narratives establish the field of cinematic visibility as a highly contested one, particularly around structures of identity. In *Photographing a Female Crook*, for instance, the moving image serves to humorously establish the failure of the still photograph to "capture" the criminal, as the subject contorts her face into unrecognizable form every time the police try to snap a mug shot. *The Old Maid Having Her Picture Taken* (1901) similarly builds its humor on the failure of photography to capture the image of a woman, presenting a number of mishaps in a photo shoot that culminate in the camera exploding in a puff of smoke. Because these cinematic texts poke fun at the work of still photography, they might seem to suggest that the moving image we are watching is more "in the know" than the photograph. However, they cannot help but also serve to humorously undermine the production of identity through visual technologies in general.[16]

In fact, while "caught in the act" and chase premises were frequent narrative tropes, misunderstanding and mistaken identity were equally as common. A variety of comedic situations in these early films are predicated on the play between visibility and knowledge (both for the films' characters and the films' spectators), particularly as related to gendered and racial identities and transgressions. The Edwin Porter film *The Unappreciated Joke* (1903), for instance, presents a man reading something comical on a streetcar who fails to notice that his companion has disembarked and has been replaced by a woman. She becomes scandalized and outraged when the man, not looking up, slaps her on the knee and otherwise physically molests her in the belief that he is enjoying a joke with his male friend.

At times, the "caught in the act" films and the misunderstanding films become one and the same: the Edison Company produced, for instance, a series of "Bad Boys" films, in which the eponymous characters engage in a number of hijinks. In one such film described by the Edison catalog, *The Bad Boys' Joke on the Nurse* (1901), a nurse sleeps while holding an infant. An old man sleeps across the room from her. As they slumber, the unblinking camera offers to the cinematic spectator what the characters are unaware of: the "bad boys" sneaking in and taking the infant from the nurse and placing it in the sleeping old man's arms. Upon awakening, the nurse attacks the older man for kidnapping and the police march them both off. The structure of the narration and the comedy are here predicated on the camera providing information to the spectator that exceeds that made available to the characters. In this case, and in *The Unappreciated Joke*, the surveillant capacities of the motion picture camera assure that, while the narrative may turn on misunderstanding, particularly as regards identity and social norms, the technology and the spectator know all, and the joke is only on the characters within the film.

But this is certainly not always the case, and the misunderstandings and mistaken identities soon developed to also make the visual mastery of the moving-image camera and cinematic spectatorship the crux of the joke. One of the most famous instances of this is Porter's *What Happened in the Tunnel* (1903), which couples a narrative of sexual impropriety with a racial punch line: in this film, a white woman on a train who is being sexually harassed replaces herself with her black maid as the train goes through a tunnel and the screen goes dark—the white male aggressor finds himself kissing the black woman as the scene becomes visible again to *both* the characters in the film and the spectators. In this case, racial visibility and cinematic technology become one and the same, and the joke is predicated on the failure and then reestablishment of both. The use of cinematic narrative and technology in this film symptomatically highlights the intersections of race, sexuality, and visibility, intersections that have been addressed in a number of contexts; within a discussion of surveillance it is clearly also salient insofar as race in particular has been historically produced as visual and visible through surveillance practices and technologies.[17]

The stakes of such production become clearer if we return to the "caught in the act" and chase films. In the context of the construction of blackness in early cinema, film scholar Jacqueline Najuma Stewart provides an in-depth analysis of the 1904 film *A Nigger in the Woodpile*, which establishes both narrativity and racialized criminality as part and parcel of the visible field offered by cinema. As Stewart describes it,

[*A Nigger in the Woodpile*] hinges upon the disguise and exposure of acts of Black transgression, as well as white retaliation, as seen by the camera, the viewer, and the characters in the film. When the film opens, two white farmers know that Blacks have been stealing their wood, even though they, and the viewer, have not yet witnessed this act; Black criminality is the already understood subtext of the action before a single Black figure has appeared. . . . The film constructs a scenario around a common slang expression, "a nigger in the woodpile," and takes it beyond its colloquial usage. The saying . . . refers to a situation involving something suspicious and/or concealed. In the film bearing this title, there are, literally, two niggers (Black men) sneaking into a woodpile; as such, there is no need to narratively motivate their criminal actions. The "niggers" presented in this film confirm the popular expression by embodying its literal and figurative meanings. These characters are not the only "niggers in the woodpile" operating in the film—there is also the sick of dynamite the white farmers have concealed inside one of the logs to expose the thieves. Thus, *A Nigger in the Woodpile* plays with the stereotype of Black criminality by multiplying the meaning of the title to signify the identity of the criminals, the scene of the crime, and the means of their exposure and punishment.[18]

In the context of "caught in the act" and chase plots, Stewart's account of the signifying work of this film shows those tropes operating alongside and through the construction of race in the United States. Stewart's description of the assumptions that go into an effective reading of the multiplied meanings within the film's title is uncannily similar to a description of the historical surveillance and policing of the black population, which served to produce identifiable visual markers around black identity, establish surveillance around an assumption of black criminality, and use that surveillance to expose and discipline. In other words, the multiplication of meaning in the film, which becomes the narrative structure, is identical with the purposes and practices of surveillance, particularly in regard to racial projects and the construction of the black subject.

Christian Parenti's history of surveillance in the United States has shown the project of identification, even before photography and cinema, to be a definitively and violently racial one, initially emerging to assist in the monitoring and capture of escaped slaves: "The *Gazette* . . . ran an average of 230 runaway notices a year during the eighteenth century, and all of them had one thing in common: they sought to identify people who, as slaves, supposedly had no identity. In other words, the master class was forced to develop not just methods of terror but also a haphazard system of identification and surveillance. The result was in many ways the imprint of modern everyday surveillance."[19] Citing slave patrols, the slave pass, and wanted posters as the three key methods of monitoring and enforcement, Parenti demonstrates that the lineage of police enforcement and the production of bodies as informationally and visually identifiable is directly traceable to the production and mainte-nance of a slave economy.[20] Surveillance is thus, at its origins, designed to produce identity along racial lines, while at the same time disavowing identity in order to maintain the racialized subject as object.

As Stewart shows in her above analysis, cinematic narratives orga-nized around race were engaged in a similar, even contiguous project, producing the black figure as an identity that is without identity: a sig-nifier upon which the narrative can turn. However, the multiplicity of meanings that Stewart addresses in her analysis of *A Nigger in the Woodpile* suggests that even in a film that explicitly seeks to establish and punish the black subject, the narrative production of criminality and discipline is predicated on meanings being multiplied, and thus, in many ways, rendered unstable. As the tropes of early cinema testify, the production of identity through surveillance narratives often betrays the ambiguity of surveillance-defined visibility, undermining the logic of both race and visual surveillance simultaneously. Close analysis of these narrative devices, themselves so intimately connected to the purposes and capacities of surveillance, can serve to expose the logic (both func-tional and failed) of surveillance practices, and their frequent, equally unstable, use as racial projects.

Cinema Studies, Surveillance Studies

With so many technological, political, historical, and structural inter-sections between cinematic form and surveillance practice, it should be clear that the history of "surveillance and cinema" is just beginning to be written, and will take many shapes. And as I will show in the chapters that follow, these intersections occur at multiple levels simultaneously, extending into technical experimentation, media marketing and con-sumption, and the cinematic writing of our own surveillance histories and futures, as evidenced by films from *The Conversation* to *Zero Dark*

Thirty, Metropolis to *Minority Report, Rear Window* to *Strange Days*. Whether one is referring to explicitly fact-based films that seek to recount the use of surveillance in specific historical moments, or films that are part of the technological and ideological fantasies accumulating around surveillance practice in different historical contexts, the history of "surveillance cinema" does not refer to a readily identifiable genre, trope, style, technology, or theme. Instead the history of surveillance and cinema must be understood as a dynamic formation through which representation and surveillance serve as mutually structuring.

Given the complexity involved in tracing such a history, one would imagine that the treatment of surveillance narratives on a critical and theoretical level would of necessity be diverse and dynamic. The surveillance narratives of the early years of film alone demand conceptual models that attend to, among many other aspects: the complexities of racial formations in the cinematic era, the technological variations of both surveillance practice and cinematic representation, and quite broadly, the political, philosophical, and scientific discourses that weave notions of "truth" in between phenomenal "reality" and aesthetic "realism."

While a great deal of scholarship on surveillance in cinema has been hampered by a certain theoretical uniformity, there has been some notable work on surveillance from cinema studies scholars on the relations between cinematic form and surveillance. Thomas Levin in particular has urged a consideration of the increasing integration of film analysis and surveillance studies through his examination of how cinematic narrative has formed itself around what he terms "rhetorics of surveillance."[21] Going so far as to suggest that "cinematic narration could be said, in many cases, to have effectively become synonymous with surveillant enunciation as such," Levin's focus on the move in cinema from a "thematic to a *structural* engagement of surveillance" is foundational for my own study, even as the structural elements on which we focus diverge.[22] Levin's analysis of the use of "real time" surveillance structures within cinematic narrative to argue that "cinema has displaced an impoverished spatial rhetoric of photo-chemical indexicality with a thoroughly contemporary, and equally semiotically 'motivated' rhetoric of *temporal indexicality*" points to the way that the discourse of and about cinema is increasingly defined in reference to principles of surveillance.[23]

Other significant facets of surveillance and cinema have been highlighted by both surveillance and film scholars, whose work serves as scaffolding for this present study. Surveillance scholar Dietmar Kammerer's essay "Video Surveillance in Hollywood Movies" reiterates some of Levin's points and argues, as do I, that the study of the relations between representational media like film and surveillance is still in nascent form. He provides instructive analyses of several films that, despite the essay's title, show how video appears in cinema as just one surveillance technology among many. The essay thus forwards an understanding of surveillance as a system not reducible to any one element, in which narratives of surveillance play a part. Even more recently, Sébastien Lefait's book *Surveillance on Screen: Monitoring Contemporary Films and Television Programs* has taken up how surveillance films serve as an "experiment on contemporary surveillance societies," "test tubes" for looking at developments and possibilities in surveillance on a broader level.[24] "Collapsing the Interior/Exterior Distinction: Surveillance, Spectacle, and Suspense in Popular Cinema," an earlier essay by John Turner, also traces the intersection of surveillance and narrative structure in a number of promising ways. Building on Guy Debord's account of spectacle, Turner looks at the elements that have increasingly come to comprise cinematic narratives of surveillance and highlights some of the attributes that tie cinematic representation to surveillance through the consumption of spectacle. In going on to argue that "spectacle and surveillance are collapsed onto one another as an effective disciplinary apparatus—a set of techniques for the management of bodies the management of attention, and for assuring the ordering of human multiplicities," Turner ultimately (if implicitly) forwards cinematic analysis as a way to explore how surveillance functions as mediation and mediation functions as surveillance.[25]

With the above works as exceptions, most other accounts of surveillance in cinema often struggle between addressing specific historical and technical formations of surveillance and relying on an increasingly universalized concept of voyeurism. Much as surveillance studies has contended with the need to move beyond the conceptual framework of panopticism that has defined the field, the discussion of surveillance in cinema (in multiple contexts) has been significantly shaped by the psychoanalytic model of voyeurism.[26] Surveillance has been addressed as a constant in cinema over and over in critical explorations as well as in the narratives themselves, and yet there is a ubiquity of references to voyeurism that tends to obscure some of what are otherwise diverse accounts and symptomatize a certain intractability around voyeurism as a framework. Norman Denzin's book *The Cinematic Society: The Voyeur's Gaze,* for instance, is explicitly a text about surveillance and cinema, and yet it is telling that not only are surveillance and voyeurism used somewhat interchangeably, but the discussion of what Denzin's own text acknowledges as a structurally complex surveillant society is rhetorically reduced insistently not just to "voyeurism" or to "voyeurs," but to a hunt for the singularized lone figure of "the voyeur": "My goal is to unmask this voyeur."[27]

Despite the manner in which Denzin's book is emblematic of the attention to voyeurism that has structured the majority of accounts of cinematic surveillance, it does important work in defining the voyeur (both cinematic and noncinematic) as a historically produced "social type," and yet few other theorists seem to have taken up a historical account of the concept. Instead, voyeuristic desire often emerges in work on surveillance, especially as it appears in cinema, as a given element that underlies other more explicitly constructed political and social formations. The related concepts of voyeurism and scopophilia in critical discourse have grown from the radical use of such ideas by feminist psychoanalytic theorists in the 1970s into a naturalized version of voyeurism that has in many instances become problematically ahistorical and overly broad in its explanatory scope. This naturalization of voyeuristic pleasure crosses disciplinary boundaries in scholarship, and joins scholarly arenas to popular. Christian Parenti's aforementioned history of surveillance in the United States, for example, is careful in its historical understanding of the construction of identity and identification as part of a surveillance project, but when the book turns to representation and entertainment, the account favors a universalized understanding of voyeuristic desire. The chapter on "Voyeurism and Security Culture" intriguingly ties together reality television shows, narrative cinema such as *Panic Room* (David Fincher, 2002), and the home security industry, but Parenti's account of reality TV, in its simplistically judgmental approach, ends up constructing voyeurism at the level of instinct: "All pander to our voyeurism and other base appetites."[28] Whether in scholarly or popular accounts, inside and outside cinema studies, it is frequent for voyeurism to emerge as a given—a "base" instinct or a "commonplace aspect" to be capitalized upon to further cement sociopolitical power formations, rather than itself a historical phenomenon.[29] A more in-depth consideration of the relations between narrative cinema and surveillance practice—and also between cinema studies and surveillance studies—can offer up the material specificities of each to elucidate how, for instance, as Denzin's work suggests, voyeurism does not just become a political tool, but may well have historically emerged as a political project.[30]

While not dismissing voyeurism as concept, I do thus want to critique it as a framework, especially when used in a manner that provides little distinction between voyeurism and surveillance and between voyeurism and spectatorship. My approach in this book seeks instead to consider (primarily) American surveillance narratives in the light of historical specificity, technological change, and political philosophy. At the heart of my critique of voyeurism as a theoretical frame, beyond its attachment to a visual model that is no longer adequate to account for surveillance in a digital era, is that it makes certain structural assumptions about the existence of a clear subject/object relationship between watcher and watched, between spectator and representation. Kevin Haggerty and Richard Ericson's assertion in their introduction to the volume *The New Politics of Surveillance and Visibility* that "[s]urveillance technologies do not monitor people *qua* individuals, but instead operate through processes of disassembling and reassembling," is only one instance of how the subject/object relations implicit in the voyeuristic account of surveillance within film studies could be usefully complicated by thinking through how the very notion of the "subject" is being reformulated not only through surveillance practice but in surveillance narratives as well.[31] And one need not necessarily turn to the Deleuzian model of assemblage to discuss the complexities of subject formation within surveillance culture—while assemblage theory is crucial to certain models of particularly informational surveillance or "dataveillance," what is more consistent in diverse studies of surveillance than a unifying theoretical model is a historical and technological specificity that of necessity attends to the variation and intersections of subject formations emerging through surveillance practice.[32]

Canonical Surveillance Cinema

Before turning to the more contemporary films at the center of this book, I thus want to briefly review the now canonical surveillance narrative, *The Conversation* (Francis Ford Coppola). This 1974 film introduces a number of formations central to discussions of surveillance and to the cinematic surveillance issues raised thus far: the historical uses of technologies of surveillance, the political and social stagings of surveillance technique, the construction of subject positions through surveillance, and the narrative structures and themes attending the cinematic incorporation of surveillance.

The Conversation serves as somewhat of an *urtext* for the more contemporary films that occupy most of this book, which centralize surveillance technology in the stylistic and thematic construction of narrative. Francis Ford Coppola's wiretapping tour de force is widely considered to reflect the explicit concerns of its historical moment around surveillance, in particular the Watergate break-ins and accompanying revelations around political surveillance within the United States. It has also been discussed in terms of how the subjectivity of its investigatory character, private detective Harry Caul (played by Gene Hackman), is structurally and politically related to surveillance practices. The film makes it difficult to separate its character-based story from a historical and technological context, and analyses contemporary to its release as well as more recent scholarship highlight this.[33] It is thus in many ways the ground on which contemporary surveillance cinema stands, perhaps best evidenced by Hackman's casting in the role of an almost identical character in *Enemy of the State* in 1998.

In its focus on the recording and interpretation of sound, and the way that both images and narrative organize themselves around sound-recording technology, *The Conversation* clearly offers a commentary on the wiretapping practices active in the politics and cultural imaginary of the 1960s and 1970s. But if we are to read the production of a visible field as a process of surveillant narration from the origins of cinema on, then *The Conversation* provides a representation of the part that sound recording also plays in the narrative conceits of cinema as they are organized around logics of surveillance. The film is structured, both formally and in its story, around Harry's efforts to make sense out of a recorded conversation by matching image and sound. It announces its own processes of narrative signification in relation to surveillance and investigation, thus suggesting the implicit relations between cinematic production and surveillance practice. In her detailed analysis of the collaboration between Coppola, sound editor Walter Murch, and composer David Shire, Carolyn Anderson writes that "sound in film is traditionally at the service of the images, usually supporting, often connecting, rarely contradicting them. . . . *The Conversation* reverses this pattern."[34] While many theorists of film sound have disputed (with good reason) the primacy of the image over the soundtrack, Anderson's argument highlights the negotiation that the film offers between visual and aural signification, and suggests that this negotiation is not only exemplified by surveillance practice, but that surveillance is based on similar mediations (much as some of the constructions of cinematic narrative already discussed are operating along the same principles as the logic of surveillance).

What might initially seem to be a standard establishing shot in the film is pulled back from its seamless omniscience by a "problem" with sound: the eagle-eye view of San Francisco's Union Square, to which we are drawn increasingly close by a slow zoom until it is interrupted by distortion in the audio recording of the street noise, is revealed by a reverse shot to be the diegetic perspective of a surveillance operator on top of a building. The following shots in the sequence also become associated through perspective or focus with various characters whose positions are revealed to be either that of a sound surveillance technician or an object of surveillance. Rather than a reversal of the "traditional" system in which sound plays a supporting role to the image, this scene (and the rest of the film) actually highlights the degree to which the smooth unfolding of the images is completely dependent on the sound engineering that *The Conversation* suggests is also the work of audio surveillance: the construction and reconstruction of sound from several sources to serve as a kind of architecture without which the narrative becomes structurally *unsound*.

This film also reflects how increasingly uniform the technologies of cinema and those of surveillance were becoming: the magnetic sound recording shown in the film as essential to surveillance practice had by that point eclipsed optical recording as a far more efficient and effective means of cinematic sound production, as was the mixing of multiple tracks.[35] And, as Mary Ann Doane has argued in her essay on "Ideology and the Practice of Sound Editing," the privileging of the image within the discourse of (and about) film is indicative not of the lack of import of sound, but of the ideological work of sound: "In an industry whose major standard, in terms of production value, might be summarized as 'the less perceivable a technique, the more successful it is,' the invisibility of the work on sound is a measure of the strength of the sound track."[36] While the industry Doane describes is the cinematic one, the same description is apposite for the investigatory technologies and methodologies of surveillance, as *The Conversation* demonstrates. Even theories of surveillance building on Foucault's account of Bentham's panopticon have overwhelmingly focused on the visual aspects of the model, even though, as Dortë Zbikowski's history of acoustic surveillance indicates, "Part of this system were bugging lines, which supported visual surveillance with complete acoustic monitoring."[37] The fact that, until recently, sound recording devices could be much more easily miniaturized and hidden away as "bugs" than could visual recording mechanisms is yet another measure of the possible invisibility of sound and another indication of how accounts of cinematic technologies are implicitly invested in the logics of surveillance technologies. The minimization of the visible work of sound recording practice, even as sound is produced as a defining element, is essential to both surveillance and cinematic narrative.

The rendering visible of sound surveillance technologies within the film, in such a way that the status of both image and sound is broken down and reconstructed, foregrounds how both the technical and ideological work of surveillance and cinematic narrative are functioning along similar premises. The deconstruction of a more expected narrative structure in the opening sequence reemerges as the *construction* of technological and narrative apparatuses through which the "truth" of the story comes out. The rest of the film follows this same trajectory: whether Harry is actively trying to engineer the sound on the tapes and the film invokes a flashback image to illustrate his engineering of the narrative that is "the conversation," or the film is exploring the larger context of the characters and the investigation, *The Conversation* reflexively demonstrates that both cinematic narrative and surveillance practice are organized not just by the production of a visual and visible field, but also by the seamless production of sound recordings and dynamic relations between sound and image. However, as the film progresses, it becomes increasingly clear that Harry's investigation and even his engineered recording of the conversation are constituted by misinterpretation of what he has heard, misrecognition of the subject positions of both his client and those under surveillance, and manipulation by forces neither Harry nor the film ever fully identify. Thus the same productions that constitute both the sound recording and the narrative eventually undermine Harry's investigative authority on multiple levels (technological, professional, and personal) and also undermine narrative coherence and psychological stability, ultimately problematizing the epistemological foundation supporting the use of surveillance in the first place.[38]

Dennis Turner's 1985 analysis of the film demonstrates *The Conversation*'s import to a discussion of surveillance cinema as a recognizable designation. Through an examination of the film's "ongoing drive to constitute itself as narrative," Turner shifts the discussion from how the film (both technically and thematically) produces a story through sound and image, to an argument that it is also constructing itself through intertextual relationships to earlier surveillance-themed films such as *Blow-up*, *Vertigo*, and *Rear Window*.[39] Turner's choice to read the film not merely as a reflection of its historical moment but as a reflection on the construction of prior cinematic narratives around investigation implies that films about surveillance are films about cinematic history as well, not just in terms of technology but also in terms of narrative formation, and that this in turn reflects back on surveillance practice.[40] The argument that "the film's reworking of material from earlier texts raises the problems of boundary and textual authority which are suggested within its own diegesis," expands to suggest that the problems raised by narratives of investigation are problems that exceed issues of boundary and authority *within* narrative—in a broader sense, the narrative's treatment of these textual issues both addresses and problematizes how boundary and authority function within actual surveillance practice.[41] Put another way, if, as Turner argues, the film's intertextual allusions to earlier surveillance narratives, as well as its numerous disruptions of narrative suture through both image and sound, enact a "drama of the disintegrating subject," I would posit that this subject refers not only to the cinematic one, but to the subject of surveillance culture as well.[42]

However, it is important to note that the disintegration of the viewing and speaking subject that Turner refers to is equally describable as the *construction* of a political subject. The film's final sequence, which presents the increasingly distraught Harry in his own carefully guarded private space now apparently under surveillance by his former clients, demonstrates how this disintegration must be viewed in terms of subject position. Having realized that the couple whose conversation he had recorded were not in fact victims but murder conspirators, and that he has misunderstood the entire purpose and scenario of his surveillance operation, Harry receives a threatening phone call warning him not to take any action. The caller states, "We'll be listening," and a recording of the music Harry was just playing in his apartment is played back for him. Harry tears his apartment to pieces, literally, trying to locate a microphone. Unsuccessful even after ripping apart the walls and floorboards, he sits in the middle of his shredded apartment and plays his saxophone. The film ends as Harry's diegetic saxophone music joins with the extradiegetic score in a kind of duet that shows that the disintegration has exceeded the space of the character and story and that even the narrative is no longer a delimited or coherent space. The camerawork in this final shot, a high-angle slow pan back and forth that imitates the automatic repetitive sweep of a video surveillance camera, also suggests that the surveillance apparatus is ultimately the film's camera, rather than a technology within the film, further eliding any distinction between cinematic and surveillant technique and technology. For Thomas Levin, the final shot demonstrates a very self-conscious example of what he describes as the "synonymous" nature of cinematic and surveillant narration: "[I]ndeed, Harry will never find the surveillant device because it resides in a space that is epistemologically unavailable to him within the diegesis: surveillance has become *the condition of the narration itself*."[43] The ambiguities that surround this film—Who is the victim? Who is being watched, and why? Is this a film about the pathology of a character or a culture of surveillance?—in the final scene become visible (and audible) as the way narrative is (de) structured through surveillance into a kind of fundamental ambiguity, which recurs in numerous significant ways in films that follow it. This breakdown of boundaries between multiple spaces at the end of *The Conversation*—diegetic and extradiegetic sound intermingling, surveillance camera and film camera becoming one and the same, the destroyed space of Harry's apartment revealing the architecture within, the psychological space of reason versus insanity—is also an exposure of the tenuous boundaries between the private/individual/ psychological and the public/social/political. The very rupturing of the narrative space demands that the psychological exploration of this principal character be viewed in relation to the context outside of the film—it is a formal demand of the narrative, as constructed through surveillance technologies and practices. But in exposing how impossible these boundaries are, the narrative also erects relations between those spheres: the possibility of intrusion on a private realm is what defines that space as private in the first place, and is one of the reasons why Norman Denzin posits the figure of "the voyeur" as central to the cinematic production of twentieth-century notions of privacy.[44] The construction of Harrry Caul's personal pathology is instructive in these terms—his obsession with his own privacy is not "ironic" given his job invading the privacy of others, as Andrew Sarris has suggested: it is a testament to the structural configurations of privacy as a contiguous production of surveillance, thus connecting their formations closely.[45] In using the narrative relations between sound and image to explore these definitionally permeable boundaries, the film also highlights how surveillance practice merges with what in another context Giorgio Agamben calls "zones of indistinction," which I explore in detail in Chapter One and Chapter Three, as I discuss the functional ambiguities and the political implications of the formations emerging from more recent surveillance narratives.

Arguably, audio surveillance is associated in particular with the 1970s and the Watergate break-ins, while the kind of information processing seen as typical of the digital era is a more common cultural reference today, but narrative formations show that these practices have developed in tandem, with intersecting structures that build on and inflect each other. The thematization of telephone surveillance in the HBO series *The Wire* (2002–2008) demonstrates that the task of audio surveillance is not simply to record all conversations and make sense of them, but to analyze patterns of who is calling whom, process times and lengths of calls, and interpret conversations specifically encoded to avoid providing evidence. Even in *The Conversation*, with its focus on a single recording, audio surveillance and the aggregation of information are one and the same. And, as Zbikowski has noted, "The problem facing the listener when monitoring telephone calls is above all a legal one," and thus such surveillance narratives are organized around the modes in which one gains appropriate authority to listen in, as well as the technological capability.[46] *The Wire's* narrative arcs of surveillance (though they are not always about surveillance in particular) are often structured by the play between technology and legality, surveillance and evasion.

Other televisual instances of surveillant narration have what would appear to be even stronger associations with surveillance than cinematic ones given that video technologies more so than cinematic constitute visual surveillance, and reality television in particular has become a central marker of popular surveillance culture. My focus on cinema (though I discuss several television series as well) does not intend to conflate television and cinema. Instead, this book contextualizes some of the narrative and technological trends around surveillance to show how the narrative codes of filmmaking that preceded television have become part of more contemporary media, while in turn techno-cultural developments in televisual representation, satellite imaging, GPS technologies, and internet mediation, among others, have become part of cinematic form.

Millennial Surveillance Cinema

In tracing several significant relationships between cinematic formations and surveillance, this book historicizes narrative trends around surveillance that popular film criticism often situates as "post-9/11," even as numerous surveillance historians and theorists have noted that such designations represent a disavowal of the fact that many of the "post-9/11" surveillance practices and ideologies were put into place prior to September 11, 2001. Surveillance cinema demonstrates that surveillance reflects United States cultural production as much or more than it represents a response to attacks on that culture. The chapters of the book are organized to highlight significant instances or trends of this cultural production through reference to developments in technology (both cinematic and surveillant), racial formations, political and economic structures, and ideological discourses around visibility, violence, information, space, and time.

The first chapter begins an in-depth analysis of these narrative trends by examining the emergence of the horror subgenre dubbed "torture porn" in the first decade of the twenty-first century and demonstrating that it is intimately related to the thematization of surveillance technologies. This chapter, titled "Video Surveillance, Torture Porn, and Zones of Indistinction," examines how video technology as manifested in the cinematic narration of graphic torture reveals the interpenetrations of torture and surveillance in the exercise of contemporary biopolitical power. The chapter focuses on a number of American torture-horror films, primarily the exceptionally successful *Saw* series (multiple directors, 2004–2010), in combination with several films of Academy Award–winning director Michael Haneke: *Caché* (2005), his two versions of *Funny Games* (1997, 2007), and the lesser-known *Benny's Video* (1992). I argue that these disparate works are joined through their narrative deployment of video surveillance technology and the violent production of visible bodies. My analysis of the films in this chapter demonstrates the interaction of torture fantasies with postcolonial politics and counterterrorist discourse in both the United States and Europe, and the central roles that surveillance and surveillant narration play in these interactions.

The chapter turns to Giorgio Agamben's political philosophy, his biopolitical analysis of the figure of "bare life," and the notion of "zones of indistinction" to show that video surveillance functions in these films as a space of narrative indeterminacy.[47] Through close analysis of American torture-horror films and their relation to contemporary politics, I demonstrate that this indeterminacy is involved in both the narrative and political production of bodies for torture. The chapter's second half elaborates why these American genre films are best understood through the films of Michael Haneke, which serve to reflexively identify surveillant mediation as essential to the ambiguous spaces of cinematic violence and the violent ambiguities defining modern politics.

Chapter Two, "Commodified Surveillance: First-Person Cameras, the Internet, and Compulsive Documentation," turns to another central formation attending contemporary narratives and technologies of surveillance: the consumer-subject in the era of home video, online networking, and digital surveillance or "dataveillance." Beginning with an introduction of Guy Debord's account of the "spectacle" as a necessary element of surveillance in a consumer economy, the chapter examines consumer-level surveillance in cinema through what I call "compulsive documentation" films—films shot entirely in first-person-camera style and based on the premise that they are composed of "real" footage shot on consumer video equipment. Such films are also, significantly, often found in the horror genre, and serve as the corollary of the more obviously politically symptomatic torture and surveillance films. With the most notable instances including *The Blair Witch Project* (Daniel Myrick and Eduardo Sanchez, 1999), *Cloverfield* (Matt Reeves, 2008), and the *Paranormal Activity* series (multiple directors, 2007–2014), I posit these films in relation to "self-surveillance," or "peer-to-peer surveillance," and use this relationship to demonstrate how commodification, consumption, and surveillance function alongside and through each other.

The chapter establishes these relationships by emphasizing both the explicit and implicit connections between the individualized and embodied structure of technological experience presented by the first-person-camera films through the video camera point-of-view shot, and the arguably hypermediated and diffuse structures of the internet and digital surveillance. Building on the work of Mark Andrejevic in *iSpy: Surveillance and Power in the Interactive Era*, which puts forth interactivity and participatory culture as deeply implicated in surveillance culture, I argue that the first-person-camera films—even as they seek to present a direct, individual experience at a bodily level—are best understood as a phenomenon through their innovative and successful interactive online marketing campaigns and their expansion of the cinematic experience into the "virtual" space of internet communities and digital economies. By tracing the formal and structural contiguities between the narrative and technical elements of these films, their marketing campaigns, social networking, and internet consumption, this chapter shows that looking at consumer-level surveillance through such narrative formations is essential to understanding how codefining subjective experience and surveillance have become in a digital economy, and the part that video mediation plays in establishing that relation.

Chapter Three, "The Global Eye: Satellite, GPS, and the 'Geopolitical Aesthetic,'" refocuses the discussions of the prior chapters to elaborate more fully how individual subject positions within a surveillance culture have been produced in relation to discourses of globalization and geopolitics, and how developments in cinematic narrative are enmeshed in this project. Unlike the films discussed in earlier chapters, and their quite implicit formulation of political relationships between individuals and systems through narratives of surveillance, these films present direct lines from the focus on an individual body to the construction of a geopoliticized subject position. Building on Fredric Jameson's 1992 analysis of the "geopolitical aesthetic," this chapter highlights the role of surveillance technologies and practices in the construction of narrative that "conflates ontology with geography and endlessly processes images of the unmappable [world] system."[48] The chapter examines the incorporation of satellite imaging and GPS into cinematic continuity systems, exemplified by films like *Enemy of the State* (Tony Scott, 1998), *The Bourne Ultimatum* (Paul Greengrass, 2007), and *Mission: Impossible—Ghost Protocol* (Brad Bird, 2011). Such films employ surveillance technology that visualizes "location" in such a way that it serves as a narrative and stylistic pivot upon which the relationships among individual bodies, transnational spaces, and broad global systems are constructed through economies of violence. Through close analysis of how what has been called "geosurveillance" has increasingly come to characterize the aesthetic of establishing shots, chase scenes, and narrative denouements within these films, I suggest that cinematic narrative has been integral to the ways that technology has participated in the production of individuals as visual and visualizable subjects of a world system increasingly characterized by various forms of *targeting*. I trace this production back to a very different cinematic depiction of surveillance and globalization, the 1993 film *Rising Sun* (Philip Kaufman), which presents the police investigation of a murder caught on security cameras at a Japanese corporation in Los Angeles. The earlier film situates surveillance as part of a global economic structure functioning as an increasingly orientalized threat, thus positioning it as both historically and generically contiguous with the rhetoric of "global terrorism" that is central to today's surveillance politics and cinematic surveillance narratives. This contiguity demonstrates how the generic development of the action-thriller since the 1990s gives insight into the shared logic between the global market economy and the violence enacted on singular bodies in contemporary geopolitical warfare.

Many of these action-thrillers address terrorism as either the center-piece of the story or as part of their broader geopolitical milieu. Those focused entirely on a single instance of terrorism tend to become narra-tive explorations of the functional logics of surveillance and counterter-rorism, in primarily symptomatic forms. For instance, *Déjà vu* (Tony Scott, 2006) and *Vantage Point* (Pete Travis, 2008) organize their narra-tives around the fantasy of preventing a terrorist attack that has already happened, and so quite tellingly exhibit a formulation of surveillance methodology and technology as both retroactive and circular—and at times devoted to past objects of threat and loss with a force that I char-acterize as a form of political melancholia.

The fourth chapter, "Temporality and Surveillance I: Terrorism Narratives and the Melancholic Security State," explores this narrative production of a temporal system through surveillance technology. The issue of temporality has certainly been raised in discussions of surveil-lance practice, most obviously in regards to the preemptive agendas of the "war on terror." Gary Genosko and Scott Thompson have usefully outlined some of the complexity of the temporalities of surveillance: a discussion of the narrative formations around surveillance in films such as *Déjà vu* offers more insight into the vicissitudes of these prac-tices, providing an almost uncanny representation of the modes of time that Genosko and Thompson outline as "a (troubled) past," "a (frag-mented) present," and "a (future) past."[49] Focusing in particular on how manipulations of narrative time are predicated on the machinations of surveillance within those narratives, the chapter shows how narrative structure, surveillance practice, and recent rhetorics of national security have become coimmersed in a construction of historical time as subject to the laws of desire and disavowal, turning politics into pure pathol-ogy. I argue that this temporal production becomes a central part of the surveillance structures explored in the earlier chapters. The chapter goes on to examine how such films—and the politics they reflect—contain the seeds of their own critique within them, as demonstrated by the more recent *Source Code* (Duncan Jones, 2011), the narrative formation of which exposes how retroactive security practice and counterterrorist fantasies are built upon a scaffolding of necropolitics.[50]

The final chapter, "Temporality and Surveillance II: Surveillance, Re-mediation, and Social Memory in *Strange Days*," joins the discussion of time in *Déjà vu*, *Vantage Point*, and *Source Code* to a consideration of the earlier *Strange Days* (Kathryn Bigelow, 1995), which allows a historically grounded reframing of both the temporality and critique suggested by *Source Code*. *Strange Days*, released in 1995 as a near-future science fiction, threads its narrative through the entangled racial tensions and media landscape of the 1990s, most fully represented by its visual and narrative references to the videotaped police assault on Rodney King. The film joins together this mise-en-scène of historicized racial violence and a millennial countdown with the mediation of a science-fictional device that can record human perceptual experience. In its historical positioning and pseudo-virtual reality fantasy, *Strange Days* represents a media and surveillance culture on the cusp of digitization, with its fictional technology multiply deployed in the narrative as memory, surveillance, legal evidence, pornography, and even weaponry. What emerges is an overdetermined narrative that weaves together individual subjectivity, social histories, and political interventions by way of a temporality of repetition and a form of what Jay Bolter and Richard Grusin call "remediation."

As the "double logic" by which new media culture can be understood through its seemingly paradoxical drives for simultaneous "hypermediacy" and "immediacy," remediation serves to reframe how surveillance and cinema work through each other, structurally, politically, and temporally.[51] I suggest that it is through such remediation that a resistant politics might be located in the cinematic narration of surveillance, in part by redefining the circularity and repetition of the political melancholia described in Chapter Four. The chapter concludes with the point that "surveillance cinema" necessarily makes clear not just the contiguities but also the *inconsistencies* between the ideological premises of surveillance and the demands of narrative form, and thus cinema can be seen, even as it functions alongside other surveillance formations, as a point of access to the often failed performances of surveillant power.

1

Video Surveillance, Torture Porn, and Zones of Indistinction

Since Alfred Hitchcock's *Psycho* and Michael Powell's *Peeping Tom* redefined cinematic terror in the 1960s, there has been a prevalence of surveillance narratives within the horror and "erotic thriller" arenas. The psychosexual slasher as offered up by those films became a central figure of monstrosity for years to come, and in these foundational texts as well as the films that followed, the violence and narrative structure are defined by voyeuristic stalking well before any knife is raised or blood spilled. From Norman Bates's peephole in *Psycho* and Mark Lewis's 16mm camera in *Peeping Tom*, on through the closed-circuit television systems of *Sliver* (Phillip Noyce, 1993) and *Captivity* (Roland Joffé, 2007), technologies of surveillance have served as a frequent narrative trope in slasher horror and have been almost invariably identified with the killer's pathological murderousness. This is certainly one reason that voyeurism has so frequently been used as the explanatory model for cinematic surveillance narratives; the fact that the analytical framework so closely mirrors the narrative structure of these films may also serve to explain why voyeurism has repeatedly been used in critical accounts in a manner that I characterize in this book's introduction as naturalizing and ahistorical.

Even as the extreme violence that characterized these slasher films has found a new, and significantly different, subgeneric home in the contemporary horror market, the use of surveillance technologies within the narratives has remained. My focus in this chapter is the postmillennial horror subgenre dubbed "torture porn" by critic David Edelstein in 2006, and its coincidence with the use of video surveillance in recent narrative cinema.[1] Generic conventions, as evidenced even in the early years of cinema by the chase or "caught in the act" films I discuss in the introduction, are a significant element of the integration of surveillance and cinema, and thus an account of the generic or subgeneric formations that have privileged surveillance is one of the most direct points of access to an understanding of the specific ways that cinema and surveillance have become mutually structuring.[2]

Best represented by the *Saw* and *Hostel* series, each of which spanned years and earned box office glory alongside widespread critical disgust, torture porn has largely abandoned the psychosexual stalker model of horror extremity. Rather than relying on the pathology and perversity of the lone psycho, torture-porn films have instead turned to the more explicitly *systematic* violence of torture scenarios and often include narrative reference to the ideological, economic, or social elements that constitute that torture as itself functioning within the logic of a broader system. The frequent incorporation of surveillance into these films thus allows for a consideration of the function that surveillance has in a narrative formation of systematic (and systemic) violence. More significantly, these narrative formations also provide insight into the extracinematic connections between torture and surveillance that I would suggest are systemic intersections—intersections that are exemplary of the political, technological, and representational aspects of surveillance in current usage.

Most simply, it is worth noting that the rhetoric and tactics of the United States' "war on terror" have since 2001 meant that both torture and surveillance have moved into a significant position in the world's political reality, not to mention its imaginary. But rather than simply noting that the intersection of torture and surveillance is symptomatic of the postmillennial political zeitgeist, my concern is to explore the way video technologies function within these narratives, and how the resulting narrative formations demonstrate the relations between surveillance and torture with greater specificity. In turn, these films and the generic conventions they exemplify become integral to a view of how cinematic narrative works within a larger system of surveillance—here understood multiply as concept, as politics, and as technology.

What might seem to be the almost insistently apolitical torture narratives of the American horror films are both structurally and politically related to certain surveillance-themed films outside of what would initially seem to be the recognizable generic parameters of American torture porn, such as the multinational productions of Michael Haneke, or

Andrea Arnold's *Red Road* (2006). Haneke's *Caché* (2005) and his much earlier *Benny's Video* (1992), in particular, serve to refocus the willfully ahistorical morality discourses of some of the American torture films into an exploration of the relations between graphic cinematic violence and the production of racial subjects in western European postcolonial surveillance cultures. The contiguities between the American and European films, based upon both violence and surveillance, are instructive for an understanding of recent narrative formations, but also serve to demonstrate that the political formations around surveillance technologies and practices are both highly coded and historically specific. The relations between these otherwise very different films also highlight the relationships between violence and visibility that are essential to an understanding of the way surveillance functions both in contemporary horror cinema and in contemporary politics.

The connections between the various films, the relations between surveillance and torture, and the political function of surveillance in cinema are best understood through reference to the conceptual frameworks offered by political philosopher Giorgio Agamben. Agamben's work on biopolitics and "states of exception" has become increasingly important for surveillance theorists (among many others) seeking to describe how the extralegal overreach of surveillance, detention, and military intervention has become the defining characteristic of democratic state power in the United States and Europe. It is Agamben's notion of "zones of indistinction," perhaps most simply understood as spatial manifestations of the state of exception, that I believe best describes the way that cinematic torture narratives are both defined and destabilized by the incorporation of surveillance. Though this manifestation is defined as spatial, it also serves to describe the type of conceptual space created by and for a violent biopolitics. These films indicate a significant mode in which surveillance politicizes cinematic narrative space by using narrative *as* a space, a cinematic "zone of indistinction."

* * *

The phenomenon of "torture porn" is frequently considered the lowest common denominator in the global reinvestment in horror in the new millennium. The ultra-graphic violence of these films, in combination with narratives that seem predominantly invested in providing the basis for incredibly drawn-out scenes of torture rather than the rhythmic suspense of a more traditional slasher film, situate them as somehow both the pinnacle and the gutter of contemporary horror. The overwhelming majority and the defining examples of torture-porn films are American productions, often connecting the threat of torture with foreign travel, as in *Hostel* (Eli Roth, 2005) and *Turistas* (John Stockwell, 2006), which present teenagers or young adults as victims of kidnap and torture during those first youthful escapades abroad that are now a tradition of upper-middle-class Americans.[3] The emergence of these narratives of American youth, frequently men, going abroad and finding themselves immersed in what often amounts to an economy of torture must be read as a tremendously projective fantasy—a fantasy in which American youth are figured as the victims rather than as perpetrators of this kind of organized violence. Particularly since the events of September 11, 2001, and the ensuing American military actions that resulted in the establishment of the detention facility at Guantanamo Bay and the well-documented abuses at Abu Ghraib, it seems striking to posit Americans as the innocent objects of torture scenarios. At minimum, the contemporary appearance of so many films about the economies, bodily experiences, and technologies of torture should be viewed in conjunction with the politics of torture that has concurrently occupied the American and world stage. That several of these films situate torture as an international affair is also telling, despite the fact that with the exception of *Turistas*, which invokes Latin American economic resentment as a rationale for the harvesting of American organs, these films disavow any explicitly political structure to the torture.

The *Saw* franchise, which emerged in 2004 and continued until 2010 (with, remarkably, a sequel released annually to enormous box office success), is one that is little marked by political commentary, and, unlike the films mentioned above, situates torture as both domestic and, though not psychosexual, highly personalized and pathologized.[4] And yet the stakes of this successful series are instructive in relation to the way torture is figured in the larger subgeneric arena, even before consideration of the way surveillance functions in relation to the torture. The *Saw* films are constituted by endless repetitions of the "games" carried out by serial killer "Jigsaw" (and, in later films, by various acolytes): each game involves the kidnapping of a victim or victims who are then placed in a scenario (frequently augmented with "homemade" torture gadgets designed to do devastating violence to the human body) requiring them to make torturous choices in order to survive and/or save those dear to them. All the victims are chosen by Jigsaw because he considers them to be squandering or abusing their own lives or those of others, and all the games are designed to teach Jigsaw's chosen victim or victims the "real" value of life: the choice at the center of the first film is that of a doctor (selected because he has been unfaithful to his wife and uncaring toward his patients) who is told he must saw off his own foot to get out of a chained cuff and kill the stranger locked in the room with him, or allow his family to be murdered. As the films progress, the "games," the torture devices, and the choices become more complex—even as the technologies of torture always maintain a sort of medieval crudeness, there is frequent attention paid to providing structural parallels or integration between the "crime" that the victims have committed to cause them to be targeted by Jigsaw, the choice they must make to survive, and the game/ technology Jigsaw has constructed to physically brutalize them. The final film, *Saw 3D*, for instance, opens with a game and a device designed to mirror and punish a love triangle between two men and the woman who has been involved with both of them without their knowledge: unsurprisingly, she ends up sawed in half.

These moralizing contraptions, even in the most extreme moments of horror and violence, create constant reference back to the framing device of Jigsaw's philosophy. Whether we view this philosophy as a nonsensical justification for elaborate scenes of violence or as an inventive narrative element that adds depth and nuance to contemporary horror film, it is clear that despite the visceral response such extreme representations might offer, the structure and purpose of the games in *Saw* refuse to let these scenes reside in the realm of pure disgust.[5] Instead, the series introduces the cinematic narration of torture as a point of entry into moral and ethical dilemmas, and demands that each torture and death scene is framed by a consideration of fundamental values and a punishment that reflects the transgression. These dilemmas and considerations join with Jigsaw's torture contraptions to create a structure through which torture, in its technologies, intentions, and effects on the body, comes to represent, in both form and purpose, a system—in this case, a value system organized around what constitutes a worthwhile life.

But the narratives do not always make these games straightforward, and the films are in large part organized by a search for the *rules* of the games, rather than a simple presentation of the games as they are played. Or put more exactly: playing the games is usually the same thing as figuring out the rules of the game, and the narrative twists and turns are representative of this type of game "play." For both the characters and the films' audiences, the narratives form around trying to determine precisely what the "game" is, what the choices are, and who is a victim and who is a perpetrator of these violences. The first *Saw* film hides the identity of Jigsaw until the surprise ending, and thus the central scenario is surrounded by a series of investigations into previous Jigsaw crimes, multiple flashbacks, and false leads for both the investigators and the audience. Ultimately, by layering the stories to show how the victims are selected, how the games unfold, and that multiple characters shift quickly between being posited as suspects and posited as victims, the *Saw* films tend to offer up every character as in some way both guilty and innocent.

This ambiguity is central to the moral-philosophical question that these films gesture toward repeatedly: is Jigsaw himself teaching something worthwhile, and are the torturous games he creates for his selected victims really "saving" them? The possibility of viewing Jigsaw as savior and moral compass is foregrounded early on in the series when one of his surviving victims from the first film, formerly a debilitated drug addict, pulls herself together after her ordeal, describes the experience as transformative, becomes his disciple in *Saw II*, and continues to figure centrally throughout the remainder of the series. This formula is repeated with other former victims; in fact Jigsaw himself dies not long into the series and his work is carried on by others who believe in his cause, further framing the torture as organized violence and part of a belief system. Thus the films, despite their over-the-top narrative contortions, still incorporate themes easily extrapolated to contemporary politics: the morality and/or efficacy of torture, definitions of life, fundamentalist belief systems, and bodily and psychological experiences of violence.

And despite the frequent critical treatment of these films as a disturbing symptom of the growing extremity of media violence, they could also be said to address some of the complexity of formations of violence (and the anger with current formulations of and responses to these violences) in a frankly less didactic way than the more explicitly political films that consider topics such as torture. At minimum it is notable that while the vast majority of films addressing the politics of torture in the United States "war on terror," such as *Rendition* (Gavin Hood, 2007) and *Lions for Lambs* (Robert Redford, 2007), lost money at the box office, the *Saw* series has proven consistently marketable: *Saw IV*, the sequel released in 2007, grossed almost two times more than *Lions for Lambs* and *Rendition* did put together.[6] It seems worthwhile then to examine some of the ways that *Saw* is speaking contemporary violences in a way that the more realistic and directly political films are not.

One aspect worth significant attention is the inclusion of multiple video surveillance apparatuses into the narratives of the *Saw* films, a repetitive narrative deployment that opens these films up to a consideration of the contemporary political relations between surveillant mediation and torture. The series incorporates surveillance as a recurrent feature of Jigsaw's methodology, one that intermingles with the games of torture in various ways; with several critical essays on the emergence of torture porn focusing to varying degrees on the prominence of surveillance in the narratives, it is fair to say that surveillance has become a significant characteristic of the subgenre.[7] The way that the *Saw* films formulate torture by introducing technological mediation and particularly surveillant formations into the rules and play of the life-and-death games insistently defines a structural relationship between narrative organization, methodologies of torture, and surveillance. This relationship is something that is of more than small consequence for a consideration of how surveillance is used politically to produce certain bodies as visible such that they may be subject to the violence of torture, and even further, of how torture, both cinematically and otherwise, produces these bodies as visible. Such production constitutes torture not just as politically consistent with surveillance or as the result of surveillance, but as a *function* of surveillance. However, as evidenced by the early films discussed in this book's introduction, the visual/visible work of surveillance within cinematic narrative, as well as the power manifested by and through such work, is often ambiguous.

A video surveillance image provides the torture aesthetic of *Saw* (2004).

The first two *Saw* films best organize a discussion of how surveillance functions in the series, and demonstrate both the direct and indirect relations between surveillance and torture. The first film begins *in media res*, with two men awakening in a filthy and apparently abandoned large industrial bathroom, and another man dead on the floor in a pool of blood. They have no memory of how they got there, and via a series of clues, primarily audiocassettes that provide puzzling instructions in Jigsaw's signature electronically altered voice, try to assess their situation and what they must do to escape with their lives. As the film progresses, it emerges for both the trapped characters and the film's audience that the men are being watched on video surveillance, or what seems more precisely to be closed-circuit television (CCTV). The film cuts from the scene of entrapment to a low-resolution video image of the same scene; the unidentified watcher of these images, shot from behind, is clearly implicated as the one orchestrating the entire scenario by virtue of his operation of the surveillance. The as yet faceless surveillance operator and his seemingly predatory gaze are clearly deployed here in the mode of stalking: the killer-to-be-named-later tradition of slasher films like the aforementioned *Peeping Tom*, *Halloween* (John Carpenter, 1978), and countless others. In and of itself, this use of video surveillance as an aspect of predation is unremarkable and would seem to be a televisually technologized version of the voyeuristic slasher—simply a high-tech version of Norman Bates's peephole.

But the surveillance and other forms of video mediation emerge in many additional places in the film, and the proliferation and variation of these moments also complicates the conceptual framework accounting for their narrative usage. The first time *Saw* presents video technology onscreen is in a flashback offered as part of a surviving victim's recounting of her trauma. The flashback begins as she awakens trapped in a head-enclosing torture mask and a video monitor turns on in front of her. An avatar puppet (another Jigsaw signature) appears on the video monitor and informs her, in the altered voice we have come to recognize, of why she is there and what she must to do escape. The video thus serves the same function as the audiotape for the two men in the film's first scene: as a means for the release of select information to the victims. On either audio or video, these recordings are a staple of the entire series. This electronic delivery of the "rules of the game," the avatar puppet that appears in the videos, the altered voice, and, most importantly, the often partial information they deliver, become integral to the torture scenarios. These elements escalate the terror of the victims and introduce what amounts to the terms of their ordeal (including the reasons they have been selected) and the conditions by which they might escape violence. Video thus comes to serve two interrelated purposes in these films: as surveillance used to monitor the scenes of torture, and as representation incorporated into the torture scenarios. In both of these uses, it is clear that video technology functions as an organizational methodology intended to produce and control responses.

The dual usages of video are in some ways exemplary of why the account of cinematic surveillance as voyeuristic must be augmented with an understanding of surveillance in its disciplinary function: Foucault's analysis of the panopticon, introduced in *Discipline and Punish*, has long served as the crux of analyses of surveillance, particularly as it is considered structurally and in regards to visual formations. Though Foucault's account emphasizes the production of "docile bodies" through a shift *away* from torture (and the spectacle thereof), this narrative production of surveillance within a torture film as a tool and form of confinement, control, and power has notable resonance with the Foucauldian account. In fact, the interaction of torture and surveillance within these films demonstrates that, despite the move away from (noncinematic) public spectacles of bodily abuse, surveillance practices are intersecting with torture in different formations, re-producing the visible, tortured body.

However, despite this narrative deployment of video surveillance and mediation as tools of bodily and psychological management and/or control, ultimately the narratives do not support an interpretation of video as a disciplinary technology, and certainly not as exemplary of panopticism (any more than it indicates voyeuristic desire). While video and surveillance serve clear purposes for the *characters* within the film that suggest such a function, the part video plays in the *narrative* formation is quite different. As a tool of surveillance and control, Jigsaw uses video as a structural element of the games of torture, organizing victims in relation to themselves and each other. But the narrative "game" for the film's spectator is different, and video frequently serves the opposite purpose: to make the roles of the characters mobile, confuse the narrative in terms of both time and space, undermine the logic of Jigsaw's morality plays, and betray the very idea of the "game" by making it unwinnable. In short, rather than reflecting or producing a clear architecture of power, video surveillance in the *Saw* films makes a very revealing mess.

In his introduction to *Theorizing Surveillance*, David Lyon cites Giorgio Agamben as a thinker whose work has shown that while "the panopticon was a distinct and bounded area; now . . . zones of indistinction are crucial, and in fact, are the locus of power," and it is Agamben's formulations that are instructive here in regard to the use of surveillance in *Saw* and other torture-porn films, even when such films might seem more immediately addressed by the frameworks of panoptics and/or voyeurism.[8] What I will posit here as cinematic "zones of indistinction" show how narrative and technology are interpenetrating in surveillance cinema in a manner that undermines the structuring elements of each in order to produce power as the function of both.

At first glance, it is not the surveillant aspects of the *Saw* films that would seem most conversant with Agamben's work, but instead how Jigsaw's games (and in some ways, the films as a whole) are predicated on reflexively defining who deserves to live, and thus become an exercise in biopower. Agamben posited the concept of "zones of indistinction" not specifically to describe surveillance culture, but more generally as a central formation through which Western politics has constructed itself around the biopolitical categorial pairing of bare life versus social/political existence. The figure of "bare life," which, defined most simply, is a life without legal or political rights, is produced by and for the discursive and literal spaces that Agamben refers to as "zones of indistinction"— the privileged example in the modern era being the concentration camp.[9] It is in the designation of "bare life" and the production of zones of indistinction that Agamben finds sovereign power in modern form, and many have turned to these formulations to describe contemporary manifestations such as the securitization of urban space and Israel's strategic occupation of the West Bank.[10] Surveillance theorists have taken up these ideas to look at the way that surveillance technologies and social formations around surveillance operate as part of these zones of indistinction in a number of ways, particularly as related to political discourse on security and terrorism and the way that heightened surveillance reflects the increasing normalization of the political "state of exception."[11]

While it is not possible to explore the full complexity of Agamben's formulations here, it is important to note that *Saw*'s torturous narrative logic parallels the manifestation of sovereign power through the biopolitical designation of bare life, and that Jigsaw's games function as zones of indistinction through which he can manifest his victims *as* bare life. Without necessarily equating the *Saw* films or their pretentious serial killer with the logic of sovereignty, it is testament to the ubiquity and centrality of this biopolitical construction that these immensely popular films, which have in many ways defined the torture porn subgenre, are themselves defined by an explicit emphasis on the use value of "bare life."

Most simply, Jigsaw's games are designed to provide access to the significance of life through a desperate fight for survival. Much as the figure of "bare life" in Agamben's account is stripped of position, rights, community—all of that which constitutes one as a social being—and exists in the outskirts or camp at a *subsistence* level, the abduction of a victim in *Saw* removes them from the context of their daily roles at work, home, etc., and relegates them to an isolated, ambiguous location (notably, the spaces of the games frequently look like nothing more than *abandoned* industrial buildings, and thus both the victim and their space of captivity are defined by various forms of abjection).

This undisclosed location also situates them in the space of the game that produces an extreme encounter with their own bodies as subject to violence and death, and ultimately an instinct-level fight for survival.[12] Absent politics, social expectation, and complex desire, they confront themselves as "bare life" at the same time that Jigsaw (via the hypermediated self-representation of a manipulated audio or video recording) instructs them that an experience of themselves *as* "bare life" will *add* significance, rather than take it away. The figure of the life that matters and "bare life" are collapsed into the single figure of the (potentially redeemed) victim in Jigsaw's games, with the contingent relationship bare life/meaningful life loudly announced.

What *Saw* lacks in such insistently individualized dramatizations of the production of bare life is an awareness of this production as a *political* act. These films, as well as some critics, are invested in the representation of these games as a kind of *pure experience*, defined as radically separate from the social factors that might interfere in experiencing oneself as, most fundamentally, a body.[13] But in the present context of more concern than these invocations of "bare life" is the role that video plays in establishing Jigsaw's games as zones of indistinction—how, in fact, surveillant mediation functions in these films to produce and define the discursive conditions out of which "bare life" emerges. Here it is the concept of "zones of indistinction" that best characterizes *Saw*'s surveillance formations, the function of such formations in the larger narrative structure, and the narrative result: torture and death. Further, the incorporation of video surveillance not only helps form Jigsaw's games as zones of indistinction within the narrative, but also allows the narrative itself to serve as such a zone. In this way, contemporary torture-horror, which frequently attempts to forward its version of "bare life" as an *apolitics*, instead becomes a marked instance of the functionality of cinematic surveillance narratives as part of a larger apparatus of surveillance and as an aspect of a broader politics—a politics that, in its current historical iteration, has made both literal and philosophical space for torture as another functioning zone of indistinction.

In his discussion of the figure of *homo sacer* (sacred man), Agamben describes the sovereign formulation in Roman law of the figure of "bare life" as that which may be killed, but not sacrificed, which is to say it is neither human nor divine (nor animal precisely); it is this "originary" zone of indistinction that Agamben suggests is the crux of a series of interrelated zones of indistinction that have become increasingly spatialized in modern politics, even as space has become increasingly politicized.[14] *Homo sacer* is excluded from legal or political rights and representation, and yet is simultaneously included by the fact that it is the power of the law that has excluded him: "He is an outlawed citizen, the exception to the law, and yet he is still subject to the penalty of death and therefore still included, in the very act of exclusion, within the law."[15] The political in-between-ness embodied in this figure is also defined by a spatial or geographical marginalization of a similarly contradictory or ambiguous character: banished (or, in more contemporary forms, interned in a detention center, concentration camp, or refugee camp), *homo sacer* occupies an area outside the legal and physical limits of the city-state, but is still defined by his externality to it. In the case of the concentration camp, this is rendered in an extreme form in which the suspension of legal limits produces the space of the camp as "the materialization of the state of the exception."[16] Even with the spatial literalization of the "zone" of indistinction, however, Agamben still seeks to describe what is above all a political formation, one that is itself not exceptional (i.e., confined to the extremity of Nazi genocide) but instead constitutes the "hidden matrix" of current Western politics.[17] It is of no small consequence that, in the words of philosopher Catherine Mills, Agamben discusses the camp not as a "simple topographical space," but as a "topological figure."[18] If we also understand the construction of narrative space within cinema as a topological project—which is to say cinematic space is not so much a *metaphor* or a *representation* of three-dimensional reality as it is a rendering of relational elements through a logic of continuity and causality—it becomes somewhat clearer how cinema and surveillance operate contiguously within a broader politics, in this instance constituting zones of indistinction through and by which a biopolitics of torture becomes part of that constitution.[19]

As was apparent in the introductory chapter's historical overview, ambiguities of various forms have attended and even defined the narrativization of surveillance in cinema from its earliest days, especially as it has related to visual surveillance and the visibility of the objects of surveillance. In large part, this was inseparable from the production of the racialized body as object of surveillance *and* cinema. And certainly in the present context it is important to note that is not just any *body* that is produced as "bare life" for and by torture. While the wishfully apolitical torture porn subgenre in part bases its apolitics on the indiscriminate production of "bare life"—with indiscriminate in this case actually meaning that the victims in torture porn are primarily white, male, and heterosexual—in the realm of actual politics, it is quite clear that biopolitical designations have been inseparable from the production of sexual, gender, and particularly racial categorization and difference. It is thus essential to understand not just how surveillance within narrative serves the spatial function of the zone of indistinction, but also how the cinematic scenes of torture are related to the production of certain bodies as visible, serving a similar function to visual surveillance. In other words, the way visibility is used to code particular bodies as "bare life" is an equally defining aspect of how surveillance and torture intersect within visual mediation, both in these cinematic narratives and in contemporary acts of torture. The narrative relations established in the films between surveillance and torture exceed a cause-and-effect understanding, and, as we will see further below, point ultimately to an increasingly indiscernible boundary *between* surveillance and torture. Viewed in this light, the phenomenon of torture porn allows for an analysis not only of how cinema produces visible violence, but more generally the ways in which, outside of the movie theater, bodies are produced as visible for, by, and through contemporary acts of torture.

This circumstance is perhaps most concretely evidenced by the systematic violences that occurred at Abu Ghraib and the degree to which they were not only documented by, but performed *through* the act of photography. The photographs from Abu Ghraib, as has been noted, were not just evidence that American soldiers had engaged in elaborate abuses of prisoners—the photography was itself a methodology of torture, designed to produce degradation of the depicted prisoners by rendering the acts of humiliation and violence visible. Jasbir Puar and Judith Butler have both highlighted the degree to which not just the act of photographing the prisoners, but the diversely mediated dispersal of the images is tied to the acts of torture. As Puar writes, "These images not only represent specific acts and allude to the procedural vectors of ever-expansive audiences but they also reproduce and multiply the power dynamics that made these acts possible in the first place."[20]

While the type of extreme violence in the *Saw* series seeks to universalize in its insistence on a basic physical experience of pain and the nearly unidentifiable meatlike treatment of the human form, Puar has pointed out that the Abu Ghraib photographs are indicative of a very specifically Muslim body designated and produced as the object of torture. The forced poses of mimicked sexual acts that characterize the abuses not only at Abu Ghraib but other recent accounts of torture are both produced and received in reference to racializing discourses: "This kind of torture directed at the supposed Muslim terrorist is not only subject to the normalizing knowledges of modernity that mark him (or her) both as sexually conservative, modest, and fearful of nudity (and it is interesting how this conceptualization is rendered both sympathetically and as a problem) as well as queer, animalistic, barbarian, and unable to control (his) or her urges."[21] Obviously at the heart of such a torture is the visual exposure of what is hailed as a Muslim body—and even further, the constitution of a specific kind of Muslim body through rendering it visible. Technologies used to produce and highlight visibility, such as the photography at Abu Ghraib, are thus serving several mutually reinforcing purposes in torture scenarios: the photography simultaneously documents the torture, serves as a technique of torture, and imagines the specificity of the body that will be/ is being tortured. Simultaneously, and through these various functions, the imaginary line between documentation and representation is blurred and the function of photography becomes—or is revealed as—indeterminate.

Thus, rather than looking at the racial profiling that has been so integral to the use of surveillance in the visual production of racialized bodies, we can use these narratives of torture both within and outside of cinema to examine what is both an indeterminacy and a *circularity* to the process and how the intersection of visual surveillance and torture have become so central to that circularity: visual surveillance marks bodies who will then become objects of torture, who are in turn re-produced as visible through acts of torture. This circularity constitutes the kind of spaces—be they narrative spaces or political spaces—in which we see the possibility and desirability of torture find a home. These spaces, characterized as they are by circular logic and thus a certain liminality, are not dissimilar to Agamben's zones of indistinction and the subject formations such zones allow for and describe.

*   *   *

In order to illustrate how surveillance serves to produce a cinematic narrative space that functions as a zone of indistinction—and how such a zone is a condition intimately related to the racializing function of contemporary torture and its mediations—it is helpful to return to the use of surveillance in *Saw* in what at first glance appears as a variation of the voyeuristic stalking recognizable from the slasher films that defined the horror genre for many years. But a more involved analysis of the narrative function of these many sequences demonstrates that they represent not simply the suspense-building *repetition* of a predatory gaze, but also a *proliferation* that problematizes an understanding of the surveillant gaze in horror as "simply" predatory.

As mentioned above, Jigsaw's identity is withheld until the last moments of the first film, but over the course of the narrative, we are presented with several possible suspects, and this accumulation of suspects is explicitly aligned with an accumulation of scenes of surveillance and several different predatory gazes, some of which turn out not to be predatory at all. Additionally, multiple characters are established, seemingly, as victims through their subjection to a surveillant gaze or to the video and audio recordings of Jigsaw's moral discourse/game instructions. It is thus surveillance, surveillance technologies, and the positioning of characters in relation to surveillance that produce characters in *Saw* as part of the aforementioned ambiguity around guilt/innocence. For instance, Danny Glover plays a police officer on Jigsaw's trail: at some point in the film he is revealed to be running an individual surveillance operation that is marked as pathological rather than legal. Holed up alone in a dilapidated apartment, mumbling to himself, and surrounded by newspaper clippings about the Jigsaw murders, the detective engages in both binocular and video surveillance that is coded as obsessively crackpotish, and is clearly not officially sanctioned. For the purposes of the narrative, this character, aptly named Detective Tapp, is shifted in his role from investigator to suspect by virtue of his operation of surveillance. Zep (Michael Emerson), a hospital orderly who has already been characterized as suspicious, is seemingly "found guilty" as the killer when we see him operating a complex video surveillance system monitoring the two victims at the center of the film, the men trapped in the bathroom; however, Zep is also the target of Detective Tapp's suspicious scene of surveillance, possibly legitimizing Tapp's surveillance operation or clearing Zep as a suspect, or neither. And through flashback it is revealed that while the two men trapped together in the bathroom are initially presented as strangers to each other, Adam (Leigh Whannell) had been following and taking surveillance photos of the other, Dr. Gordon (Cary Elwes). The question of whether Adam is now implicated as a suspect or remains a victim of the scenario is rendered unclear by his surveillant acts. The film's climax reveals that none of these people are actually Jigsaw, and all of those who appear to be suspects are themselves pawns or victims, suffering their own fates at Jigsaw's hands; even so, these and other moments that posit the victims as less than completely innocent also function in some small way to legitimize their selection for torture.

Not only is there a guilt and a pathology associated with the operation of surveillance technology here, but more significantly it is surveillance that is used repeatedly as the plot device that blurs the distinction between who is the subject or object of the games of torture and establishes the victims as themselves guilty of *something*. To point out that this reverses the general forensic point of surveillance—which is to establish guilt (or innocence) on the side of the surveilled subjects—is clear. But what is significant is that the narrative structure of the horror, as well as the torturous choices that the victims must make, becomes wrapped up not with a sadistically voyeuristic or panoptic model, but with blurred boundaries, the production of ambiguity, and the formation of what I would suggest are narrative zones of indistinction through the introduction of surveillance technologies and practices. More simply put, there is a turn here away from the classic horror formulation that "someone is being watched and there is danger there," to "someone is being videotaped, and we don't quite know what it means, who is operating the technology, and what the association with that technology implies."

Video surveillance technology is used to similar effect in several other films from the torture porn subgenre. *Captivity* (Roland Joffé, 2007), for instance, represents a return to the psychosexual slasher film, but with an explicitly torture-focused scenario that emerged as part of the postmillennial surge in that subgenre; as such the video surveillance technology follows a trajectory that demonstrates how even the most "traditional" formulation of surveillance within a sadistic voyeuristic model becomes necessarily complicated by the indistinctions circulating through video. The film's first segment presents a young model as she is stalked—this stalking is presented through and as a video camera point-of-view shot, a clear harkening back to Michael Powell's *Peeping Tom*, which has been a defining instance for discussions of the coincidence between moving-image technologies and psychosexual violence. But just as I have argued in an earlier essay that the use of the small-format camera in Powell's film fails to produce clear subject/object relations, the multiple incorporations of video technology within *Captivity* serve to complicate the sadistic voyeur trope even as they remain central to the torture scenario.[22] After the abduction of the female target of the video point-of-view shot, Jennifer (Elisha Cuthbert), the majority of the film takes place in the torture chamber, which is outfitted with myriad forms of surveillance technologies, including video monitors, two-way mirrors, and audio microphones, as well as video screens for playback.[23] The narrative unfolds as Jennifer is subjected to a series of terror-inducing experiences and what appears to be physical torture. However, much as within *Saw* the surveillance technology is used to *mis*lead, here as well the video is also primarily used as *representation* to heighten her confusion and fear, rather than as only a methodology of voyeuristic excess or as a monitoring tool. She is, for example, shown a video of a prior victim, strapped down exactly as she is, while acid is poured on her face. The same process unfolds for Jennifer in the present, with a spigot beginning to pour the same ominous liquid as that on the video. Jennifer thus experiences the video as a kind of anticipatory mirror, showing her what she is going to experience just moments into the future. But the liquid we see pouring onto Jennifer turns out not to be acid: after a fade to black, she awakens with bloody bandages on her face, but discovers as she peels them off that she is physically unharmed.

These "games" grow even more complex as another captive is introduced into the scene: Gary (Daniel Gillies), a young man, from whom at first she is physically separated and who is also surveilled on video by the as yet unidentified watcher. The romance and sexual encounter that develops is captured and enjoyed via video surveillance by a wine-drinking, but as yet unidentifiable, figure. Rather than the surveillance constituting another level of voyeuristic enjoyment for the lone director of this basement play, it turns out that Jennifer's new romantic interest is a co-conspirator, and the entire development of the traditional heterosexual romance narrative between the two captives is in fact part and parcel of the torture and surveillance—a manipulation. Video once again moves firmly into the role of *representation* that stands outside its understanding within a surveillance logic as a method of pure documentation. And though it appears that video as representation still performs a disciplinary role, it seems clear that it can do so only by virtue of its status as a highly ambiguous form. *Vacancy* (Nimród Antal, 2007) builds its narrative in the reverse trajectory but toward the same end: the realization from two motel guests that the videos in their room are not just disturbing horror films left for their entertainment, but documents of prior violent murders in their motel room that serve to escalate their fear as they become the objects of the production of a new "snuff" video.

The snuff film premise, which has numerous connections to the torture subgenre, is also common and can be found in such varying forms as *My Little Eye* (Marc Evans, 2002) and the ensemble film *V/H/S* (multiple directors, 2012). Though neither are representative of torture porn per se, they both indicate different ways in which video surveillance works in the production of a functional ambiguity that is essential for different torture scenarios. For instance, both films use videotapes to generate confusion for the characters (and occasionally for the audience) as to the status of the images as reality or fictional representation, and this ambiguity often serves to define the moments of horror as in *Captivity* and *Vacancy*. *My Little Eye* extends this to the digital era through the premise of a (faked) internet reality show and a filmic narrative structured in the form of such a reality show. The film makes surveillance even more integral by presenting virtually the entire narrative through video surveillance point-of-view shots—the *Big Brother*-or *Real World*-styled show turns out to be a sadistic game in which the contestants are psychologically tortured and eventually killed.[24] With such centralization of surveillance in both form and content, the ambiguities and contradictions multiply: the characters are told they are being broadcast to millions through the internet, but it turns out the video signals are merely going to a private server; certain characters appear to switch back and forth between victim and conspirator; finally, and perhaps most significantly, though we are insistently presented with surveillance video point-of-view shots, the film never reveals who is watching or orchestrating this sadistic spectacle. The surveillance becomes a question that is never answered. Ultimately of course it is us—the film's audience—who are actually watching, and the surveillance point-of-view shots thus also indicate a lack of distinction between the surveillance, the sadists who have organized this scenario, and the cinematic spectator; this in turn suggests a lack of distinction between the surveillance cameras and the film's cameras, between the surveillant gaze and the cinematic.

The reflexive structure of *My Little Eye*'s narrative serves to render all of these ambiguities in exaggerated form. Even in the less explicitly self-referential narratives, scenes of surveillance tend to produce a narrative that appears ambiguous and open to interpretation (perhaps a more sinister version of what Umberto Eco described in literature as an "open text").[25] Surveillance figures centrally in torture-themed horror as an organizational model predicated on the production of uncertainty, ambiguity, instability. But while these narrative effects might well produce a degree of openness to spectator interpretation, they also serve to delimit the narrative space of surveillance as a *zone* of indistinction that often functions alongside the narrative logic of torture in ways that are indicative of the contemporary integrations of surveillance and political violence. Extrapolated to Dietmar Kammerer's broader account of how Hollywood surveillance narratives are related to video surveillance practices, the notion of the surveillance narrative as a zone of indistinction offers more shape to one of his essay's concluding points: "It is not a question of 'conspiracy' or 'complicity' but rather of 'complication' and 'complexity.'"[26] What *is* clear is that the generic and subgeneric parameters of horror have at least in small part been defined and redefined by the function that surveillance has within the narrative. It is thus perhaps to be expected that the recent comedy-horror *Cabin in the Woods* (Drew Goddard, 2012), a metanarrative that bases its satire on the generic construction of horror films, suggests the production of horror narrative to be predicated on an elaborate surveillance and control operation designed to placate ancient gods. The video surveillance is used to monitor the subjects of this "ritual" and to facilitate the subgeneric choices (zombie, ghost, axe murderer?) determining how the victims will meet their ends, and thus serves as a testament to the degree to which the multiple cultural codes of horror have become intertwined with a surveillant structure that is itself operating on multiple structuring (and destructuring) levels.

However, while "ambiguity" or "reflexivity" may well describe certain aspects of what I am describing as zones of indistinction within cinematic narrative, neither is an exact synonym for indistinction in Agamben's sense. The type of formation I am referring to, of which ambiguity is only a part, would be more accurately described as the liminal space that emerges when contradictory states exist simultaneously and often as mutually defining. For instance, Agamben speaks of the "originary zone of indistinction" in the figure of *homo sacer*—excluded from the law, but simultaneously included by virtue of his exclusion. This formulation (which is of necessity offered here in shorthand) is in both form and effect rhetorical, structural, political, and *violent*—in fact, it shows how integrated all of those aspects are in certain formations of power. What I am calling *narrative* zones of indistinction in these films are ambiguities or paradoxes that structure the codefinition and contingencies of surveillance as trope, form, function, technology, and, ultimately, politics.

The insistent use of video and televisual surveillance in torture porn highlights some of the structural specificity of narrative zones of indistinction, and demonstrates why such zones of indistinction figure centrally in torture porn narratives. The second *Saw* film, for instance, pivots on the indistinction between past and present that is constructed out of video's use as both live transmission and prerecorded representation.[27] *Saw II* organizes its entire torturous narrative around a policeman watching his son on closed-circuit television attempt to survive various tests in a house along with other victims. Late in the film it turns out that this is not *live* CCTV, but a recorded video, and the "test"/torture is not the son's, but the detective's. And here, in the particular uses of video, we are provided with a clearer sense of how a zone of indistinction does not refer simply to a misrecognition or an ambiguity, but to something that is also fundamentally, ontologically indistinct. The video is a live event, as it unfolds for the police officer and the film's audience—but it is also a past event, both within the narrative and, again, for the spectator. The power of the video within the narrative is in these very zones of indistinction.[28]

What become the multiple, endlessly repeatable narrative "resolutions" foreground why the political formation of "zones of indistinction" is apt for a discussion of these films: the indistinctions produced by surveillance in all of the above films are almost necessarily punctuated by acts of incredible violence, illustrating how the cinematic incorporation of surveillance here relies on the logic of torture for both narrative and ideological structure. The closing montage sequence of the first *Saw* film is particularly instructive. The sequence serves to organize all the prior narrative incoherence in a crescendo of violence in both content and form: as Jigsaw's identity is finally revealed, a series of increasingly fast cuts joins together prior scenes of investigation and violence until a door is literally slammed on the narrative and the credits appear. All the prior ambiguities are revealed as manipulations organized by Jigsaw, and the "truth" of the various characters' positions is demonstrated here not only by the more traditional narrative revelation of the "real" killer, but also stylistically. The high-speed reintroduction and reorganization of a series of images represents the production of narrative clarity: but it is more than incidental that this ostensible clarity is offered through a violent collision of the film's earlier images. The very provisional narrative closure and the production of clearly defined subject positions—the sense and sensibility that are produced here—are much more about the systematic reproduction of violence than about narrative resolution. Or, more to the point, the resolution here requires violence reorganized into, and as, a system. This system, of course, demands a sequel. It is thus both intra- and extradiegetically that these films signify power through the production of torture not as resolution, but as repetition and proliferation.

The point here is not simply that surveillance becomes a part of the torture, which is also very much the case, but that the narrative formation around surveillance *asks* for torture, hailing it in order to turn narrative zones of indistinction into accumulating deployments of power. John Turner has suggested that films frequently "integrate the use of surveillance as a narratival device to promote suspense and, subsequently, violence," and thus demonstrates the narrative relations between sur-veillance and violence even outside of horror.[29] And while I agree that surveillance serves to build suspense, I am less concerned here with its use in the *Saw* films (and other torture porn) as what Turner calls a "harbinger" of violence, and instead focus on how surveillance as zone of indistinction becomes the *condition of possibility* for the torture to serve the purposes it does: as organization, as meaning, and as a nar-rative resolution defined by the possibility of repetition. It is this last aspect that indicates another significant element of why the ostensibly apolitical torture of the *Saw* films must be read politically: the systematic repetition and proliferation of violence defines not just a "serial killer"; in this case, it also defines Jigsaw's games, the narrative organization of the films, and the production of these films as a media franchise. Jigsaw's character occupies the films not as the lone pervert of *Psycho* or the figure of indestructible and abject evil represented by Michael Myers or Jason in the *Halloween* or *Friday the 13th* series, but most fully as the organizational principle of generic production around torture in contemporary horror. As such, Jigsaw's games become not merely ex-pressions of violent pathology, but an integrated system of surveillance and torture that bears greater similarity to organized political power and violence than the perversity of a cinematic monster.

This political interpretation is furthered by Jigsaw's yammering bio-moral lectures that serve to structure the films, the games, and even the devices of torture that are ritualistically reproduced by the *Saw* se-ries. While there are occasional references to the pathological origins of Jigsaw's (and his followers') murderous motivations, the films and the games within the films are dominated by discourse on what con-stitutes a life that matters. Paired with their immense popularity in a decade politically and culturally saturated by the "war on terror," they resonate with analyses of biopolitical power formations. The narrative power of the games in *Saw* works as an (albeit over-the-top) parallel to Agamben's increasingly apt account of sovereign and contemporary state power insofar as all are defined by their ability to designate subjects as "bare life." Certainly outside of the cinema, it has become increas-ingly hard to ignore the indistinctions between the functioning of the U.S. war on terror and the exercise of sovereign power given the 2012 disclosure that U.S. president Barack Obama has taken it upon himself *personally* to pass judgment on who will be subject to assassination by drone and, redefining the rule of law, "has reserved to himself the final *moral* calculation."[30]

Beyond the fact that such films evidence the popular resonance of the biopolitical formulation of power embodied by the current U.S. president, their narrative organization must be taken into account to fully understand the relevance of torture-porn film to Agamben's argument that the state of exception "tends increasingly to appear as the dominant paradigm of government in contemporary politics."[31] The zones of indistinction that characterize and manifest the state of exception are essential to the current practices of torture employed by the United States, exemplified by the detention center for suspected terrorists at Guantanamo Bay and the designation of CIA "black sites" within other nations. These literal zones of indistinction where torture occurs are inseparable from the state of exception around surveillance introduced in the U.S. by the Patriot Act, and thus represent a correlation between the form of surveillance tropes in torture narratives and the very real ways surveillance and torture are tied together within current legal and political discourses. The Patriot Act, passed by the United States Congress in 2002 (as well as the more recent National Defense Authorization Act for 2012) is primarily known for its creation of an extralegal space for an expansion of surveillance and detention, and is cited by Agamben as exemplary of the state of exception.[32] The discursive production of the already ambiguously situated political/legal Patriot Act in the service of the (now endless) state of exception known as the "war on terror" ends up also producing indistinction between the space of extralegal surveillance and the production of suspects without legal rights, targeted for indefinite detention and torture. Just as the torture serves to resolve and repeat the zones of indistinction produced by surveillance within the cinematic narratives under discussion, so the designation of suspects for detention and torture by the Patriot Act produces a justification for the surveillance that has designated them as suspects in the first place. The zones of indistinction, both narratively and politically, demonstrate that the ambiguities produced by surveillance do not serve to undermine the logic of the use of torture, but create a space where torture is what "makes sense" out of the system.

Thus, at the risk of overestimating the ideological value of these films, there is certainly sufficient rhetorical and political motivation to view the zones of indistinction around surveillance in *Saw* as crucially tied to the film's primary narrative construction around the production/elimination of a life through structural games of torture. And it is not necessary to argue that there is any *direct* parallel between Jigsaw's use of the games in *Saw* to designate "subjects" that must consider the meaning of their lives by exposure to torture and death—making decisions about both their value systems and their very bodies in attempts to escape from various deadly contraptions—and Agamben's discussion of how the designation of "bare life" by a sovereign can be thought of as "something like the originary 'political' relation."[33] The intentionally apolitical torture film has proven exceptionally marketable at the same time that surveillance and torture have expanded within the state of exception of the United States' "war on terror." This state of exception is the political context for torture-porn cinema; in the world of these films, much like in the actual "war on terror," "The first foundation of political life is a life that may be killed, which is politicized through its very capacity to be killed."[34]

This is to say that insofar as the *Saw* films narrate torture as an ideological project that defines lives that matter by designating life to be exposed to death, they are definitionally operating in a highly political sphere. But it is important to deemphasize Jigsaw's selection of victims as the film's construction of a political relation, with him in the role of sovereign and his victim as subject produced as "bare life." It is, more significantly, the narrative formation—which combines the ambiguity and indistinction of surveillance and mediation with Jigsaw's ideological discourse and the presentation of extreme, graphic violence—that produces for the films' spectator a sense of who onscreen is deserving of life, and thus is indicative of the kind of (de)structuring relationships upon which biopolitical violence is predicated, and out of which it emerges. The indistinctions of the narrative ambiguities are just as central to an interpretation of these films as biopolitical as the explicitly ideological discourse of Jigsaw, the film's representative of power. What might in other generic examples appear as the use of a surveillance trope to promote suspense—a narrative temporality defined by deferral—in torture films functions in many ways as *spatial*—a zone of indistinction between guilt and innocence, subject and object, representation and reality, life and death. Even the temporal function of surveillance within narrative is also subject to the space of indistinction, with present and past rendered as simultaneous, and resolution as simply the possibility of repetition. This is the narrative space of torture, and the generic formation of torture porn. Thus the selection of victims by Jigsaw is only part of the biopolitical formation: the torture, the surveillance, and the narrative all function together in the films as biopolitical technologies serving to produce and sort out "bare life."

And certainly it is not only Agamben's philosophy, nor the concept of zones of indistinction, that describe how the mechanism of torture is predicated on indeterminacy. As Elaine Scarry writes in her seminal discussion of torture in *The Body in Pain*, "[I]t is . . . precisely because the reality of [a regime's] power is so highly contestable, the regime so unstable, that torture is being used."[35] Similarly, a surveillance culture, far from serving as a highly controlled deployment of political power, is both producing and reflecting such deeply unstable zones of representational, temporal, technological, and ultimately political indistinctions that torture becomes the mode through which power realizes itself. Stated somewhat differently, and as the closing montage of the first *Saw* film forcefully demonstrates, surveillance in both cinematic narrative and contemporary politics serves primarily to precipitate a kind of consolidating violence that will provide a definitive meaning to that surveillance. Surveillance theorist Sean Hier's analysis of urban surveillance and CCTV argues a parallel point about discourses of social order and disorder. Rereading Foucault in combination with recent work on the Lacanian "Real," Hier describes a number of instances in which the discourses around CCTV serve to develop a series of projections in which a "sense of social order" is constituted "through the visualization of social disorder."[36] He suggests how the culture around surveillance (in large part the media coverage of surveillance, of which I would argue surveillance narratives are a part) "can be understood to incite emotive conditions for the imaginary constitution of a disorderly social world."[37] This account of the affective politics of CCTV discourse, though a differing theoretical model, describes yet another framework in which the conceit of stability is produced out of representational instability, certainty out of ambiguity.

The temporal ambiguities in torture porn demonstrate how some of the technological indistinctions of video surveillance have a direct relationship to the production of "bare life" as reified power: the "liveness" of an event is produced by the terrible presence of a body in pain, a fight for survival, or the moment of death. As Agamben argues in *Homo Sacer*, "Until a completely new politics . . . is at hand . . . the 'beautiful day' of life will be given citizenship only either through blood or death or in the perfect senselessness to which the society of the spectacle condemns it."[38] The *Saw* series hyperbolically reflects how "blood and death" and the "society of the spectacle" are not just parallel options, but contiguous formations: as the bodily violence repeatedly resolves the narrative ambiguities accumulating around the proliferation of surveillance and video technology, blood and death give a horrible grounding sense—and sensation—to the senselessness of rampant and incoherent specularity.

*   *   *

It is the way that both torture and surveillance practices in contemporary politics are racially inflected that further makes the narrativized apolitical and presumably non- and/or postracial representations of the torture and surveillance narratives discussed thus far so clearly a disavowal and a fantasy. The films, both in their narratives and at times in critical analysis, posit a universalizing and even liberatory human experience through the reduction to a pure biology of pain and survival. But, as noted above in regard to the torture at Abu Ghraib, the surveillance that is so central to how these narratives of torture are produced cannot help but lead back to a visual field that is actively engaged in the coding of bodies as racialized and gendered such that violence may be enacted upon those bodies.

This would seem to be a sweepingly negative statement about the relations between surveillance culture and forms of political violence, and to a great degree it does characterize the implications of the narrative structure at the heart of the American torture films. However, it is worthwhile, if not necessarily hopeful, to note that these surveillance models and their resulting formations of violence can also complicate and unravel the functioning of such ideological and political projects, even as the narrative incorporation of video is very similar. A film such as Michael Haneke's *Caché* (2005) makes this clear through its explicit emphasis on the narrative indeterminacies of video surveillance within a cinematic space.

* * *

Caché could be considered to have a somewhat tenuous relationship to the wave of American torture films discussed thus far. However, Haneke's earlier films such as *Benny's Video* (1992) and *Funny Games* (1997) can easily be seen as the artsy predecessors of the American horror market in the first decade of the twenty-first century—a point driven home by the release of the American remake of *Funny Games* in 2007, directed by Haneke himself, and making the earlier films now retroactively inseparable from the trends in American film of the following decade. *Benny's Video* and *Funny Games*, both in their own ways, intermingle video surveillance and representation with traumatic, graphic violence and point in some highly revealing ways to the use of video as a methodology of torture and a means of exaggerating cinematic violences. But *Caché*, with its much more subtle meditation on video surveillance as aggression, constructs a narrative space that reveals how the implicit politics of the American torture narratives become more explicitly postcolonial and racializing. *Caché* reveals the political and racial disavowals at the heart of the films discussed above (as well as Haneke's earlier films), and shows how subjective, political, narrative, and even generic formations are working through each other in surveillance models.

Caché tells the story of a bourgeois host of a literary television show and his family who are sent surveillance videos of their home with no clear origin or agenda. For a variety of reasons, some seemingly internal to his own guilty associations, the TV host, Georges (Daniel Auteuil), suspects he is being targeted by an Algerian French youth from his childhood, Majid (Maurice Bénichou), whom Georges's family was considering adopting until Georges caused him to be sent away with manipulative lies. Georges tracks down the now-grown Majid and violently accuses him of the present video aggressions; Majid compellingly asserts his own innocence, as does his adult son (Walid Afkir). The spectator's growing view of Majid as now the victim of Georges is somewhat complicated by Georges's later receipt of a videotape that recorded the encounter between Georges and Majid at Majid's apartment.

This confusion extends through the remainder of the film and not only remains narratively and affectively unresolved, but grows increasingly more complex. The narrative indeterminacies are, however, almost secondary to the extended visual indeterminacies that set up the film and continue throughout, resulting in what Thomas Levin characterizes as "the nervous and unsettling quality of what could be described as a *panoptic undecidability.*"[39]

Film scholar Ara Osterweil's account of the opening shot describes how quickly *Caché* introduces its complex visual affect, which is primarily associated with an inappropriately surveillant look: "Filmed with a static camera, uninterrupted by editing, and lingering longer than most viewers are accustomed to, this mysteriously ominous glimpse of French street life immediately sets the mood that is the hallmark of Haneke's work: discomfort, suspicion, anxiety."[40] It turns out that we are watching not just the film's establishing shot, but a video within the film; the film's opening shot is revealed—through a sudden fast-forwarding—to be the videotape that Georges and his wife, Anne (Juliette Binoche), are watching after it has been mysteriously delivered to them. Critic D. I. Grossvogel describes further indeterminacies established by the film's opening: "Only after this single take lasting nearly three minutes are we made aware that we are not *outside* the house but *inside* the Laurents' television room, looking with them at the first tape."[41] The purpose and obviousness of what is usually considering an "establishing shot" of a film's setting is undermined by duration (long take), temporal manipulation (fast-forwarding and rewinding), and the confusion of spatial parameters (outside is inside). The film's opening here shows how the temporal indistinctions particular to video surveillance can emerge as contingent with spatial ones, and sets the terms for the way that the introduction of video surveillance immediately destabilizes coherent or defined structures through the indistinctions raised by narrative and visual interpenetrations.

The spatio-temporal indistinctions introduced by the film, both in this opening and as they develop throughout the film, are inextricable from its presentation of unstable subject positions, especially as established through surveillance and mediation. As Levin suggests (adding to the layers of reversibility and indeterminacy already apparent in the film's opening), "One could say that what we see in the first scene of *Caché* is somebody discovering by watching the fact that they are being watched."[42] These uses of video technology produce indeterminate narrative effects and affects that refer back to the systems of torture in the *Saw* series, connecting the American series' solipsistic and self-contained scenarios to the more explicitly politicized implications of Haneke's film. *Caché*, importantly, makes all of the questions and indistinctions that emerged in the *Saw* series more explicit by removing explication: guilt and innocence, temporal ambiguity, and the momentary resolution of graphic violence—all figure in this film as centrally as in the torture porn examples, but without the ostensible clarity provided by the more traditional narrative structures of the American films. The narrative zones of indistinction become defining and unresolved, and tied to subject formation on multiple levels, especially as understood through the visuality and visibility specific to video surveillance. Because *Caché* has a tremendously complex unfolding of affect and politics based in what is in some ways a profoundly simple plot formation, it provides a space to explore how the *Saw* films are indicative of larger political formations—formations that either began as or have become racialized in quite specific ways.

One of the crucial aspects of the way video functions in *Caché* is how it provides both the instability and the punctuation of the film—and how this punctuation is not definitional and organizational, but instead elliptical and circular. The opening scene sets the terms for this: not only do we not know who is watching or why someone is being watched, but it is also unclear what the technology is that is producing the image, and whether that technology is intra- or extradiegetic. The inside/outside boundary permeated by the incorporation of video is not simply that of the Laurent's house, but the narrative space of the film. At first we think we are watching "the film," which of course we always are, but then it turns out that we are (narratively, as well as technologically) watching the video within the film.[43] This use of video surveillance dissolves borders between representation and surveillance, interior and exterior, film and video and so on, and demonstrates how simple it is for the inclusion of video surveillance to constitute cinematic narrative as a zone of indistinction. What in *Saw* is a narrative feint—are we watching this live or is it recorded, and what does it mean that a character is conducting surveillance?—is similarly deployed in *Caché* through this opening long take, but here also produces an indistinction between whether we are watching this film or a video within the film, and whether the POV is subjective, technologized, or omniscient. This will be repeated in the film's closing shot, which not only refuses to resolve the question of who or what is watching, but also whether the look is a threat. *Saw*'s unstable narrative could be considered simply (and perhaps unintentionally) incoherent and *Caché*'s narrative more meaningfully ambiguous, but it is not just coincidence that they both produce narrative space as a zone of indistinction in a way that is inseparable from video's unclear status as representation or contemporaneous surveillance. In *Saw* the temporal ambiguity opens up the space for—even demands—torture as a wishfully ahistorical call to presence through bodily violence. But as we will see below, in *Caché* the ambiguous temporality introduced by the video calls attention to the historical productions of both pathological and political violence.

The punctuating moment in the opening sequence—when the tape begins to fast-forward and we realize we are watching video—provides an answer of sorts to the questions raised by the extended length of the opening take.[44] But it also raises more questions and begins a circuit and accumulation of videos with implicit and explicit references to graphic violence. The repeated video punctuations continue to structure the narrative with contradictions and ambiguities. The Laurents receive more tapes, along with drawings made in a childlike scrawl (which indicate to Georges that Majid has sent the tapes, insofar as they seem to reference the lies Georges told about him when he was a boy), continuing the thread of the mystery amid Georges's growing agitation and providing a narrative defined more by anxiety than suspense. The next unmistakable moment of narrative punctuation occurs when Majid kills himself in front of Georges during Georges's second aggressive visit to the now increasingly beleaguered seeming Majid. But, as Osterweil succinctly puts it, "When a videotape of this clandestine meeting is sent to Anne and Georges's television producer, all bets are off."[45] Shown twice—first from Georges's subjective position, and then from the perspective of what was apparently a hidden video camera—the suicide exemplifies how video surveillance and graphic violence work together to process zones of indistinction in a different manner than that of American torture porn. "On the one hand, the footage, which shows Georges as a belligerent, threatening presence, is a potentially incriminating piece of evidence that calls into question the audience's (and Anne's) initial assumptions about the true identity of the victimizer. On the other hand, the very fact that a tape has been made by a hidden camera within his low-rent flat suggests the impossibility of Majid's innocence."[46] Here, the violence does not serve to even momentarily resolve the slippages of culpability and narrative coherence produced by the video, but to produce more, and to do so in conjunction with the surveillance and re-presentation of this moment. Majid's suicide would seem to place an almost primordial guilt firmly on the side of Georges, in both his past and present aggressions against the Algerian. His sudden cutting of his own throat is so affectively shocking to both Georges and the film's spectator that the entire pace and tenor of the film is ruptured at this point into a moment of horrible presence. However, the implication that somewhere in Majid's apartment there is a hidden surveillance camera capturing the whole encounter on tape would seem to prove him guilty in the sequence of video aggressions against Georges that led to this moment. Once again, the introduction of video has established everyone and no one as both guilty and innocent. While in *Saw* and other torture-porn films the violence is presented as a moment of clarity defined by either survival or death, here that moment of clarity is merely reintroduced into the video gaze to highlight the circuit of violence and surveillance that is fundamentally unstable and constantly recoded. In other words, as soon as the cinematic plot would seem to provide some clarity or even resolution, a videotape reemerges to circle the narrative back into a state of total questionability around subject positions and their relationship to enactments of violence.

The film's open-ended conclusion firmly establishes this as the defining formation of the entire narrative. Another long-take gaze, an extreme long shot (mirroring and circling back to the beginning of the film), presents us with Georges's teenage son (Lester Makedonsky) on the steps of his school. There he is approached by what appears to be Majid's son, and the two have a discussion, which we do not hear from the distanced position of visual surveillance. The camera's position is in fact so distant, and the action in front of it so seemingly incidental, that it is not entirely clear what we are watching—who the objects of the camera's (and our) gaze are—and it is easy to miss the encounter between the two boys entirely. If one does notice the meeting of the two boys, the initial question it raises about the possible relationship between them is quickly followed by another, perhaps more confounding question: if Majid's son is in front of the camera, and Majid is dead, with whom is this look from the video camera to be connected? Catherine Wheatley's work on *Caché* emphasizes how narratively irrecuperable its surveillant perspectives are: "One problem that poses itself is that the vast majority of the taped scenes are shot from seemingly 'impossible' angles: filmed from outside walls where bookcases stand, or from a position too high for a handycam operator unless they were standing very conspicuously on the roof of a car."[47] Thus what is repeatedly suggested to be a diegetic video camera within the film both isn't and can't be explained by diegetic means. At the end of the film, the ambiguity of all that had preceded finally announces itself as a kind of *impossibility*: the production of an apparently surveillant video gaze (and its corollary visual field), formally coded as a diegeticized, technologized "real," becomes also highly metaphorical and testament to the incoherence of the accumulated surveillant gazes. The video point-of-view shot is a recognizable visual code (voyeuristic, disciplinary, violent) that here decodes itself into abstraction.[48]

In this way the film ultimately offers up the surveillant gaze as both the primary structuring and destructuring force, suggesting that sur-

The final shot of *Caché* (2005) presents another ambiguously surveillant gaze.

veillance, even at its technological basis, often deconstructs its own premises. Video surveillance establishes nothing but its own codes, until another logic (in many cases a violent one) turns those codes into systems. Clive Norris and Gary Armstrong explore some real implications of this on the sociological and criminological level in their detailed study of closed-circuit television in the United Kingdom. With the U.K. deploying more video surveillance cameras than any other nation in the world, Norris and Armstrong note that on the most basic level, "While we are all increasingly under the camera's gaze, what this means in practice is that its implications for social control are dependent not so much on the cameras, but on their integration with other technologies, and the organizational environment in which they operate."[49] When compared to the functioning of a system of surveillance, the narrative abstraction away from the material realities of surveillance video in *Caché* appears not as a metaphor of a totalizing gaze but as a demonstration of the very real fact that surveillance technologies are not, on their own, systemic or even functional. Or, as Norris and Armstrong put it in relation to the putative panopticism of closed-circuit television: "The extent to which CCTV produces an 'automatic functioning of power' is questionable."[50] And yet to say that video surveillance becomes dispersed, abstracted, and metaphorized is not to say that surveillance is in itself "neutral" until it is applied—rather it is a non-system that accesses visual, social, and historical codes of power and violence. The non-system will often be resolved into a system through the repeated deployment of violence, as in the *Saw* films, or point back to its coding, as with *Caché*, in a manner that opens up multiple points of access to the violence of surveillance and of the surveilled situation: in this case the postcolonial European bourgeois family.

The violence against and within that familial space achieved a kind of crescendo in Haneke's 1997 *Funny Games*, the film that most explicitly connects the director's work to the American torture films by virtue of Haneke directing his own faithful remake for the American market in 2007. In these films, two teenage boys, coded by their matching tennis outfits and polite demeanor as privileged white youth, at first insinuate themselves into and eventually forcibly infiltrate an upper-middle-class white family's country home. They mount a campaign of psychological and physical violence, and finally murder the entire family (once again, a family composed of two parents with a single male child), one by one, in Haneke's characteristically shocking matter-of-fact style. Neither version contains explicitly narrativized surveillance and both are insistently limited to the bourgeois domestic space, but here also Haneke refuses to engage in a "straightforward" narrative of violence without reference to mediation and spectatorship. Occasional direct addresses to the film's audience from the perpetrators of the violence imply complicity on the part of the spectator in the unfolding of the scenario. And it is with the television blasting (almost as if it were a primary character in the scene) that the film reaches its horrifying pinnacle: the child of the family executed with a shotgun. What the spectator is offered visually in this scene, however, is not the boy being shot, but the blood-splattered television screen in the aftermath—a none too subtle connection between the television's images and the violence of the film we are watching. But even more notably, when one of the aggressors is surprisingly shot and killed, the film ruptures its already somewhat reflexive diegetic space entirely: the other perpetrator, traumatized at the death of his partner in crime, grabs a remote control and rewinds the film we are watching as if it were a videotape. Reclaiming mastery over the narrative, the boy takes the narrative back in time and "rescues" his partner from (prior, now erased) death, for the continuation of their "funny games." This rewinding is of course a similar gesture to that of the opening shot of *Caché*, when the otherwise cinematically realistic shot is interrupted by a fast-forwarding, reframing (literally) the narrative as a video narrative rather than a cinematic narrative. The gesture also similarly signifies the temporal instability of the video image discussed earlier. Here, however, there is no narrative explanation serving to recuperate this rupture back into narrative coherence: not only is video used to undermine a clear temporal location, but its invocation is now also used to undermine both visual and narrative realism.

Funny Games, in both its pre–and mid–torture porn incarnations, is clearly more invested in a direct critique of media violence than it is in the political complexity of circuits of surveillance (which is not to say that these are unrelated issues—the intersection between representation and surveillance is clearly central to this discussion). However, of greater interest is the casting of the scene of torturous violence as that of the highly mediated bourgeois home and the perpetrators of the violence not as outsiders to that environment, but themselves white, educated, "proper" young men. The way in which even a home invasion narrative is posited as one in which the invaders seem more like insiders than outsiders highlights how inherent this violence is to that domestic space.

In *Caché*, the brutality within the European bourgeois family unit that is at the heart of *Funny Games* (and virtually all of Haneke's films) assumes a more explicit focus about what some of that violence contains: the family unit is extended to reveal the repressed element—the "adopted" (colonized) North African who has simultaneously been implicated in and ejected from the white "family." The infantile, pathologized jealousy, guilt, perversity, and aggression that make up the personal narrative of *Caché* is also the circuit of racialized violence and projection of contemporary Europe in a postcolonial and now "post-9/11" era. Or, as Osterweil aptly sums up, "Haneke suggests that First-World talk of 'post'-colonialism involves denial and attempted self-exculpation—an effort to defend against any acknowledgement of continuing internal and international oppression and injustice."[51] The way these issues focalize around the video gaze and a lack of clarity about the origin, production, control, meaning, and use of the videotapes suggests not only how mediation functions to both produce and obscure the particularity of these social relations, but specifically the way that technologies of surveillance—so weighted with signification around power relations and the visibility of truth—become a point of access, if a violent one, to the circuit of projection and injustice around race in "post"-colonial Europe.

Haneke's 1992 film *Benny's Video* introduces racialization as a disavowed production of surveillant violence in almost the reverse direction, which proves illuminating for a reading of the structure of the later film. This film, which takes place not in France but in Austria, quietly tells the story of white, bourgeois teenager Benny (Arno Frisch), whose obsession with violent video imagery causes him to organize his life around video rentals, the repetitive viewing of a video recording showing his family's participation in the slaughter of a pig with an air gun, and the setting up of video cameras to monitor both the world outside his apartment window and within his darkened room. After inviting a young girl home from a video store with no clearly identifiable intent, Benny shoots her with the air gun in what seems like an only vaguely aggressive manner (they are playing a half-hearted game of dare with the gun when Benny impassively decides to fire). As she screams in pain and tries to crawl away, Benny struggles with her and then, in an apparent panic, reloads and shoots twice more until her screaming stops. The scene is presented largely as caught on his video camera, and eventually he shows the videotape to his parents, who, with stunned complicity, try to figure out how to manage it. As his father cleans up the mess, Benny's mother takes him on a subdued tourist expedition to Egypt, a "vacation" that serves to reframe the mediated events at home significantly. Although the televisual and videotape imagery is clearly the centerpiece of the film, and suggests, like *Funny Games*, a rather straightforward indictment of a contemporary culture so inundated with television violence that, as if by sleepwalking, Benny simply reproduces, it is the family's cover-up of the crime that marks the colonial production of race in those circumstances, one that does so in the interest of sustaining the bourgeois family unit.

It is the aftermath of the violence that is most telling in this regard—while the father buries the evidence of the murder, the son goes to Egypt with his mother and returns: tan, with a shaved head, and wearing a knit kufi. Benny's visual transformation remarkably shows how the sociopathic violence at the heart of the bourgeois European family has become cast as racial other during the cover-up, with a gesture as

Teenage sociopath Benny shows off his home surveillance project in Haneke's *Benny's Video* (1992).

direct as a vacation. Most simply, Benny's act of violence leads to his production—*visually*—as racialized other. While the television news shown earlier in the film focuses on the ethnic violence in collapsing Yugoslavia, here Benny is cast off and reemerges as a more particular remnant of western European ethnic violence. The danger within is sent abroad and returns, as if it had always come from there. What effectively becomes an erasure of the evidence of the crime within the narrative, also becomes an erasure of that erasure—the film's audience goes on vacation with Benny and his mother, while, as Brian Price and John Rhodes describe, "[t]he image of the father back home hovers as a potentiality. . . . To grant us the vision of the father's violence would be to privilege and restrict our understanding of violence to this gross corporeal display. By rendering Egypt in its isolation, Haneke asks us to consider violence in more nuanced terms, even to understand how cultural tourism itself—the desire to produce a picture of oneself in a culture not one's own—is itself an act of violence."[52] While this is already a powerful critique of the projection and disavowal of white European violence, the fact that Benny comes back from this trip and turns himself and his parents in to the police recasts the issue as a return of the repressed in the form of culpability.

Benny's visual coding as the colonized other brings the responsibility home to roost not because he *truly* represents the "other" that highlights the structural violence of his culture, but because he represents the very process of visual coding and recoding, as Price and Rhodes imply, that has marked the violent production of racialized subjects in colonial and postcolonial Europe: a production, as has so often been noted, tied both historically and experientially to mediated visibility. Frantz Fanon's famous account best communicates the violence in the circuits of visualization at the heart of the colonial enterprise, particularly in relation to mediation: "I cannot go to a film without seeing myself. I wait for me. In the interval, just before the film starts, I wait for me. The people in the theater are watching me, examining me, waiting for me."[53] The fact that for Fanon the experience of cinematic spectatorship is also an experience of the intensive surveillance of him as a racialized object highlights how even narrative cinema, a media form less associated with surveillance, becomes enmeshed in that project specifically through the production of race in the colonial context.

In *Caché*, we find visual coding, recoding, and, crucially, *decoding* operating far more explicitly as a function of the surveillant gaze, but with the racial and postcolonial issues more centralized. The repeated and ultimately unresolved introductions of the videotapes and video point-of-view shots as simultaneously accusatory, exculpatory, evidentiary, irrelevant and, finally, simply impossible, forces the issue: the idea of social identities and relations as produced by a visual-cultural field, particularly one defined by surveillance, makes sense only if we understand those productions as also irretrievably destabilized by that same visuality. Put simply, every time a video image appears in the film it undermines any prior stability of form or content offered by the narrative. Insofar as race is also often visually produced as a marker out of that same surveillant field, it too becomes a coded position that is here also decoded even as it is centered and centering in the zones of indistinction of modern politics and media.

* * *

To be clear, such narrative uses of video surveillance, and their relation to ambiguous designations of violence, guilt, and subject formation exceed the genre of horror and horror-adjacent, and further demonstrate the structural indeterminacy enacted by the cinematic use of video surveillance. Countless thrillers and crime/caper movies such as *Ocean's Twelve* (Stephen Soderbergh, 2004), *Femme Fatale* (Brian De Palma, 2002), and the earlier *Rising Sun* (Philip Kaufman, 1993), which I discuss in detail in Chapter Three, use the potential slippages between real-time surveillance and recorded video, or between documentation and representation, as the pivots upon which the plot turns. Other films focused on surveillance have, like Haneke's, used surveillant formations to open up their narrative to a series of thematic and structural meditations designed to foreground ambiguity and violence (and the ambiguity *of* violence). Andrea Arnold's *Red Road* (2006), for instance, focuses on a female CCTV operator within the United Kingdom, the nation, as mentioned above, with more CCTV cameras operating than anywhere else in the world. The film's central character, Jackie (Kate Dickie), develops an obsession with a man on her video screen: she follows him both with her cameras on the job and, after work hours, on foot. Were the gender roles reversed, the trope would read as suspense and automatically suggest the model of the voyeuristic predator; by reversing the more expected gender roles, *Red Road* decodes the received understanding of the voyeuristic model of surveillance narrative by highlighting that gendered subject positions determine that reading far more than the surveillance structure ever could—as it is, the film's spectator follows the follower with little understanding of the purpose, or even the affect, of the investigative gaze. At the end of the film it is revealed that the man Jackie has followed and now become involved with has recently been paroled for killing her husband and child while driving under the influence of drugs. What we now understand as a desperate and ambiguous vengeance mission, however, is complicated by her final admission that it is *she* who in fact feels responsible for the death of her family, having sent her husband out in the car after a fight. Not only does *Red Road* highlight the dynamics between gender and surveillance, but it shows that even a film explicitly about crime and punishment (and some of the very literal uses of video surveillance in contemporary law enforcement) uses the surveillance trope as the basis of ambiguity and indistinction. In fact, the narrative purpose of video surveillance seems, across genres and nations, to be more about the production of indistinctions between past and present, guilt and innocence, surveillance and mediation, watcher and watched than the basis of factual documentation or clearly mapped subject positions, whether they be racialized or gendered identities, or structural subject positions within narrative or juridical discourse.

* * *

In the end, that now clichéd phrase "caught on tape" appears deeply ironic. Both narratively and politically, video as surveillance ultimately "catches" nothing, but opens up spaces for a series of violences; some of these violences are those of surveillance and surveillant narration serving functions within a system of biopower, others demonstrate the use of surveillance and mediation as an assault on their stable integration into such a system. The narrative figuration of the *Saw* films suggests not only that video surveillance is part of the methodology of torture, but that the production of torture and the grounding function of the brutalized body is hailed as an endlessly repeatable (non)resolution to ambiguities within the field of surveillance. In a related formation, which is (somewhat frustratingly) neither "on the other hand" nor "similarly," *Caché* implies that the video surveillance model is so deeply unstable that when followed to its (il)logical conclusion, it deconstructs its own functions in a manner that also problematizes the political, technological, and narrative systems that intersect in the visual field of video surveillance.

The choice to read the ostensibly new genre of "torture porn" through reference to Haneke's work is a suggestion that the generic codes of cinema are not separate from the coding of subjects by and for video surveillance—this coding is itself a constant decoding. The narrative zones of indistinction that spatialize these codes offer a manifestation of recognizable boundaries; this manifestation in turn only points to interrelated systems that have no clear boundaries. Torture porn thus *must* be read as trans- and international, trans- and intergeneric, trans- and intertechnological, simply because the narrative formations of surveillance and torture insist on the production of boundaries only to blur them, and the introduction of indistinctions only to produce (un)stable resolutions. This is to say that despite the hyperbolic insistence on the recognizability of graphic, bloody torture as monitored and produced by video surveillance in American postmillennial horror, that very subject matter opens up to the complexity of the international political and media stages that are in fact the more literal (non)location of torture and surveillance in current times.

2

Commodified Surveillance

First-Person Cameras, the Internet, and Compulsive Documentation

The spectacle is the existing order's uninterrupted discourse about itself, its laudatory monologue.
—Guy Debord, The Society of the Spectacle[1]

As people share more, the timeline gets filled in more and more with what is happening with everything you're connected to. The pace of updates accelerates. This creates a continuous stream of information that delivers a deeper understanding for everyone participating in it. As this happens, people will no longer come to Facebook to consume a particular piece or type of content, but to consume and participate in the stream itself.
—Mark Zuckerberg, founder and CEO of Facebook[2]

Despite the historical understanding of surveillance as an instrument of institutional or political power, it is by now commonplace to note that surveillance—in practice, in representation, and in critical discourse—is no longer something that can be discussed in the mode of a purely unidirectional or top-down activity in which surveillance is something done *by* the state, the market, or the voyeuristic predator *to* the citizen, the consumer, or the victim. While it is certainly true that state authorities surveil individuals and that companies track consumer activity, the proliferation of these practices are attended by the corollary, though far from equal, production of citizens surveilling the state, consumers participating in the surveillance economy with their own surveillant behaviors, and individuals producing new practices and technologies to undermine and resist the economy of surveillance.[3]

Rather than this diffusion of and resistance to unidirectional surveillant activity necessarily serving to reduce the more traditional power models of surveillance, the dynamic play of surveillance has caused it to become increasingly definitional of contemporary culture. Similarly to Kevin Haggerty and Richard Ericson's remark in their introduction to *The New Politics of Surveillance and Visibility* that "[resistance] can foster a dynamic back and forth of evasion and official response that tends to ratchet up the overall level of surveillance and control," the supply of surveillance to a consumer market in an ever-expanding variety of forms has simultaneously made surveillance less exclusive to domains of institutional authority and reified surveillance as a structural component of daily life.[4]

Theorists of surveillance have addressed this proliferation in a variety of ways, both extending the critique of surveillance and at times recuperating surveillance as empowerment. "Synopticism," introduced into the conceptual framework by Thomas Mathieson in his 1997 essay "The Viewer Society," suggests that while in many cases the panoptic structure still describes much of modernity, increasingly there is also a synoptic structure in which the many watch the few.[5] David Lyon has furthered Mathieson's point, arguing more recently that "surveillance—which at its social and etymological core is about watching—is easily accepted because all sorts of watching have become commonplace within a 'viewer society,' encouraged by the culture of TV and cinema."[6] Such a generalized critique of a broadly scopophilic culture that bolsters the securitizing aspects of surveillance is also embraced by Christian Parenti in *The Soft Cage*, where he includes a chapter on "Voyeurism and Security Culture" in which he similarly suggests that an urge to gaze is pandered to and capitalized on. I have suggested in the opening chapter that such approaches problematically naturalize voyeurism, situating it at the level of human instinct. There are, however, also numerous examples of work that examines other aspects of the diversification of spectacle and surveillance, such as the essay by Hille Koskela on webcams that argues that the ability to broadcast oneself introduces a sense of power and agency that destabilizes, among other things, traditional gender roles; Caren Kaplan's work on the militarization of the consumer through the marketing of geoinformational technologies (which I discuss more fully in the following chapter); and most centrally for the current context, Mark

Andrejevic's analysis of the relation between the discourse of "interactivity" and surveillance, that as we will see below, intersects with cinematic narrative in some revealing ways.[7]

While Foucault's accounts of panopticism and discipline have been essential to critical thought on how surveillance functions, Guy Debord's discussion of the "society of the spectacle" is also necessary for an understanding of the commodification and consumption of surveillance as cultural form, particularly in its visual modes. On the most general level, Debord's text is a critique of twentieth-century commodity culture, and on what he himself describes as the most "superficial" level it is an evaluation of the role of mass media in that culture. However, his work defines and redefines the term such that "spectacle" exceeds a reference to television or film, and comes to signify the systemic social and political conditions organizing and organized by the construction of the world into visual representations. Debord's definition of spectacle as "not a collection of images, but a social relation among people, mediated by images," serves as a surprisingly lucid account of the dissemination of surveillance technologies and practices throughout consumer culture and their increasing coincidence with technologies and practices of representation that serve myriad interrelated purposes for the "average" consumer (ranging from mobile phone cameras to automobile GPS, reality programming to nanny-cams, online social media to parental control software), and demands that we consider the commodification of visibility as integral to the politics of surveillance.[8]

It is certainly clear that the saturation of film, television, computers, and other screen media reflects and produces a culture (in fact many different cultures) of spectatorship, broadly defined. Films such as *The Truman Show* (Peter Weir, 1998) and *EDtv* (Ron Howard, 1999), as well as science-fictional instances like *The Running Man* (Paul Michael Glasser, 1987) and the cinematic adaptation of *The Hunger Games* (Gary Ross, 2012) and its sequels, have taken up the issue of commodified surveillance as spectacle most explicitly by providing cinematic narration around the phenomenon of "reality TV." In its production of daily life as spectacle, reality programming is in many ways the most straightforward packaging of surveillance culture for a consumer market. Certainly such programming, as well as its cinematic representation, deserves (and has received) in-depth critical attention, and yet the cinematic narratives of such spectacle and spectatorship are weighted heavily toward reproducing "spectacle" in the sense of "a collection of images."[9] To explore fully the relations between surveillance and consumption, it is also crucial to examine the specificities of the "social relation" such images mediate. And even while spectatorship does not itself describe a single or clearly defined activity, "spectator" is not the only role a consumer plays in regards to the spectacle or other forms of commodified surveillance, particularly when "spectacle" (as images *and* as social relation) is being reframed by digital technologies and the redefinition of production and consumption in a digital economy. There has been and continues to be a great deal of variation within consumer-level surveillant activity, as well as the social relations and market politics manifested in such activity. As Debord states, "The oldest social specialization, the specialization of power, is at the root of the spectacle. The spectacle is thus a specialized activity which speaks for all the others."[10] This rather oblique comment implies that dynamics of social power are represented by and even organized through the mediation of spectacle, a description that appears even more apt if one considers the widespread diversification and commodification of surveillance technologies and practices for a consumer market.

Accordingly, cinematic representations of surveillance have incorporated the "everyday," consumer, or "peer-to-peer," side of surveillance practice into both aesthetics and narratives in ways that exceed and complicate references to a "viewer society." Most representative of consumer-operated surveillance in cinema is the rise of the "first-person-camera" narrative, made famous in 1999 by *The Blair Witch Project* (though earlier examples exist).[11] The first-person-camera film is both style and trope, characterized by the diegetic incorporation of (at least one) video camera into a feature-film narrative, with the entire film presented as shot through that camera. Usually the trope is attended by the strongly related conceit that the film is composed of "real" footage. The trend and success of these films has continued and expanded, most notably in the horror genre, with varying forms of diegeticized cameras and "found-footage" contexts. *Cloverfield* (Matt Reeves, 2008), *Diary of the Dead* (George A. Romero, 2007), *[REC]* (Jaume Balagueró and Paco Plaza, 2007) and its American remake *Quarantine* (John Eric Dowdle, 2008), *Home Movie* (Christopher Denham, 2008), and the *Paranormal*

Activity series (multiple directors, 2007–2014) are just a few of the *many* films that picked up where *Blair Witch* left off, and show the degree to which the torture trend in horror (and its surveillance aesthetic) discussed in the prior chapter has been matched by an equally strong trend toward incorporating the video gaze on the side of the protagonists and spectators.[12] The use of surveillance as part of the systematic structure of torture scenarios is here reorganized in equally violent form, but this time in a manner that more often than not represents violence toward the surveillant apparatus and its user.

These films incorporate first-person video style in several ways—as faux documentary or news footage (*Blair Witch Project*, *[REC]*, and *The Bay*), found amateur video (*Cloverfield* and *V/H/S* [multiple directors, 2012]), or amateur home surveillance (*Paranormal Activity*), among other narrative constructs.[13] While there are an extraordinary number of films that incorporate video footage as a small or large part of their narrative, what makes the first-person-camera films distinct is that they present such footage as the *only* point of access to the film—whether it is just one camera and one person behind the camera or multiple cameras and various footage edited together, these are films in which there is no camera that is outside the narrative context. What all the aforementioned films have in common is the look of an "amateur" or low-budget video production: frequently hand-held and thus unstable cameras and low-resolution images, all distinguished from a more "transparent," cinematic image.

The style of the first-person-camera film is intended to simulate the ubiquitous amateur video gaze provided by consumer electronics ranging from video cameras to mobile phone cameras and webcams, and either shared online through YouTube, Facebook, Vimeo, and a number of other internet forums, or presented on television as reality programming. What these films thus best represent is the increasing ubiquity of visual recording technologies in the hands of the "average" person and the drive to *record*, on such consumer-level technologies, virtually everything: to document, represent, share, and spectacularize the world as it unfolds before each individual. The films are essentially organized by a direct address to and from a cinematic spectator mediated by personal electronics. The first-person (or, more accurately, first-camera) gaze of the diegeticized video camera becomes the first-person perspective of the film's spectator, and reproduces what has now become a highly recognizable aesthetic of reality representation. Since these are narrative films that are usually shot on video (though many are filmed on professional equipment rather than the consumer-grade video of the diegetic camera through which we are supposedly looking), they also represent the convergence of "cinematic" representation (as a generic rather than a technical term) and surveillance at the level of technology. What the first-person-camera films offer is not just an aesthetic of the real as defined by contemporary forms of video representation (home video, reality TV, etc.), but an *identification* with the *process* of self-representation—a drive toward insistent documentation of one's experiences—that is one of the definitive elements of contemporary formations of surveillance, particularly in its consumer forms. Thus the realist and experiential claims of the films are themselves implicated in the structuring of subjectivity and surveillance as mutually defining.

The convergence of (self-)representation and surveillance is evidenced by the fact that a number of the first-person-camera films are also what I call "compulsive documentation" narratives, which suggest that recording technologies in the hands of consumers means (among many other things) that both ordinary and extraordinary events might increasingly be visually documented by "anyone," rather than surveillance and media representation existing solely as the domain of institutions, authorities, or production companies. Compulsive-documentation films demonstrate how any characterization of diffuse surveillance practice would be incomplete without an analysis of the multiplication of spectacle, the use of consumer video as representation, documentation, and surveillance, and thus the mingling of explicitly subjective perspectives with more traditionally "objective," evidentiary representational forms.[14]

Taking up Debord's account, John Turner has argued that spectacle and surveillance have become increasingly merged in pop culture, and examines the way that surveillance practice has become commodified as spectacle and entertainment in explicitly surveillance-themed films like *Enemy of the State* and *The Conversation*, films addressed elsewhere in this book.[15] The films under discussion in this chapter represent a slightly different form of this production of spectacle, centralizing the consumer as simultaneously a consumer and producer of surveillance, rather than just spectator, a formation best summed up by Christian Fuchs's analysis of the rise of the producer-consumer or "prosumer" in the internet economy.[16] And while the films that build their entire premises upon consumer-level video production and surveillance are predominantly in the horror genre, the incorporation of occasional video moments into narrative film spans genre and is equally likely to emerge in comedies ranging from *American Pie* (Paul Weitz, 1999) to *It's Complicated* (Nancy Meyers, 2009).

First-person-camera films, which organize their narrative around the production of the very images we are watching, represent perhaps the most overtly metacinematic or self-reflexive form of surveillance cinema, and thus are useful in thinking about the intersections of cinematic representation and surveillance that are less explicitly pronounced in other surveillance-themed films. But more centrally here, first-person-camera films indicate how formalized structures of surveillance are unthinkable without the dissemination of surveillant practice into the hands of consumers, who in turn forward surveillance as a marker of self through repetitive self-documentation and documentation of events around them from their subjective position. Even further, such documentation serves as an entry into contemporary forms of exchange and interaction that are inextricable from a surveillant economy, for better or for worse. This chapter reviews the common stylistic and narrative elements of first-person-camera films, and explains how this trend in narrative cinema is contiguous with practices of online self-documentation and their place in social networking sites, particularly the overarching example of Facebook, as well as broader trends in digital surveillance.

*   *   *

Arguably, online social networking is the most quotidian form of consumer, or peer-to-peer, surveillant activity, and is structured around producing artifacts of one's life as visible to, in the case of Facebook, one's "friends" (who may or may not be coincident with non-Facebook friends), and the monitoring of this information by others as a form of social interaction. As Fuchs has noted, the very functioning of a social networking site (as well as any user-generated media site characteristic of Web 2.0) is predicated on the exchange of information by users, and is thus inextricable from a discussion of data tracking/surveillance. But it goes further than this: Facebook's literal economy (as well as that of multiple other dominant internet businesses, most obviously Google)—their ability to *monetize* the activities of users—is also based on the collection and exchange of information about users' identities and behaviors (both with and without their knowledge), establishing users as consumers targeted for advertising and further monitoring. Fuchs thus argues in no uncertain terms that "the combination of surveillance and prosumption is at the heart of capital accumulation on web 2.0."[17] These forms of "dataveillance" are representative of consumers participating (often willingly) in practices of surveillance in such a way that they produce themselves as subjects and objects of surveillance simultaneously.

This most obvious of instances is but one representative of the broader economy of surveillance and marketing that attends "interactive" or "participatory" media, an economy which Mark Andrejevic, in his exemplary study *iSpy: Surveillance and Power in the Interactive Era*, has demonstrated is a defining characteristic of contemporary digital culture. Andrejevic conceives of a "digital enclosure," with the internet as its prime example: "the creation of an interactive realm wherein every action and transaction generates information about itself."[18] Within such an enclosure, which is increasingly difficult to avoid, submission to tracking becomes, essentially, the very price of admission to enjoy the convenience of online shopping, use a "free" service such as Facebook to connect with friends, or even to look up the definition of a word.[19] When I refer to a surveillance economy, it should thus be understood that in many ways this is meant to be literal: a formation in which surveillance not only attends virtually all exchanges, but in which surveillance also occupies the positions, in increasingly fluid forms, of commodity and capital.[20]

If consumer tracking, data mining and information aggregation and analysis are the dominant forms of contemporary surveillance, it is essential in the present context to understand how narrative formations in cinematic practice contend with this form. First-person-camera films, as much as they represent consumer-operated and self- or peer-to-peer monitoring, also share much common ground with commercial surveillance *of* consumers in the digital era.[21] These films thus reveal a great deal about how individual consumers are enlisted as active participants in the commercial surveillance apparatus in its current form.

That the most famous of these films are notable in great part because of their innovative and tremendously successful internet marketing campaigns is reason enough to explore their relation to digital cultures. Such marketing is more than an incidental relationship: what appears to be the insistently analog formal structure of first-person-camera films—an almost primitively visual formula of signification—is also incredibly instructive for understanding the forms that consumer-subjects take in digital surveillance. The relationship between the first-person camera, online interaction, and monitoring of consumers by marketers is something that indicates such coextensivity on both associative and structural levels that it becomes a more telling instance of the consumer relation to surveillance than the more obvious examples of surveillance technologies directly marketed to consumers for home security, personal uses, and entertainment. Perhaps counterintuitively, the insistently individualized and subjective vision of a first-person-camera film is actually inextricable from the diffuse mediation and virtual sociality that characterize digital cultures, thus providing a useful thread to follow between more "traditional" visual models of surveillance and digital surveillance/dataveillance.

*   *   *

The dominant style of the first-person-camera film is that of the fictionalized found-footage horror film, defined early on by *The Blair Witch Project*. As noted above, central to this type of narrative is the diegetic incorporation of the video camera as the defining perspective on the action and as privileged signifier of reality in moving images. With a few exceptions in which the cameras have more stable placement, the aesthetic and experience of the films has remained remarkably similar to *Blair Witch* despite multiple variations in theme—the look of the handheld video camera gaze varies little between its zombie, witch, ghost, possession, and alien invasion iterations. The shaky camera provides a sense of instability, vulnerability, and limited visibility, all contributing to what is intended to be an immersive experience in which the gaze of the video camera offers the spectator a first-person sense of horror that is inseparable from the attendant narrative conceit that the events we are watching are *real*. Rarely is it questioned that the "reality" effect is produced by the specificity of the video gaze; it is merely taken for granted that the video and found-footage premises of the film afford an aesthetic that is consistent with both perceptual experience and realism, which are themselves assumed to be consistent with each other.

The lack of distinction in these films between the cinematic point-of-view (POV) shot meant to offer the spatial perspective of a character and the identification with the video camera gaze is crucial. The formulation, though not always logical, is simple: to identify with the camera of the protagonists is to identify with the protagonists themselves. Subjectivity is signaled through the shaky, often disorienting camerawork and poor image quality in addition to the camera's consistent presentation as a prosthetic extension of a character's body. While much mainstream narrative cinema relies on editing and cinematography that is so unobtrusive that we rarely question our perspective on the action, the video image in the first-person-camera film loudly announces its presence with its lack of distance and transparency, and signals a situational relationship to a character within the film. Alongside and because of this use of subjective style, video is coded as more *material* than film, with materiality signaled by the marks of the technology on the image.

The inadequacy/materiality equation represented by the video image (as compared to a more traditional cinematic style) also serves as essential to the reality effect of narrative films defined by their use of first-person video camera. While smaller-format celluloid technologies (particularly Super 8) have occasionally been used for a related effect (and the smaller format registers similarly given its grainy, handheld quality), the specificity of the video technology used in first-person-camera films is central to the way the films are constructed for and received by viewers. The definition of video as reality representation forms the aesthetic and historical ground for the way such video images hail the film's spectator at the level of a very narrowly defined materiality and embodiment. This spectator, as we will see later in the chapter, functions as a corollary to the virtual subject of digital social networks, and the relationship between these two figures is a significant element of the dynamic structure of surveillance in the consumer market.

Before moving to the specific manner in which the video gaze is incorporated into narrative film as first-person perspective, it is instructive to review how the video medium has been characterized historically.

Its marked discursive history has contributed to the way video comes to bear the weight of loaded and at times contradictory definitions of mediated realities: video as material and objective, video as subjective and personal, video as evidence, diary, direct experience, filtered reality, and so on. A consideration of the medium's multiply coded status is especially called for given that the incorporation of video has been, as is implicit in much of the work on surveillance in cinema, one of the more insistent signifiers of "surveillant narration," even if it is not necessarily the dominant mode of surveillance in actuality.[22] Much as Jean-Louis Comolli noted that the camera had become an ideologically laden metonym for the entire cinematic apparatus, within surveillance cinema it is frequently the video image—highlighted as such—that signifies the presence of a surveillant gaze to the spectator.[23] The phenomenal and aesthetic particularity of video images is thus salient, particularly at a historical moment when informational surveillance, or dataveillance, is in many ways the larger surveillance apparatus of which video serves merely as a more visualizable representative. And, as we will see below, in works ranging from early video art to contemporary narrative cinema, the medium has been inseparable from the type of self-documentation that constitutes a substantial portion of consumer-level surveillant activity, perhaps even more so than the use of video as amateur surveillance of others.

The proliferation and increased dominance of reality programming, which has been the privileged example of the diffusion of surveillance into commodified spectacle, has been made possible almost exclusively by the use of video technology, first analog and now digital, and video imaging has come to be regarded as synonymous with reality representation in common understanding. While the development of digital video has advanced to the degree that to a layperson high-end DV is indistinguishable from 35mm film, an investment in *less* highly resolved video images has been crucial for video in its claims to authenticity. Historically, it has seemed almost as if the credibility of video's status as "real" increases exponentially with its decreased quality of image. If the video experience does not represent either an accurate mimesis of human visual perception or the idealized/idealizing gaze provided by 35mm or even 16mm film, it must instead offer some other quality of the "real" that can explain the medium's ongoing investment in that subject. The use of surveillance video as forensic evidence makes the matter even more crucial, since the medium loses a great deal in translation, and particularly in its digital forms is subject to elaborate manipulation. Its frequent admissibility in both civil and criminal legal proceedings (most famously in the case of the police assault on Rodney King in 1991, discussed further in the final chapter of this book) demands that both narratively and in relation to the politics of surveillance we interrogate how the various forms of video technology have established themselves as "real" to the point of being evidentiary, especially in the face of images that are so obscured by the markings of the medium that at times what they represent is almost totally unrecognizable.

Clearly the materiality and sense of physicality offered by everything from the low-resolution imagery to the handheld camera and the object-status of the videotape itself goes far to explaining the status afforded to video as reality. But even that materiality requires further explanation, especially as it comes to signal subjectivity and self-documentation in surveillance cinema formed around the first-person camera. The version of materiality offered by video is augmented and supported by another definitive element of video's representational specificity: the link between television and video, especially in terms of claims to immediacy and authenticity. Pre-YouTube and internet video sharing, David Antin traced the acceptance of video-as-truth to the founding mythologies of television, which, though not synonymous by any means, is historically and technologically intertwined with video. Antin suggests that television's ideology of realism is most understandable in relation to "live" imaging, as the main claim of television in its beginnings was the transmission of signals in an immediate manner. Instantaneity was the hallmark of television's claim to truth: this scene is happening elsewhere, and you can watch as it unfolds on television before your very eyes.[24] This rhetoric of immediacy is still paramount, perhaps even more so, in relation to digital imaging, with the seemingly instantaneous production and transmission of an image via mobile phone and internet. But even as this immediacy produced a kind of "presence" coded as reality, the technology of both television and video provide imagery that falls short of resembling the world as visually perceived: "The medium maintains a continual assertion that it can and does provide an adequate representation of reality, while everyone's experience continually denies it."[25]

Video's temporal claims to the real were also the subject of an essay on early video art by Rosalind Krauss, and for her are tied to the questions of subjectivity and self-documentation that also define the use of video in the narrative context of first-person-camera films. For Krauss, video's instantaneity is notable because of what she considered at that time to be the primary mode of video art: the use of video as a mirror. Unlike Antin, who implies that video's instantaneity is only a myth generated by its relation to television transmission, Krauss notes that video artists are fascinated with the possibilities of this instantaneity and exploit the fact that one can be filmed at the same time that one sees the recorded image of oneself.[26] Quite pointedly, Krauss criticizes the medium as "narcissistic," at least as represented by some of its earliest artists and their exploitation of the temporal attributes of video to produce representational feedback loops. Less judgmentally, but with reference to a conceptual framework that similarly posits video's relationship to reality as that of a mirror or double, Evangelos Tziallas has more recently argued that "[v]ideo surveillance is reality's uncanny."[27] In very distinct contexts, both of these characterizations suggest that at historical, technological, and discursive levels, video mediation produces itself and its subjects, jointly, as a project of self-reference.

Krauss cites several influential artists who exploited the use of video as a mirror, from Bruce Nauman to Richard Serra, in work all remarkably similar, but her introductory example of the work of Vito Acconci asserts her account of this sort of reflexivity the most emblematically: Acconci simply videotapes himself pointing to the center of a video monitor.[28] As described by Krauss, in multiple instances the medium of video becomes a tool for immediately referring back to one's self; or more precisely, to point at the video monitor *is* to point to one's self. Even in considerably later work, we see such equivalence abiding, perhaps most directly stated in the title of Peter Campus's 1999 series of works: *Video Ergo Sum*.

Given the tendency of video artists to use the medium as a form of direct self-reference, it is notable here that in the first-person-camera films, the video camera point-of-view shot also serves as self-representation for the character (supposedly) behind the camera. In fact, the video POV is offered in these films as a more direct representation of a character's authenticity within the space of the narrative than showing that character onscreen, even as it is also an erasure of that person by both removing them from the image and presenting a video recording as synonymous with that character's subjective experience. It is for this reason that I refer to the point-of-view shot of these films as self-documentation, even as it does not always serve the more explicit mirroring function of the video artworks Krauss discusses: whether the person associated with the video camera is onscreen or behind the camera, or both, the "subject" presented is so fully self-referential that it is hard to know the usefulness of making such a distinction.

Krauss sums up what for her are the stakes of this self-reference: "The nature of video performance is specified as an activity of bracketing out the text and substituting for it the mirror reflection. The result of this substitution is the presentation of a self understood to have no past and, as well, no connection with any objects that are external to it."[29] This assessment highlights the connection between temporal immediacy and self-containment, pointing to an ongoing trend in video art: that which conflates video technology and an embodied self-representation characterized as alienated and alienating, "self-encapsulation—the body or psyche as its own surround."[30] The result of this self-encapsulation has often been a highlighting of the self-as-object, a hyperphysicalized representation of one's own body that emphasizes the isolating effects of self-reference: the body as object rather than subject.

A number of feminist video works from the same era Krauss discusses—such as those of Valie Export, Joan Jonas, or Hannah Wilke—used video's gravitational pull toward the body for critical or ironic commentary on how signification has attached to bodies, and given the variation within the medium we should not assume that the video-body equation is always or necessarily a reductive one. However, the tendency toward using video representation as a tool of reduction has been pronounced. The correlation of video with an alienated body reaches a pinnacle in Gary Hill's installation *Inasmuch as It Is Always Already Taking Place* (1990), in which his entire body becomes separated into pieces and disorganized by video monitors. Each monitor represents a separate body part, and the parts are highlighted as separate through their removal from the context of a lived, perceptive body: an ear sits next to a foot next to a groin, etc. Hill here uses the technology of video as representative of his self-as-body, but a deeply objectified version. This piece's collection of incoherent physical parts presents video's relation to the body as one of isolation and fragmentation rather than embodied subjectivity—not only is the body isolated from the world, its parts are separated even from each other.[31]

These artworks demonstrate how the aspects of video used for self-documentation are joined to the materialist elements, but the resulting subject-form is one that renders embodiment almost as ossification. Even if one rejects the grimness of this formulation—and certainly treating one's own body as a material object need not be self-destructive nor unethical, but at times profoundly enabling—it is an account that demonstrates how particular instances and aesthetic forms of video mediation, as well as the broader economic structures surrounding a video-mediated culture, become increasingly resonant with Debord's summation of the society of the spectacle as "separation, perfected."[32] The alienation produced by commodity culture that Debord describes is echoed in an associated form in works such as Hill's by a video mediation that renders materiality as objectification. The self-representation frequently emerging from the exploitation of video's technical specificity—in early artworks as well as in narrative cinema, as we will see below—thus appears in a subject-as-object formation; such a formation itself serves as an individualized mirror for a societal condition by which mediation and commodification have become mutually defining: "The spectacle cannot be understood as an abuse of the world of vision, as a product of the techniques of mass dissemination of images. It is, rather, a Weltanschauung which has become actual, materially translated. It is a world vision which has become objectified."[33]

It is thus not surprising that with the increasing dispersal of video technology into the hands of consumers, and the move from analog video to digital that supported such dispersal, there is consistency in the use of the now more broadly defined video medium for self-documentation (again referring to both the self behind the camera and the self on camera). Such uses have achieved a quotidian ubiquity with the incorporation of cameras into mobile phones and direct connection to the internet for immediate sharing of such media. When smartphones were innovated to incorporate a lens on both the face and back such that users could train the camera on themselves and look at their image onscreen simultaneously, the feedback loop was complete enough that mobile phones are now often used simply as mirrors, and can easily produce oneself as both subject and object of the camera's gaze with absolute ease: a representation now dubbed, with gleeful infantilization, the "selfie." The fact that the use of these phones for self-reference is tied to their use for communication and networked engagement as such images are shared online exemplifies how the frequently self-referential imagery of video now circulates seamlessly with engagement in social media. Self-referential imagery integrates with the surveillant elements of online social networking and demonstrates one way that the "social relation among people, mediated by images" functions in the present context.

*   *   *

Like the move from analog to digital, the incorporation of video into narrative cinema has done little to change video's position as representative of the self-as-body, or what could more simply be called a form of "hyperembodiment," though in somewhat different form from non-narrative art. While the video artworks discussed above offer the video monitor as the representative portion of the video apparatus, their narrative counterparts in first-person-camera films are almost exclusively structured by the thematization of the video camera as insistently presented by the definitional POV shot. Regardless, there is a consistency in how different aspects of video technology in markedly different contexts are similarly used to present the body as extreme immediacy—self-present to a fault. However, the hyperembodiment characteristic of early video art is presented in first-person-camera horror less as narcissistic isolation and more as experiential vulnerability, often using narrative in the direct service of emphasizing bodily materiality and mortality.

The Blair Witch Project (Daniel Myrick and Eduardo Sanchez, 1999), though certainly not the first to use the conceit of the first-person camera, has come to define the genre in a number of ways. The film is exemplary of the faux-found-footage film, the faux documentary, and first-person horror, but also of the online/viral marketing campaigns that tie the definitionally singular perspective of the first-person-camera film to the diffuse, arguably disembodied or multiply embodied perspectives of online communities. The film presents a group of three student filmmakers embarking on a camping trip to film a documentary on the myth of the Blair Witch. They get lost and experience a series of eerie events, all of which they record on their two cameras, and are never seen again. The film opens with a caption that tells us that what we are about to see is their footage, discovered a year after their disappearance. *Blair Witch* thus represents both of the most frequent narrative premises of the first-person-camera film—the found-footage film and the fake documentary—and the film's imagery has become synonymous with the video point-of-view shot, particularly in horror. While one of their cameras is video and one 16mm film, the difference in their uses is telling: while the video is used as a personal diary and record of their experience, the 16mm film is reserved for limited "professional" representation in the form of the documentary they are ostensibly shooting (the film within the film). What is considered the most frightening aspect of the film, its particular brand of horror, is the direct experience of fear and vulnerability provided by the first-person video camera; the most notable aspect is that the hand-held video point of view that constitutes the spectatorial point of access to the film is *always* aligned with one of the film's characters, and thus always presents what is suggested to be an embodied perspective.[34] *The Blair Witch Project* and the majority of other first-person camera films are in this way distinctive from more traditional narrative films in which we often watch the film from a position not associated with a character or object within the diegetic world, not necessarily attached to any one perspective. Within traditional narrative film, although many shots are periodically associated with characters, often we are watching from "nowhere": simply the camera's perspective, usually specifically structured to eliminate awareness of the camera.[35] This allows the viewer a periodic sense of removal from the scenario of the film; the spectator is often distant from the action and, more crucially, *mobile*—moved from perspective to perspective within not just the film at large, but even within a single scene. A point-of-view shot is a common mechanism in much narrative film, but it is generally a punctuation and rarely lasts for very long. Thus however he or she might psychologically identify with characters, *structurally* the viewer is frequently offered an outside and varying position, and while in a sense the spectator is central to the action, this is often a perspectival centering rather than a situational one. The relative originality of *The Blair Witch Project* lies in its total lack of non-character-identified point of view and the total alignment of character point of view with an explicitly marked video record. Or to use Christian Metz's terminology: in this film, primary identification with the camera is always secondary identification, with a character; there is no seemingly disembodied gaze, no omniscient camera-eye.[36] In *The Blair Witch Project* there is no single moment that is not clearly the ostensible point of view of one of the characters in the film, as represented by a video image.[37]

The Blair Witch Project highlights how the hand-held camera and the POV shot have become almost inextricably identified with video in particular, and what this reveals about the developing aesthetics of self-representation and consumer uses of surveillant media. Hand-held video imagery has been common in popular discourse since the late 1980s, with the emergence of such television series as *Cops* and *America's Funniest Home Videos* (both first airing in 1989), and video's portability and use of point-of-view shots have led to an easy identification with this apparatus as a form of a physically "realistic" point of view. While this hand-held aesthetic exists in cinema proper as well, the video apparatus brought it to the fore in a way that has become definitive of the medium, while for film it was merely a digression from the norm. This accounts to a certain degree for the easy connection made in these films between the body of the character-subject and video technology: as "hand-held," it exists in what, in another context, Don Ihde has called an "embodiment relation" to its user. For this reason, video images frequently refer back to the person shooting the images as much as what is in front of the camera, and are often used as self-representation on the part of the videomaker. Vivian Sobchack has argued in her seminal phenomenology of cinema, *The Address of the Eye*, that such embodiment relations are an essential part of the cinematic experience, that filmmaker, film, and spectator are "engaged as participants in dynamically and directionally reversible acts that reflexively and reflectively constitute the *perception of expression* and the *expression of perception* [emphasis in original]."[38] This argument demands that the relay of looks at play in the cinematic experience be seen as fundamentally grounded in a series of embodied perceptions that put the camera and the filmic text in an embodiment relation to both filmmaker and spectator. Sobchack's cinematic analysis focuses on the relay of visual perception/expression and thus, at least structurally, applies equally to video. Add to this the common usage of amateur video as hand-held, especially as deployed within narrative cinema, and the embodiment relation becomes even more direct and often exaggerated. With camera attached to hand and held to eye, the jolting point-of-view shots of *Blair Witch* intend the camera to see as our own eyes might, for instance, as we run through the woods—a direct representation of perceptual experience. This is furthered by the ease of synchronous sound recording offered by video, so that the voice of the person provides dialogue with such intimate proximity to the microphone that it frequently mimics an internal monologue.

However, if we go beyond the straightforward structure offered by the film, which works under and strives to reify the assumption that subjective experience = the video point-of-view shot, and actually describe the look and experience of its point-of-view shots, it is clear that in fact they bear little relation to the experience of embodied perception, particularly visually. Phenomenologically speaking, vision does not appear so unstable and disorienting when we move our bodies. Our visual field is far more fluid, and less overwhelming, by virtue of its relationship to the rest of our body and our body's relation to the world around it. The embodied view expressed by the handheld video point of view is, despite the seeming directness of this type of viewing experience, not a body that is similar to a perceptual body. It is presented as a hyper-eye: almost pure vision—without the mediation of a full bodily context—thus more vulnerable, more unstable, and suggestively, more subject to violence.

Not only do first-person-camera films objectify the far more complex nature of perception and sensation, but in the reduction of embodied being to a largely visual representation of "pure" experience, such films also serve as an erasure of the *differences* of lived bodies. The use of a video POV shot as a stand-in for subjectivity suggests that perception is an absolutely uniform and generalized experience, even as it is presented as intensely individualized; in the first-person-camera film, one's experience is not informed by gender, class, race, physical capacity or incapacity, and so on. The identification of experience with video documentation is a vast leveling off, and (not dissimilarly from the representation of the extreme experience of violence in the torture films discussed in the preceding chapter) such an identification serves as a disavowal of the fact that certain bodies are constructed such that they are more subject to violence than others.

So even while it is apparent that this type of imagery is radically different from "actual" experiences, the violent insistence on the physical materiality of the perspective detracts attention both from its inaccurate mimesis of human vision and the fact that subjective and bodily experiences, *especially* in relation to violence, are historically and culturally informed. Like many of the earlier video artworks, the first-person-camera film invests in the pure physicality of embodied being, at times effectively substituting an object for a subject, technology for embodiment. It is this objectification that constitutes the hyperembodiment of the first-person-camera film, connecting the technology to the character through a constant reference to materiality. This materiality, however, is not consistent with the materialist phenomenology through which Sobchack accounts for cinematic experience as a relay between expression and perception, nor does it situate embodied experience as social, historical, or political. It is a materiality with no understanding of historical materialism. It is a materiality that subsumes all such dynamic engagements to the physically identifiable, objective grounds of experience: hyperembodiment rather than embodiment.

To put a finer point on it, *Blair Witch* ends as soon as the final camera falls to the ground, further accentuating the character-identified POVs presented throughout the film. There is no explanation, and for *Blair Witch*, no possibility of filming without a character behind the camera. The end of the film corresponds with the end of the characters' filming, and the end of the characters. This seals the identification with the characters and their cameras that had been briefly ruptured by their (presumed) deaths, and yields an eerie result: a striking lack of narrative closure that produces a remarkable abandonment of the spectator. The absolutely immersive identification of spectator with character and camera results ultimately in its flipside, the lack of the contextualizing space of narrative that might exceed the bodies and technologies that have now simply run out of functionality. *Blair Witch* thus suggests that to reduce a film *entirely* to the camera point-of-view shot is to render representation subject to the laws of the purely physical, bringing a simultaneous death of the human body and an end to the images associated with the perceptual experience of the characters. The first-person-camera aesthetic, which produces a marriage of character point of view to video point of view, is, in this and so many of the films that follow, inevitably deadly.[39] The narrating function of narrative cinema in this formation hides itself behind the pretense of merely creating a record, and the creation of a visual record as an end in itself becomes a narrative style.

While an in-depth reading might not be strictly necessary in order to describe the perspective of these films as violently and insistently embodied (as any nauseated spectator could attest to their experience of the film as such), it highlights how this definitional example of the first-person-camera film is predicated on a rendering of perception as housed in a technology that relates to lived bodies and subjective experience, but exaggerates the elements of those bodies that crudely signify "objective" existence: physicality, inadequacy, mortality. A phenomenological account of the status of the first-person-camera aesthetic and narrative structure also clarifies their relation to consumer surveillance: specifically, how the hyperbolically embodied subjectivity that characterizes a film such as *Blair Witch*, as well as much of the video corpus that preceded it and the first-person-camera films that follow it, are a perhaps counterintuitive corollary to the types of subject formation that have come to dominate discussions of digital culture and informational surveillance. Digital subjectivities are more likely to be discussed in terms of virtuality and disembodiment, and yet their relation to the first-person camera, in its emphasis on materiality and a violently produced objective subject, is pronounced in a variety of ways.

First-person-camera films strive to relate us directly to character experience, but what they in fact point to is the technology that is doing the filming. The camera and the character are processed as one and the same in these films—the task here is to produce an embodiment relation to the camera that is so strong that the distinction between character point of view and camera is lost, eliding any distinction between signifiers of subjective being and those of objective being. The result is that the technologies of documentation are reflexively positioned as stand-ins for existence itself. Recording is what it means to remain alive.

Such films show how producing a constant record of oneself simultaneously overidentifies forms of being-in-the-world with technological documentation of that being, constituting many of the films as "compulsive documentation" narratives. Perhaps the most direct relation to be made between *Blair Witch*, the similarly structured films that have followed it, and the form of consumer-level surveillance represented by online communities lies within such compulsive documentation. This compulsivity is evident in *Blair Witch* in the refusal on the part of the characters to abandon the cameras at some point of stress. *Blair Witch*, and virtually every other film of its type, includes a scene that provides a psychological or otherwise narrative rationale for the characters' continuing to film their experience beyond when many audience members might find it reasonable to do so (in *Blair Witch*, one of the characters who had previously yelled at another for continuing to film when their situation had become dire, states that he understands why she keeps doing so upon taking up the camera himself: it makes things "not quite real").[40] Such preemptory defensiveness on the parts of the films seems to indicate an anticipation that the audience will find the ongoing video documentation of the characters so compulsive that it would create a challenge to the suspension of disbelief. However, as has been borne out by the particular combination of video recording and online media, particularly social media, compulsive documentation of self and others has become one of the defining elements of digital cultures, and characterizes one of the most dominant forms of peer-to-peer surveillance practice: the near constant projection of self and the equally constant monitoring of others through such forums as Facebook, Twitter, Instagram, YouTube, etc. Though this could be described as an exhibitionist culture that is the necessary corollary to a voyeuristic culture, it is of more use to think of it in terms of the consumption of surveillance as pleasure, or what Alice Marwick puts forward as "social surveillance."[41] This peer-to-peer, consumer surveillance practice in turn produces surveillance *of* the consumers as the information users post about themselves is organized for more precise online marketing. Consumers thus participate in surveillance at the level of their social interactions *and* in producing and consuming information that serves targeted marketing.[42]

As Nicole Cohen points out in an early article on the political implications of Facebook, the website, both in its monetizing strategy and its social function, engages in a "valorization" of surveillance that harnesses the "producer-consumer" (or in Fuchs's term, the "prosumer") as both subject and object of that surveillance: "By uploading photos, posting links, and inputting detailed information about social and cultural tastes, producer-consumers provide content that is used to generate traffic, which is then leveraged into advertising sales. By providing a constant stream of content about the online activities and thoughts of people in one's social networks, Facebook taps into members' productivity through the act of surveillance."[43] While by now it is not unusual to critique online social media, particularly Facebook, as sites of surveillance, it is nevertheless notable that the valorization of which Cohen writes has been so markedly successful. While complaints and some resistance about what users consider breaches in privacy emerge frequently, the shift toward acceptance of and pleasure in things that earlier registered as problematic demonstrates how effectively Facebook has commodified the surveillant aspects of social media. For instance, Cohen's 2008 article discusses the user outcry over the introduction of the News Feed to Facebook in 2006, which "generated negative feedback from Facebook members, who called the feature 'too stalkeresque.'"[44] Facebook incorporates this resistance into its very functioning, as it "provides the tools for members to speak out against the site itself, and then responds to this dissent through the creation of new policies of amendments to this policies," effectively turning online organizing into consumer feedback and market research.[45] But even further, the "stalkeresque" News Feed has in fact become the definitive element of Facebook, and is what allows both for increased production, consumption, and interaction between users *and* more integrated advertising into the flow of information: the ability to constantly update others as to your location, thoughts, and activities (both on- and offline), augmented by photographs, videos, hyperlinks to other media, etc., and to see the activities of others. This stream of information—some of which users can control and customize and some of which Facebook does for them—is the social version of a stock ticker, and in the end there is little to distinguish a friend's description of the movie he or she just saw from a targeted advertisement placed within the News Feed. In other words, what was initially introduced as something that registered as surveillance to a large number of users, has now been turned into probably the most desirable aspect of this form of social media, and thus the compulsive documentation aspect of Facebook is in fact one of the most effectively marketed forms of Web 2.0 to date.

The most obvious point to make here, then, about the relations between first-person-camera films and the surveillant aspects of a social media site such as Facebook or Instagram is that the seemingly "virtual" production of identity/identities that constitutes an online profile, and the nauseatingly hyperembodied vision of the first-person-camera film are structurally inseparable, in function, but also in form. However, such films are designed to provide a vision violently centered through a first-person perspective, while online identity has often been characterized as an amalgam of media and information that produces a virtual, "decentered self" (in Sherry Turkle's words).[46] Or as Judith Donath of the MIT Media Lab presented this opposition in 1998:

> In the physical world there is an inherent unity to the self, for the body provides a compelling and convenient definition of identity. The norm is: one body, one identity. Though the self may be complex and mutable over time and circumstance, the body provides a stabilizing anchor. . . . The virtual world is different. It is composed of information rather than matter. Information spreads and diffuses; there is no law of the conservation of information. The inhabitants of this impalpable space are also diffuse, free from the body's unifying anchor.[47]

Since these early-ish pronouncements of the ostensible free-form virtuality of online identity, there has been a great deal of theoretical intervention by such scholars as N. Katherine Hayles and Mark Hansen illustrating the numerous ways in which the body is not simply shucked off and left behind in digital realms (and that information itself is, in fact, not opposed to matter but stored in and processed by technologies composed of matter), but the virtual/real dichotomy seems to have stuck.

In the present context, it is essential to first reduce the distinction between the virtual, digital, online self and the representation of an embodied, "real" experience of the first-person camera, by highlighting that the ability to document oneself visually, in the first person, as it were, using consumer electronics (most obviously phone cameras), is much more structurally similar to the production of one's online identity than critical accounts might initially suggest. With social media as just one formation among many where one is encouraged to digitally contribute more and more information about oneself, it becomes apparent how what I am calling compulsive documentation is implicated in a broader drive toward "ubiquitous computing," which is increasingly where technology companies are putting their developmental resources.[48] The effort to integrate computing into every aspect of one's life, which for marketers means greater ability to individuate and target a consumer, is represented in oversimplified form by the first-person-camera film, in which the insistently highlighted video mediation is packaged as that which most fully signifies "experience." In other words, subjectivity and mediated representation are one and the same in the compulsive documentation film; it is the dream of ubiquitous computing distilled into cinematic form. As Warren Beatty taunted Madonna in all his superior snobbishness in the (preinternet) paean to Madonna's narcissism, the documentary *Truth or Dare*, "Why would you say something if it's off camera? What point is there existing?" Beatty's mocking question "seems terribly quaint in these heavily documented times," as noted by internet gossip/news site Gawker in 2012.[49] The question has bled over into the now multiply asked question: "If it's not on Facebook, did it happen?" Compulsive documentation, as represented by the first-person-camera film, as insistently visual as it may seem, and as tied to a kind of visceral and direct experience of the world as it feels, is as much a representation of digital media as cinematic. Further, ubiquitous computing means that at the level of consumer electronic use, the technologies utilized to (a) produce and reproduce an aggregated virtual self through constant information feedback about activities, location, consumption, and communication, and (b) visually document one's embodied perspective with video, are now often one and the same or seamlessly integrated (with the smartphone as the clearest example). For this reason alone, the "subject" they are to represent becomes a complex figure that must somehow be understood as defined both by such singularly embodied self-representation and the diffuse patterns that come to represent a subject in the schema of information.[50]

* * *

But beyond the technologies, there is an even more central connection between the overly embodied vision of the first-person-camera films and the diffuse dispersal of information on the web at large as well as in narrower formations of online communities. The structural conditions of the first-person-camera films are far more complex than the simplicity of the point-of-view shot might suggest, and the "direct experience" of such films is belied by the degree to which such films are dependent on the extratextual conditions of their marketing campaigns. It is instructive here to look at *Blair Witch* in conjunction with *Cloverfield*, which followed in its footsteps, so to speak, fairly directly. *Cloverfield* (Matt Reeves), made in 2008, represents an urbanized and recognizably post-9/11 version of the more traditionally rural horror of *Blair Witch* and offers an updated version of a single-camera found-footage film. In this case the footage is that of a series of friends recording a going-away party when a never-quite-visualized overwhelmingly destructive force visits itself upon New York City, in what the film eventually suggests to be an apocalyptic alien invasion. Like *Blair Witch*, *Cloverfield* insists on an identification with the camera without pause for relief, demonstrates an inability on the part of the protagonists to just stop recording and deal with an increasingly life-threatening situation, and refuses to ever fully reveal the threat or provide narrative closure in the form of explanation or resolution. We don't exactly know what we have seen, we don't know exactly who has died and who has lived, and the premise of the film is that the footage we are watching has been discovered by a third party (the Department of Defense) and re-presented to the public. But the other central connection to *Blair Witch* is the marketing of the film: it is not coincidental that both films, so defined by the first-person experience of vision, are also both known for exploiting internet discourse as a marketing device in a manner structurally related to their narrative form.

Blair Witch's high-powered marketing campaign was outrageously successful in both its more traditional forms and in its creative use of the internet to further those methods, but it is especially noted by both scholars and marketing experts for the internet-specific discourse around the film that served as a new media "mirror" of the film's narrative devices. J. P. Telotte demonstrates in his account of the film's internet presence that "[t]he selling of the *Blair Witch Project* and the *telling* of that film, its narrative construction, were from the start a careful match or 'project,' one that better explains both the film's success and why that success was so quickly and easily laid at the door of the now almost equally famous web site."[51] The "mythology" around the film lent itself to the structure of the internet as, if not more, easily as it did to the film's first-person-camera experience. Telotte points out that while it had already become standard by 1999 for films to have their own website as part of their publicity materials, *Blair Witch* moved beyond what other sites were doing, which ranged from being simply "digital press kits," to offering more interactive devices such as electronic giveaways or plot-related games for site visitors to enjoy. *Blair Witch* went further, and extended the narrative conceit of found footage into the campaign for the film: rather than speaking of the film extradiegetically, the marketing was designed to enlarge the diegesis to incorporate the internet into it. The website "stays in character" as it provides additional immersion into the fiction of this found documentary footage, such as additional background on the film's characters, the legend of the Blair Witch, and so on. Every item on the website, rather than framing the film from outside its narrative, encourages us to see *The Blair Witch Project* "*not as film*, but as one more artifact, along with the materials gathered together at the Web site," making it clear that rather than marketing the filmic text as a recognizable form of entertainment commodity, the "project" of the website is to "suggest, in effect, that this particular film is as much a part of everyday life as the Internet, that it extends the sort of unfettered knowledge access that the Internet seems to offer, and that its pleasures, in fact, closely resemble those of the electronic medium with which its core audience is so familiar."[52] It is thus significant that *The Last Broadcast*, a first-person-camera, faux-found-footage film released a year before *The Blair Witch Project*, achieved little of the same success. *The Last Broadcast* is recognized primarily as the first broadly released feature shot and edited entirely on consumer-market digital video equipment. Without entering into a comparative review of the two films, the fact that *Blair Witch* stands out historically while *The Last Broadcast* has faded into oblivion, despite the degree to which the earlier film has a greater claim to historical significance at the level of its production, highlights the import of the marketing campaign to *The Blair Witch Project* as a phenomenon. The internet figures centrally for both, but while *The Last Broadcast* thematized the internet intranarratively, *Blair Witch* disseminated both its narrative and aesthetic form via the internet and, more specifically, employed the structural form of the internet for marketing innovations. It is clear which has had a more lasting effect.

Tellote completes his analysis with the suggestion that similar to the meandering experience of the characters within the film, the marketing materials encourage a relation like that produced by a hypertext, "a text of many fragments but no whole, no master text. . . . [T]he hypertext invites us to find our own way, even to find some pleasure or profit in its very decenteredness."[53] Of note here is the connection made between what I have described as the hyperembodied experience of first-person-camera films, and the fragmented and decentered experience of internet interactivity. Arguably, the first-person-camera film is the *opposite* of decenteredness, insistently placing the spectator into a direct relation with one single perspective. And yet this singular perspective experientially produces a decentered and fragmented sensibility more characteristic of the discourse around digital media, and thus suggests that an overidentification with a single visual perspective and the dispersal of a field of information across a web of interactive media are entangled in ways that illustrate how consumerism is posited in relation to surveillance as both an abstract fact and a subjective experience. The film experience of *Blair Witch*, beyond addressing the spectator directly through first-person camera, also incorporates the spectator via a level of interactive engagement with the information amalgam of the internet as medium, all bound increasingly tightly together by the thread of synergistic marketing.

The concept of "media convergence" further illuminates how *The Blair Witch Project* circulates in multiply mediated forms that seem to simultaneously diversify and unify the phenomenon of the film. Media critic and scholar Henry Jenkins has pointed out that "convergence" encompasses multiple concepts describing several different cultural and technological aspects of contemporary media; the version of media convergence that he defines as "cultural convergence," particularly in the form of transmedia storytelling, aptly describes the marketing of *Blair Witch*. More importantly here, Jenkins also shows how cultural convergence functions with "social or organic convergence," in which a consumer utilizes multiple platforms of media in an either simultaneous or integrated manner, and thus produces convergence quite explicitly at the level of their own body and experience. Viewed in this way, media convergence produces a "body" of work that is simultaneously more diffuse and more unified—the structural relation between the first-person-camera experience of *Blair Witch* and its transmedia marketing campaign is exemplary in this regard. Convergence in this context describes both the method of marketing employed and the way a consumer-subject (mirrored by the first-person-camera form) emerges from a discombobulating circulation of information. While theoretically this could place the consumer-subjects in a privileged position in which their experience and perspective filters and defines a world of value, there is an equally strong argument to be made that the reverse trajectory (or at least the effort to make the trajectory reversible) is gaining sway, and that the algorithm that aggregates their activity and experience in order to sell a product to them in multiple formats and on multiple levels is working to replace the body as the unifying structure of a subject. If it can be sold to you, you exist.

* * *

To appreciate more fully the structural relationships between the first-person-camera films and the construction of the consumer-subject, particularly in terms of marketing, we can turn to Daniel North's analysis of how *Cloverfield* takes up the "project" of first-person camera and internet publicity.[54] Like *Blair Witch*, this later film is known both for its elliptical first-person-camera structure and its equally famous innovative use of fan-driven online interaction for its marketing. And though *Cloverfield* and *Blair Witch* have each received attention for their marketing campaigns, the commonality between the two and thus the relations between the form of narrative and the form of marketing require more discussion. Notwithstanding the lack of connection made in his article to *Blair Witch*, North does an excellent job of showing why we must look at the narrative and aesthetics of *Cloverfield* in relation to the form of its marketing campaign. In demonstrating that both *Cloverfield*'s first-person-camera style and its publicity campaign are characterized by a play between display and concealment—a series of partial views—North shows how the visual representation of a single hyperembodied view is not opposed but *parallel* to the structure of the consumer in the film's marketing. Noting that the imperfect and incomplete visuals of the imagery and narrative exceed the frame of the film, he writes, "The film's obstructed views extend to the whole fabric of the movie, including its pre-publicity campaign and its framing narrative."[55] *Cloverfield*'s marketing campaign was able to harness the notoriously difficult to anticipate force of viral media on the internet, and use the controlled dispersal of incomplete information through enigmatic trailers, MySpace, blogs, and a variety of other "breadcrumbs" that were not necessarily marked as publicity materials, to generate fan participation and data. Here not only is the first-person camera representative of the kind of literal technologies of documentation one might find presented by a user on YouTube, Instagram, or Facebook, but the play between information and subjectivity within the film is also employed as a method of interactivity: "Even as they are invited to 'experience' the attack through a single camera's lens, the spectators are prompted to assume the position of investigators watching a piece of documentary evidence. . . . Spectators were not constructed as passive consumers awaiting the film's release, but as participants in a search for the information necessary to pre-imagine it and then to unravel its mysteries."[56] Thus beyond the embodied POV shot, the broader "body" of the film produces the spectators as active consumers—the identification with the video camera point of view is configured alongside an identification of the consumer with the processes of digital surveillance by structuring disparate pieces of information into a pattern. These dual identifications happen not *in spite* of the dissimilarity of those two modes, but because they are in fact increasingly structurally integrated.

Cloverfield's marketing harnesses precisely the type of interactive/participatory marketing that Andrejevic posits as central to the functioning of what he calls "iCulture": not only do potential audiences perform the labor of disseminating information about the film; they are encouraged to experience such labor as part of the identificatory pleasure that (this) film offers. "If the commercial mobilization of the promise of interactivity is that consumption can be creative, its cultural corollary is that creativity is being made more accessible to a new generation of 'prosumers'—or, in the parlance of media studies, 'active audiences.'"[57] In many ways this is an interactive campaign that could just as easily be for shoes or phones. However, the first-person-camera films add a dimension to an interactive campaign by creating a kind of narrative tutorial on how to be an active consumer of media, as well as priming internet audiences on how to understand their investment in the cinematic experience that they haven't yet had.

> Traditional publicity campaigns rely on the carefully timed release of authoritative information from a central source to a mass audience. Viral campaigns, in contrast, depend on relinquishing control: releasing key pieces of information in carefully chosen places, in the hope and expectation that it will spread organically through the target audience, as a virus spreads from person to person within a population. . . . The studio's presentation of its product is augmented, developed and mutated by a swarm of online input as fans comment upon, study, and transmit clues around networks of users. Unable to examine every facet, one is required to locate patterns in the data.[58]

The fact that these viral campaigns, which incorporate consumers as marketers through various kinds of social networking, have been used for the three most notable "first-person" films—*The Blair Witch Project*, *Cloverfield*, and, as I will discuss in greater detail below, *Paranormal Activity*—is perhaps the most direct connection between the reductive, partial, and often violently subjective view of consumer electronic surveillance (digital video cameras, computer webcams) and the diffuse, multiple, and pattern-oriented subject of online surveillance constructed primarily for marketing purposes.

The value of such participation to the consumer is hard to gauge; there is some evidence that audiences are engaging in critical spectatorship that exerts a degree of influence over the shape of media culture, as Henry Jenkins has suggested.[59] But there is also ample evidence that the primary benefit is to the media companies using such participation to gather market data and increase their economic power over the consumer. As Andrejevic argues convincingly, through participation in interactive campaigns, we supply not only labor but information about ourselves that can be further traded upon: "The danger of the emerging model of interactivity as cybernetic feedback is that it teaches a form of participation that amounts to actively staging the scene of our own submission: helping marketers—both political and commercial—increase their leverage over us."[60] Particularly in the context of horror, "staging the scene of our own submission" could not be more apt to describe a first-person-camera film, which deploys consumer electronics within the narrative, and a corollary campaign external to the narrative, to engage spectators in an identification with a position of extreme vulnerability and objectification, even as they appear to be given a more fully subjective experience through the use of the point-of-view shot. Discussed in somewhat different terms: the formal properties of the first-person-camera film complement the carrot dangling at the end of the contemporary marketing s(ch)tick: the willingness of the consumer to surrender to increased tracking online is bolstered by "the promise of individuation" that such customized marketing proposes to provide.[61]

The virtuality of online identity, as defined by the advertising economy that in large part structures internet experience, thus works desperately to offer deep recognition to individual consumers of their singularity. The hyperbolic, material "I" of the first-person-camera film finds its virtual body double in the aggregated consumer-subject that internet commerce offers as the "promise" that conceals the threat. The threat, however, is loudly announced via the cinematic horror of the I-camera, and yet is still successfully packaged as authentic experience. The "payoff" of horror film for the spectator is too involved and contentious of a discussion to fully entertain here, but certainly there is no dispute that the viscerally affective thrill produced by both psychic and bodily engagement is a significant part of the horror appeal.[62] To find ways to engage that experience makes a horror film what it is—in this case a viscerally stimulating narrative form is utilized by marketers to refine their process and exploit the consumer's various levels of engagement with the ever-expanding filmic text. The film and its distribution, taken as a whole, thus mirror the surveillance aspects of digital culture in multiple aspects: a constant and compulsive gaze, the processing of information into a pattern, and consumer-spectators who end up marketing all of this to themselves through notions of their participation and particularity, in the process producing more personal data about themselves online. This will, of course, subject them to further marketing that becomes simultaneously more refined and more expansive. The result is that this kind of "direct-experience" cinema, one that is reduced to a hyperbolically visual model that may seem outdated in contemporary discussions of surveillance practice, is structurally integrated and even dependent upon the informational and pattern-driven models of digital surveillance.

* * *

The material singularity proposed by both the first-person-camera film and the individual consumer, as evidenced by the marketing of these films, also shows how social media and online communities (which might at first glance seem contradictory to the customized, hyperindividualized subject) are absolutely consistent with the "promise of individuation" beyond the simple fact that the social forum of Facebook has become synonymous with target marketing. The POV shots of the first-person-camera films refer to a vulnerable, *partial* view that constructs the singular body of the spectator in relation to the myriad partial views of a broader, digitally enabled "community." Viewed in conjunction with the kind of experience produced by both the first-person-camera films and their interactive marketing campaigns, such a community could be more closely related to the word's Latin origin, *communitatem*, which refers less to an actual group than to a shared sense, a community of relations or feelings. As Daniel North argues,

> Consumers of viral marketing campaigns *become an interpretive community sensitized to media* [emphasis mine] that may or may not contain relevant information about the forthcoming film, supposedly heightening their awareness of other potential messages until the puzzle is solved. It is not difficult to see why this kind of marketing might be advantageous: It distributes the task of publicizing the film by urging spectators to become participants, entering into the narrative space of the film, and drawing others in with them in order to collaboratively construct its meaning. . . . This networked publicity campaign does more than just promote the finished product; it complements the tenor of the film, which thrives on the paranoid space of obstructed vision and partial knowledge.[63]

Thus a first-person experience becomes the most direct point of entry to a shared experience. Understood in this way, the integration of the first-person-camera narrative formation and the marketing campaign draws yet more direct parallels between a technologized visual-perceptual model of experience and an informational model of social interaction, reducing the distinction between the two. In some ways, this is remarkably similar to a materialist phenomenology in which our individual perceptual bodies become our point of access to the world and others: being is always being-with and being-in-the-world. And in many ways it really is that, in variously mediated forms, and yet all the productive possibilities of that account of embodiment are not what appear to be the result of this construct. Being-in-the-world has been "brand hijacked," robbed of the majority of its ethical dimensions, with perception repurposed as surveillance and community redefined as a market segment, in many cases as a free labor force for both capitalism and its attendant security state.[64]

The participatory and interactive marketing campaign of *Cloverfield* is addressed specifically in relation to labor models in the digital economy by Emmanuelle Wessels, who draws a direct line from the film's marketing to the production of consumers as "citizen-subjects" in a securitized post-9/11 environment.[65] Her analysis builds on the work in Michael Hardt and Antonio Negri's *Empire* in such a way that the various threads of my prior discussion, especially the relationship among first-person-experiential narratives, social media, surveillance, and consumption might be further bound together through the notion of affective labor in the digital economy:

> Dealing with computerized devices, according to Hardt and Negri (2000), has become a central component of what life means today. As human beings become more integrated with computers, the nature of the work done changes as well, moving away from the production of tangible goods and services to work with information and symbols. This type of labour is crucial in the creation of brands, advertising, and other commodity symbols. The "entertainment industry," Hardt and Negri (2000:292–293) also demonstrate, is implicated in this system of immaterial labour insofar as it is "focused on the creation and manipulation of affect."[66]

"The creation and manipulation of affect" is almost comedically exaggerated, at the same time that it is narrowly defined, by the use of first-person camera, especially in horror, which makes far-too-easy equivalencies between experience, subjectivity, technology, and visual representation. But, as Wessels points out, the formal elements of the film feed directly into the already discussed interactive marketing campaign, which builds layers upon the affective elements in play, in particular the online contest soliciting fan-made videos imagining their own *Cloverfield*-esque response to a monster attack as captured on their consumer electronic equipment. The identification produced by the film through both its narrative and marketing is not just the traditional character identification of cinematic signification, but identification with oneself as a user of consumer-level electronics—an exemplary prosumer—and the use of those electronics as a point of (literal) entry into an internet fan community and the media economy. Ultimately, all of this is capitalized on by the film studio, which gained the exclusive rights to the fan videos that were used to market this and future films to those same fans, as well as led to the next solicitation of consumer participation in the film's marketing: the fan vote to determine the winner of the fan video contest. As Wessels notes, "Although participants in the *Cloverfield* vote do, presumably, enjoy the affective pleasures of agency in selecting their favorite video, they also labour to consume advertising and promotion for Paramount, and supply an email address likely ensuring future monitoring and advertising reception."[67]

What was presented as a sponsored contest in *Cloverfield* is, unsurprisingly, naturalized by what we might call the "postmarketing" phenomenon of the 2012 film *Project X* (Nima Nourizadeh). This first-person-camera film, a comedy about a group of aspirational teenage boys who document on video their rise to local popularity and minor fame by throwing what the film poster calls "the party you've only dreamed about," spurred a number of actual copycat parties and video recordings of the parties. These copycat events and videos (while denounced by the studio) demonstrate the degree to which the film successfully marketed video self-representation as a road to social significance and media notoriety.[68] Most of these copycat parties were able to attract enormous numbers of attendees by utilizing Facebook, Twitter, and other social media, and the parties were then covered by both national and local news, which in their coverage of course referred back to the original film *Project X* (often including scenes from the original film as part of the news story), thus (re)producing the series of reflexive layers that have become common with video narrative. Here the first-person-camera film, in combination with the "wild" possibilities of viral internet exchange and growth, dovetails neatly with an American dream of equal opportunity translated as a consumerist ideology in which the fantasy of economic and social success is the free gift accompanying every purchase. Or, put somewhat less cynically, the ability to assert a self-representation through consumer video has joined with the communicative possibilities of the internet such that the structural specificity of each is more fully defined by reference to the other. Seen in this light, the hyperembodied first-person camera, as it morphs, integrates, and generates through digital community, is actually less about direct visceral experience and is in fact more consistent with the diffusion of affective investments through the multiplication of media in an online community, which also serve an affective purpose to "generate a feeling of belonging or fulfillment."[69] And yet such participatory culture unavoidably generates more information about the participants to be aggregated later for further profit to someone other than themselves and, as Wessels argues about the case of *Cloverfield*'s clearly "post-9/11" imagery, also marshals the anxiety and vigilance of a "security subject" alongside other affective investments.[70]

The circular logic of surveillance discussed in the preceding chapter (and to which I will return in the final chapter) certainly applies to the present context, but it is also accurate to characterize the formation at work here as a reflexivity of both structure and content, a refracting process of mediated self-identification. The video camera point-of-view shot maps the form by which we might identify a self that is both subject and object of one's own gaze: a chain of mediation follows that ends up with one finally identifying with oneself as consumer, with access to media commodities and technologies that further perpetuate that very self-identification—a "world vision which has become objectified." While these films are in still in some way about lived bodies as presented through visual mediation, the materiality of perceptual experience—as represented, defined, and commodified by contemporary media—has become fundamentally inseparable from the variations on the form that Wessels and Cohen discuss in relation to "immaterial labour," Marwick as "social surveillance," and Andrejevic as "interactivity." All of these concepts, in their distinct meanings as well as their interrelations, are integral to consumer surveillance, and all are deeply implicated in the first-person-camera film, which ultimately is a networked and multilayered formation masquerading as direct, bodily experience.

*   *   *

The nexus of first-person-camera films, interactive/viral marketing, and the construction of the reflexively self-identified consumer achieved what may be its crescendo with the phenomenal success of the *Paranormal Activity* franchise, and yet intriguingly, the first film (Oren Peli, 2007) skipped the parallel form between the narrative and the marketing that both *Blair Witch* and *Cloverfield* capitalized on. Rather than generate mythology around the film's content and mirror the narrative structure with marketing techniques, here the marketing campaign, instituted after the film was acquired by a studio, went directly toward generating buzz about its own distribution and reception. The marketing campaign hailed a participatory consumer who could literally produce "demand" to see the film. After a selective release started a buzz around the film, the online marketing utilized Facebook, Twitter, and most centrally, Eventful.com, where potential audience members interested in seeing the film could click the "Demand" button.[71] The promise was that one could request a screening in one's own town, but that if the demand hit one million, the film would go into wide release. In some ways, the consumer/spectator was thus put into the position to identify not just with the camera and the characters, but also with the filmmaker, distributors, and the idea of making a success out of a little-film-that-could. Of course, it is no coincidence that identifying with the filmmaker *is* to identify with the camera and characters, since the director starred in the film, and thus his first-person camera within the film and the making of the film are even more pronouncedly one and the same.

While *Blair Witch* and *Cloverfield* asked their audiences and potential audiences to situate their terror in relation to the experience of the characters within the film, the marketing campaign of *Paranormal Activity* asked audiences and potential audiences to *identify directly with themselves as audience*. This is to say that the most iconic images of the marketing campaign were not from the film, but were clips and stills of audience members reacting in terror at a screening of the film.[72] As Josh Greenstein, the copresident of marketing at Paramount, which distributed the film, summed up, "Traditionally, when you cut TV spots or a trailer, you show the scariest parts of the movie, you build suspense, and then you actually have visuals from the movie to support it. . . . But because the movie works so well as a truly slow build into terror, we didn't want to show your usual kind of scenes and cutting-style horror movies have been using. We wanted to use an experiential sell to help dictate how and where it rolled out to the consumer." Greenstein goes on to explain why the distributor opted for a supposedly "honest" approach, as opposed to the extension of the narrative that its viral predecessors banked on: "Audiences are so sophisticated now, pretending this movie is something it's not would feel false to people. . . . We really want to sell it for what it is. The truth is, the experience of watching the movie is terrifying, and it's an absolute communal type of experience best seen in the movie theater."[73] The emphasis here on both truth and experience is of course the same rhetoric of the earlier films, but this one, according to the distributor, is *more* true: the experience that is privileged is now quite explicitly the *shared experience* of the consumer/audience, rather than that of the characters. Thus the first-person experience of these films migrated to the internet to become shared, interactive experience, and returned to the theater as a communal sensation of terror. The "genius" of this formula is that it harnesses the interactivity and sense of shared experience of online social media in order to get the consumer *back* into the theater at a moment when online and/or home film viewing is moving toward dominance. And, as Wessels notes in regard to *Cloverfield*, an appeal to affect is central here.

The result of this, of course, is an audience who, identifying now with themselves as both *individually* (dis)empowered consumers *and* a *community* of shared experience, subject themselves (in the sense of being both subjects of and subjects to) through and to the informational flow of social media and the resultant market segmentation. This subjection narrows them down into a highly individualized and vulnerable target, once again ready to "Demand" for themselves an experience that the market will of course provide.

*　　*　　*

Identifying with the audience: the marketing of *Paranormal Activity* (2007).

Given that the marketing and compulsive documentation elements have produced such close ties between the first-person-camera film and the internet, it is not surprising that these largely single-perspective, individual-experience films are generically joined with films that augment the first-person-video-camera aesthetic with an accumulation of digital media and perspectives. Films such as *My Little Eye* (Marc Evans, 2002) and *The Bay* (Barry Levinson, 2012) utilize diegeticized video cameras and the found-footage premise alongside explicit references to the internet. In doing so, their video-camera gazes become multiple and in the case of the latter, the physicality of the first-person-video gaze is incorporated easily into a multimedia faux internet documentary. In their presentation of both the first-person-video POV as their primary look *and* the accumulation of media and perspectives, such films highlight the relationship between the hyperbody of the subjective video camera and the hypermediation of the internet: the diffuse virtual subjects and community structures of online representation and interaction.

While *My Little Eye* is structured as a Big Brother–style internet show that turns out to be a snuff film, *The Bay*, again in the horror genre, approaches web mediation quite differently, as a faux internet documentary exploring the conspiracy behind an ecological disaster in a small Maryland town that results in the production of ocean monsters and a deadly virus. It is, most insistently, *not* about a single embodied POV, though it utilizes the hand-held video form frequently to increase its experiential aspect; it is, instead, about the collection of information and the accumulation of multiple perspectives (largely using the internet as source) to form narrative coherence out of a constantly surveilled world. Like many documentaries, it assembles various forms of documentation in the service of the what we might call a new realist aesthetic, one defined by a reflexive structure that makes explicit reference to the manner in which any event or understanding of an event is multiply mediated (webcam interviews, news footage, surveillance video, internet research, text messages, voice mail, phone camera video, Google image search, and so on). The narrative construction weaves together the first-person-camera shots with internet mediation seamlessly, and highlights that such subjective videos are most likely to be seen on the internet, either as YouTube videos or reframed and repurposed on other sites. The fact that not just on a generic but on an aesthetic and experiential level such a film is easily categorized alongside the overly centered first-person-camera film shows how strongly these two sides are connected, at least at the level of representation; the personal, the individual, the hyperem-bodied are increasingly indistinguishable in aesthetic and function from the social spectacle, the virtual assemblage, and the hypermediation of networked communications.

* * *

All the films under discussion, from *Blair Witch* to *Cloverfield*, from *Paranormal Activity* to *The Bay*, might simply be grouped together by virtue of their formal and narrative premises of "realistic" footage. But this would ignore the degree to which the single-camera, character-identified realism, what I am calling the hyperembodied film, flows into the diffuse multimedia presentation of the hypermediated inter-net narrative and social spectacle, with affective investment serving as a transitional device. Looking at the extranarrative elements of the mar-keting practices discussed earlier foregrounds the interrelations of these structures. In fact, the references to realism that bind these various films together are primarily self-reflexive references to the technologies of their making. Rather than the cinematic realism championed by André Bazin in the 1950s—which privileged the indexical nature of cinema to such a degree that Bazin seemed often to be describing a magical revelation of reality uncovered by the film camera "freed" from the subjective taint of the "artist's hand"—this new "realism" focuses instead on the ever-accumulating layers of technological mediation, both in the way the narratives develop and in the way they are marketed, and marks authentic experience as that which is accessed through technological documentation: "pics or it didn't happen."[74] This increasing technologization of not just subject position but acts of perception is thus predicated on an identification with surveillance and documentation as that which defines us as individuals, or at least that is how it is being sold to us, quite literally.

The phenomena of the first-person-camera films and their marketing campaigns is really just a fragment of the complex and in some ways overwhelming matrix within which consumer culture and surveillance intersect and expand, but such films evidence that cinematic form, even as it distills it, serves as a structural element of that matrix. What the distilled version provided by these films offers is a *vision* of how our lived experience as individual subjects is hailed through consumer electronics (and, importantly, hailed as highly vulnerable and contingent) in a way that incorporates us more fully into the shared experience of online social media and an internet economy increasingly driven by the commodification of surveillance. The almost absurdly literal subjective experience of the first-person-camera/compulsive-documentation films, which would seem to be antithetical to a digital virtual self constructed through information patterns, actually serves as a structural double for the endlessly defined and redefined producer-consumer-subject-spectator (and as the hyphens accumulate, the distinctions between the separate terms dissipate) of the internet. Such is the scenario that naturalizes the language behind something like the following offer-demand to a user from Hulu.com (current dominant provider of television online) that would otherwise simply be bizarre: "Answer a question to help us improve your ad experience."

And yet even given such a critique, it is worth noting that video technology, since its very beginnings, has allowed those outside the existing power structures of the cinema industry to enter the field of production as well as provide the possibility of self-representation, as feminist and queer videomaking history can attest.[75] And the makers of *The Blair*

Witch Project demonstrated with their first-person-camera film that limited resources can foster a compelling, and ultimately profitable, aesthetic. Perhaps more importantly, consumer video in combination with expanded media distribution has also allowed citizens to turn the cameras back on authorities to document abuses of power and circulate the resulting imagery such that in certain instances overwhelming collective affect has demanded and produced some accountability. Similarly, digital media hold the political promise of a more participatory process, as social media sites such as Facebook and Twitter have proven invaluable for grassroots political organizing. But as Andrejevic and others have demonstrated through various analyses of interactivity, participatory marketing, and surveillance, while the possibility of power sharing certainly exists, the current trend is in the opposite direction. My critique is thus not of the filmmakers, consumer-subjects, new media innovators, and active spectators who have produced *work* that on many levels is radically empowering, and at times technologically transformative, but of the integrations of capitalism and surveillance by which traditionally corporate powers have been so easily able to commodify and profit from such work, almost seamlessly assimilating what could be resistance back into an increasingly totalizing system.

3

The Global Eye

Satellite, GPS, and the "Geopolitical Aesthetic"

The source of Hollywood's power extends far beyond the history of cinema, to the cultural-communications complex that has been an integral component of capitalist exchange since the end of the nineteenth century. In the second half of the twentieth century, Third World activists, artists, writers and critical political economists nominated that complex as cultural imperialism. By the late twentieth century, it became fashionable to think of this power in terms of globalisation, a maddeningly euphemistic term laden with desire fantasy, fear—and intellectual imprecision. "Hollywood" appears in nearly all descriptions of globalisation's effects— left, right and third ways—as a floating signifier, a kind of cultural smoke rising from a US-led struggle to convert the world to capitalism.
—Miller et al., *Global Hollywood 2*[1]

For it is ultimately always of the social totality itself that it is a question in representation, and never more so than in the present age of a multinational global corporate network.
—Fredric Jameson, *The Geopolitical Aesthetic*[2]

Political action-thrillers such as *Eagle Eye*, *The Bourne Ultimatum*, and the *Mission: Impossible* series, which make extensive aesthetic and structural use of satellite imaging and global positioning systems to construct tales of international espionage, constitute some of the most recognizable examples of surveillance cinema. And unlike the great majority of the films discussed in the prior chapters, they also seek to widen, rather than narrow, the focus of their surveillant gaze. At every level—massive budgets, expansive international distribution, casts of A-list celebrities, explosive action designed for a large-screen theatrical experience, the grand scale of their thematized surveillance operations and technologies, and the construction of geopolitical narratives with stakes as high as presidential assassination or nuclear apocalypse—such films "go big" with their incorporation of surveillance into cinema. However, the thread connecting their stories, their style, and their selling also constructs a map of the relation of an individual subject to political and economic systems, and indicates the role surveillance plays in establishing that relation.

In virtually every analysis of surveillance, and as is evident throughout this book, it has been either explicit or implicit that modern surveillance has always served simultaneously (and in often interdependent ways) to frame an individual and to function as part of a broader system in which that subject might be positioned. From the institutional discipline of the prison and hospital or the cataloguing of mug shots to high-speed computer information processing, to watch one has meant to watch many (and vice versa). Accordingly, surveillance technologies have followed a trajectory through which tracing the relations between the singular and the social has often meant that those technologies have been integral to the production of ever more complex and far-reaching systems into which each individual might be incorporated. This has been the case from the realm of market demographics to counterterrorism, and stops at nothing less than the geopolitical pinpointing of one person in relation to an entire "world system." This chapter explores the ways that cinematic narrative structure and the generic development and marketing of the contemporary action-thriller both illuminate and contribute to those systems concerned with the construction of a "global subject"—an individual posited as a functional element of a globalized economy and a strategic figure in a geopolitical landscape.

As argued by Fredric Jameson in *The Geopolitical Aesthetic*, a number of films of the 1970s and 1980s were already actively processing the relations of the individual to a mapping of the global system. Jameson focuses on such "conspiratorial films" as *Three Days of the Condor* (Sydney Pollack, 1975), *The Parallax View* (Alan J. Pakula, 1974), and *All the President's Men* (Alan J. Pakula, 1976) to argue that these conspiracy films, beyond reflecting literal technologies and politics of the time, were also functioning as allegories serving in the "cognitive mapping" process attending a subject's maneuvering through what Jameson aptly refers to as an "unmappable world system."[3] Conspiracy, in this case, is not merely the political gestalt of the 1970s, but an allegorical function serving to map the *form* of the global in late capitalism.

The films discussed in this chapter are the clear heirs and/or "evolution" of the conspiratorial narratives Jameson writes about: political action-thrillers such as *Enemy of the State* or *The Peacemaker* (and more recently the Jason Bourne series, *Eagle Eye*, the *Mission: Impossible* film series, and the television series *24*), as well as the more realist political drama-thrillers *Body of Lies* and *Syriana*. All of these films produce their conspiracy narratives in conjunction with the explicit visualization of a global system most fully represented by both satellite imaging and satellite-enabled GPS (global positioning systems). The cinematic production of narrative around such technology is both the culmination of the allegories Jameson describes, and, I would argue, an ongoing move to simplify and literalize that unmappable world system by continuing to distill those allegories into surveillance technologies and practices. In so doing, the cinema of surveillance finds yet another way to produce and reproduce surveillance as not only the privileged formation of contemporary politics and culture, but as structurally necessary to the functioning of any so-called "world system": a system predicated on producing "the global" as both visible object and a principle of relationality between individual subjects.

Jameson's account of the "geopolitical aesthetic" highlights how that aesthetic seeks to envision the world as a political, economic, and social structure, constructing a metaphorical "map" that will allow maneuvering through an extensive and unrepresentable system of power and exchange that is cognitively challenging at the level of embodied experience. The allegorical function of geopolitical cinema from the 1970s and 1980s that Jameson describes makes a great deal of sense: such films ranging from *All the President's Men* to *Videodrome* (David Cronenberg, 1983), both of which Jameson foregrounds in his discussion, propose the possibility of conspiracy as a way to frame an understanding of what he calls "totality." The narrative form of a totalizing system is conspiracy: everything is related, interdependent, mutually informing—ultimately what Jameson calls an "unconscious, collective effort at trying to figure out where we are and what landscapes and forces confront us in a late twentieth century whose abominations are heightened by their concealment and their bureaucratic impersonality."[4]

The Geopolitical Aesthetic describes films from a time, though not before satellite imaging and locative technologies were in use, certainly before they had found their way into cinematic narrative. In fact, Jameson argues that conspiracy narratives seek to map the mode of production that satellite imaging *cannot*—within his argument surveillance images are merely "caricatures of the mode of production itself (most often called late capitalism), whose mechanisms and dynamics are not visible in that sense, cannot be detected on the surfaces scanned by satellites, and therefore stand as a fundamental representational problem."[5] Now that such images as Jameson refers to have fully made their way into conspiracy narratives—have in fact become their privileged aesthetic in the action-thriller genre—his argument seems to have come to full fruition: all the technologies of both visualization and narrative are being deployed to make sensible and make sense of an increasingly information-based world system that does not otherwise lend itself to perceptual and cognitive registers. However, in many ways the forms of narrative allegory Jameson describes have culminated in and been superseded by that element he describes as "caricature": an effort to produce us all through geographical imaging systems as visual and visible geopolitical subjects.

Caren Kaplan has suggested in her analysis of the role of GPS in producing U.S. consumers as militarized subjects that, "[i]ndeed, the centrality of geographical images in information sciences helped to create the visual logics of contemporary U.S. subjectivity."[6] Media scholar Lisa Parks has advanced similar arguments in her discussion of "satellite television," which she defines as the "convergent practices of live international transmission, remote sensing, and astronomical observation."[7] In *Cultures in Orbit*, Parks discusses televisual mediation as neither technology nor text, but as "an epistemological system derived through the alternating discursive modalities of commercial entertainment, public education, military monitoring, and scientific observation."[8] Chad Harris's detailed analysis of the technological, systemic, and ideological use of satellite and aerial surveillance in the United States' waging of the first Gulf War in 1991 argues that such tactical usage is "where surveillance is most directly attached to concrete purposive action: the pre-cise application of force and violence for organized warfare, perhaps the ultimate act of purposive agency."[9] To formulate how the very *form* of the convergence between surveillance, targeting, weapons, and media representation of the Gulf War reflects a tactical logic, Harris turns to the military use of the term "interoperability," which describes systems not just working in conjunction with each other, but fusing together into an "assembled unity whose operational goal is greater than the sum of its parts."[10]

With a view to Harris's suggestion that this assembled formation is "held together by imagery," I argue that it is cinematic narrative struc-ture that provides the connective principles through which images can serve such a purpose: thus the visualization and narrativization of sat-ellite and GPS imagery in cinema is deeply enmeshed in these "visual logics" and "convergent practices," functioning as an element of the "in-teroperability" of what James Der Derian calls the "military-industrial-media-entertainment network."[11] Parks suggests, with reference to Jameson, that such recognizable forms of satellite imaging as "Earth-shot" images "work to synthesize, contain, and transform the world's irreducibility into an iconic expression of global totality," and thus serve a discourse of globalization that emphasizes unification and organic de-velopment.[12] While the cinematic uses of satellite surveillance in geo-political action-thrillers would seem to focus instead on the tensions and violence of globalization, such surveillance narratives highlight the structural components of the move toward a visually and visibly situated world system. Even further, the structure of these films evidences how even the principles of unification and connectivity in idealized versions of a global totality are consistent with and even an aspect of the drive toward seamless operational fusion that defines the contemporary mili-tarized United States.

*　　*　　*

Most generally but most straightforwardly, surveillance narratives rely-ing heavily on satellite and GPS imagery indicate the place surveillance technologies have come to hold in the formations of geopolitics, particu-larly through the integration of system and subject. This integration can be traced directly to the manner in which surveillance is incorporated into a film's storyline, but, perhaps more importantly, also to its increasingly privileged place as an aspect of cinematic continuity systems. What one finds in films that incorporate locative technology and satellite imaging is that both systems serve dual and interrelated purposes: to visually establish an individual subject from a great distance, and to find a technological means *within* the narrative for motivating crosscutting between shots that construct elaborate plot connections between spaces, people, events, and actions. Whether they include a liberal surface critique of surveillance in their narrative, or unabashedly celebrate the spectacle of global surveillance, such films work to legitimize that caricatured element of the "world image" by demonstrating how central it is to the narrative allegory of totality explored by Jameson. There are myriad examples of these dual purposes: in the seminal example of such films, *Enemy of the State* (Tony Scott, 1998), the numerous shots coded as satellite images, targeting the protagonist from high above, visually situate him in a variety of complex urban spaces. These shots are then "put into play" as they are crosscut with shots of the satellites themselves in orbit, the satellite operation center, and other figures in the political drama that unfolds. Similarly, *Body of Lies* (Ridley Scott, 2008) begins a scene with a close-up of its white American protagonist (a CIA operative), sitting in a desert in North Africa; as he looks up, the scene cuts to what we might call an extreme reverse shot—ostensibly from the perspective of a satellite—of the protagonist's tiny form in the center of the bare desert expanse. The following shot brings us to the control room and thus situates the satellite image as part of a larger CIA operation overseeing and interacting remotely with the action "on the ground" as it unfolds. *Syriana* (Stephen Gaghan, 2005), an ensemble narrative that uses its parallel and intersecting plot threads as an analytic and critique of the politics of oil and American interest in the Persian Gulf, largely avoids the narrative or aesthetic use of surveillance as a method of establishing connections in its multilevel story. Nevertheless, the film culminates narratively in the satellite-enabled targeting and rocket assassination of an Arab political figure by the CIA. Several central characters previously operating in separate threads come together in this scene, which crosscuts (as is now standard) between the scene on the ground, with its personal character development and investment, the satellite control room, and satellite images of the characters from high above. Thus the intersections of violence and conspiracy in the world oil economy, which were managed almost entirely by parallel narrative development for the majority of the film, find their eventual expression in a tactical aesthetic of violence familiar from the televisual presentation of the 1991 Persian Gulf War—a war "at a distance" enabled in large part by geosurveillance.[13] The relations between the characters and their narrative threads simultaneously become evident and reach their conclusion through the introduction of the narrative and aesthetic device that is the satellite imaging system.

Many films that do not directly employ satellite imaging have borrowed the ubiquity of its unmistakable overhead angle as aesthetic and signifier. For instance, *Untraceable* (Gregory Hoblit, 2008), a film that pits the FBI against a serial killer murdering people live on the internet, uses several establishing shots of cities from directly above—not the more traditional high-angle extreme long shot from a helicopter, but instead a shot from absolutely, directly above, an angle that borrows from and evokes the satellite gaze. Similarly, *The Call* (Brad Anderson, 2013), which pits a 911 operator against a kidnapper as she attempts to locate one of the abductees, opens with an establishing shot of Los Angeles from directly above. This perspective has become increasingly common, and reveals a move toward a satellite-referential cinematic model, in which the traditional panoramic city shot is replaced with a direct overhead shot. This is especially true of films in which tracking and investigation are central, regardless of whether satellite imaging is explicitly incorporated or not.

GPS imaging, a digitally animated rendering of a figure in a given space enabled by satellite locative technologies, serves a similar purpose in these narratives, and is used both alongside and interchangeably with satellite photography.[14] The image, though this time arguably more mediated by digital animation than photographic images, is designed to show a point on a map from above. These data visualizations appear in the same cinematic genre and with an almost identical narrative function as the satellite photography—to visually pinpoint a singular figure within a broad narrative and visual context—and thus GPS also provides a tie between the general and the particular, an individual body and a system.[15] Satellite and GPS images, as might be clear from the above examples, often serve the function of establishing shots, providing the context for the individual storylines that will develop either within the entire film, or within the scene that shot is establishing. Here, however, the establishing shot is a continuous presence, insistently tying the individual's image and action to its context—a context that includes not just the space the satellite provides an image of, but the space that *includes* the satellite—a world system in which satellite technologies have an integral part, both symbolic and literal. The cinematic satellite image is, like many surveillance moments within these narratives, a type of point-of-view shot—an image that, insofar as it is highlighted as a technologized vision set apart from the other cinematic images, insistently refers back to itself as much as it refers to the objects it provides images of.

Thus these satellite (and GPS) images not only provide a broad view of a subject within space and position that subject in relation to other characters and plot elements within the film, they also represent an image of the very production of a global system—or at least a system predicated on the conceit of the global. While Jameson perhaps rightly refers to a satellite image as a "caricature" of an actual, unmappable world system, nevertheless the cinematic insistence on providing an image that represents the *point of view* of the global system represented by the film's narrative encourages the spectator to assume an identification not just with subjects within that system, *but with the system itself.* In doing so, these films also suggest that a character's import can be measured not just by the degree to which they are emphasized, as is traditional, in close-ups and dialogue but also, and even instead, through their visual portrayal from a vast distance and through the technological mediation of broad, networked processes. The implication is that, at least in the visual and narrative logic offered here, identification and subject formation for both film characters and cinema spectators are globally defined.

The satellite and GPS images within these films also clearly function as a narrative device, a technique that motivates crosscutting or establishes other cinematic forms of narrative connectivity. The satellite or GPS image almost never exists as a signifying image in and of itself; instead it is used as a mode of producing narrative relationality across very broad fields, and almost inevitably, in a manner that highlights the individual as a geopolitical subject. Most frequently and simply, this will take the form of a chase scene, in which we see not only what is happening on the ground but also the third and broader term in the chase—

the larger agency monitoring and directing the chase through satellite and GPS, an agency that represents the broader political context of the smaller, individual actions below. Thus what is otherwise simply another type of image-making technology becomes integrated into a *system*—in this case both a narrative system and a system of surveillance that comes to organize the world in certain relationships of power and exchange, showing that system's increasing centrality in the allegorical totality of the "global." Within these scenes, the surveillant image and the surveilling agency are frequently the narrative touchstone, the fulcrum of the scene, as much if not more than the protagonist (who is rarely aligned with the surveillant gaze) and in this way we see the further invitation to the film's spectators to identify themselves with both the system of surveillance and a globalizing visual logic, even as they are also identified with a character subjected to that system.

The fact that the great majority of scenes utilizing satellite and GPS are chase scenes that culminate in destruction and often death (though rarely of the protagonist) is crucial to understanding exactly what kind of global system this is: all the films use surveillance technology that visualizes "location" in such a way that it serves as a narrative and stylistic pivot that constructs relationships among individual bodies, inter- and transnational spaces, and broad global systems through economies of violence.[16] The agency and world citizenship of the protagonists of current political action-thrillers is offered only in relation to a violent targeting, even as they gain increased value within a larger symbolic economy of "global" politics. The frequent result, as we will see more fully later in the chapter, is that these films follow both a narrative and spatial trajectory that frequently establishes Americans as geopolitical subjects through monitored immersion in globalized urban locations, while simultaneously isolating and challenging the perceived threat of the "anti-urban": the orientalized desert.

This triangulated visual-narrative system of surveillance and its use in constructing a relation between individuals and a complex geopolitical milieu reached a (probably momentary) crescendo in the 2007 *The Bourne Ultimatum* (Paul Greengrass), the final film in the original Bourne trilogy (though the *Legacy* has recently continued on).[17] This series, based on the Robert Ludlum novels, follows Jason Bourne, an amnesiac rogue CIA assassin, as he tries to evade his former employers (who are now targeting him) and discover his own identity and his part in the espionage intrigues that develop. The twin objectives of the narrative—the identification of Bourne (unpacking his mystery) and the insistent tracking of his every move—could not do more to highlight the manner in which contemporary action-thrillers structure individual subjectivity as part of a global system. The identification of Bourne as a distinctively global subject is established in the original film, *The Bourne Identity* (Doug Liman, 2002), even and especially through his loss of identity. His search for himself begins with the discovery that he has approximately ten different passports, from nations ranging from the U.S. and Canada to Brazil and Russia, each covered in stamps from around the world. While the intrigues explored in the film series range from cold war espionage to contemporary counterterrorism, the politics of such global relations are reduced almost entirely to the question of "Who is Jason Bourne and what part does he play in all this?" As Klaus Dodds has written, in the Bourne films, "The geopolitical is always personal—and vice versa."[18] According to Dodds, the representation of Bourne's mastery as a resistant operative in geopolitical battles is intimately connected to his interpersonal relations and a recuperation of his masculinity. In the Bourne films, the politics are secondary to Bourne's search for himself—thus both he and those chasing him are engaged in essentially the same operation: the need to locate Jason Bourne. Accordingly, the narrative structure remains insistently tied to the GPS/CCTV/satellite-enabled chase scene as its almost total form. Rather than chase scenes and their insistent fast-paced crosscutting through a surveillance system serving as punctuations in between other narrative developments, *Ultimatum* uses the chase scene as its primary method of developing plot (with only a few brief pauses in between to introduce information in some other form). It is no accident that films wholly based on the relation between an individual subject and a complex and far-reaching geopolitical system would choose as their defining aesthetic, and even their entire plot structure, geolocative technologies and surveillant mediation. Even in scenes where it is not entirely clear that satellite imaging and/or GPS are being used by the characters, the aesthetic remains, foregrounding the visual coding of a "global subject" as one defined by contemporary structures of geosurveillance.[19]

What develops then, in between the geopolitical conspiracy films of the 1970s and 1980s that Jameson discusses and the surveillance-heavy geopolitical conspiracy films addressed here, is a shift from narratively oriented allegories of totality to an almost compulsive visual production of a total, global system through surveillance technologies: an extreme rendering of the geopolitical aesthetic that fully embraces its own caricatured forms. These simultaneously broad and specific visions of the world in turn organize the narrative such that personal, social, and political relations between characters and systems are motivated by and dependent on this visual production, rather than vice versa. The rising dominance of these imaging systems within both daily life and cinematic narrative appears to be both "the triumph and the grave" of allegories of totality.[20] Surveillance technologies and practices attempt to organize the global such that the world system and images of that system appear now so completely aligned that the distance between the literal and the figurative becomes difficult to conceptualize.

It is this simultaneous hegemony and collapse of allegories of globalization that will come to structure the films under discussion in the

Enemy of the State (1998) exemplifies the now standard action sequence, crosscutting between the chase, the surveillance operation, the satellite, and the satellite point-of-view shot.

remainder of this chapter, which vacillate between the celebration of the new global subject and the targeting of this subject for death. In a century defined as much by world war as by global capitalism (which is not to suggest that those are discrete phenomena), it is thus of use to augment Jameson's account of the geopolitical aesthetic as an allegory of late-twentieth-century capitalism with an understanding of the more literal intersections between geosurveillance and cinema (as technology, as structure, and as industry). Harris writes of the "interoperability" through which the distinctions between intelligence gathering, targeting, and weaponry are minimized such that the process of conceiving, planning, and carrying out an assault in the 1991 Gulf War became "essentially a technical and bureaucratic feedback system" that serves primarily to produce, reproduce, and reflect U.S. global military power.[21] But the technical and systemic merging of surveillance and targeting did not begin with the Gulf War, as Harris points to with examples from both World War II and the Vietnam War.[22] Paul Virilio has traced an even earlier foundational history of visual mediation in industrialized warfare, and his account makes it clear that the coextensive technologies and discourses of surveillance (especially overhead imaging) and cinema have been inseparable from the practices of warfare over the last one hundred years. Arguing that "[t]here is no war, then, without representation, no sophisticated weaponry without psychological mystification," Virilio sketches the shared history of war and cinema most directly through reference to aerial surveillance photography and film, which of course are the aesthetic and functional precursors to satellite imagery.[23] His discussion of technical, discursive, and ideological formations presents numerous surveillant intersections of the cinematic and the tactical, from technical developments in cameras to the study of movement. Most importantly for this current context, Virilio shows that the narrative contiguity I have been describing between a "globalized" subjectivity, surveillance, and targeting for death is grounded in historical, technological, and ideological coextensions established long ago.[24] Noting that in World War I air reconnaissance there was little practical difference between taking a photograph and firing a gun ("The pilot's hand automatically trips the camera shutter with the same gesture that releases his weapon"), Virilio offers a description of an operation from one hundred years ago that might easily be an account of the multiple functions of today's aerial reconnaissance, satellite systems, or drones: "For men at war, the function of the weapon is the function of the eye."[25] The production of cinematic spectacle that Virilio sees as consistent with these other operations, especially at the level of defining a cinematic system (aesthetic, industrial, and social), continues as well. And in the generic formations of the contemporary political action-thrillers, these spectacles foreground surveillance as an integral element of narrative structure, and, perhaps more significantly, show how the principles of cinematic storytelling establish "the cinematic" as a connective tissue between surveillance and death.

*　*　*

Enemy of the State, as suggested above, has come to serve as the model for more recent films that incorporate satellite imaging as an integral part of the narrative, and Tony Scott (before his suicide in 2012) was becoming somewhat of a surveillance auteur, continuing these themes and aesthetics in the 2006 action-sci-fi-terrorism-thriller *Déjà vu*, discussed in greater detail in the next chapter. *Enemy of the State* tells the fictionalized story of the political intrigue surrounding a bill that allows the U.S. government broad powers of surveillance, pitting corrupt National Security Agency leadership against resistant members of Congress and unwitting citizens. The political tale is told through the filter of one of these citizens, a labor attorney played by Will Smith, who, like Matt Damon in the Bourne films, had been established in the prior few years as one of the most marketable, on-the-cusp-of-A-list actors. With the casting of Smith, *Enemy of the State* establishes itself as an action-based political film with a personality-based narrative, even before the narrative unfolds. While it is "set" entirely within the U.S., both the political stakes around national security and the use of GPS and satellite within the narrative make this a film that presents domestic concerns (in a number of senses) as on the cusp of global political significance.

Smith's character, Robert Dean, finds himself by pure happenstance at the center of this intrigue when an old college buddy surreptitiously drops a computer disk into Dean's shopping bag as he runs for his life. The disk contains surveillance footage of a congressman's murder, which Dean's friend, a wildlife researcher, captured unintentionally with a hidden camera intended to record birds. This series of purely accidental encounters, though equally as unlikely as the complex conspiracies of the Bourne films, similarly results in a large-scale manhunt (already begun with the chase of the friend who slips the disk to Dean), with the massive technological and political power of the NSA unleashed upon Dean by those responsible for the videotaped murder. The narrative is organized around Dean's discovery that he is being tracked and then targeted, followed by his attempts to extricate himself from the multiple "framings" used against him as weapons: the constant visual frames of the surveillance he is now under, and the information technology–enabled frame-up in which his professional, financial, and personal life are destroyed such that he will have no credibility should he go public with the video. By using the NSA's access to massive amounts of personal data as the method of targeting Dean alongside its elaborate geo-surveillance operation, the film already effectively elides any distinction between its surveillance system and the myriad economic and social systems through which daily life functions in the contemporary United States. Here *Enemy of the State* suggests the dependence of a subject's position on the "correct" functioning of multiple systems (computer systems, legal systems, financial systems, etc.), which a surveillant narrative structure produces as integrated and thus unstable—a threat to one's very identity.[26] Ultimately, the film goes to great lengths to demonstrate how an individual's life, in this case bourgeois domestic life in particular, is inextricably linked to geopolitical concerns; in no uncertain terms, it also makes clear that the tie that binds these realms is a network of surveillance systems.

Similarly to the visual system described above in which the pinpointing of an individual is tied to a representation of global totality through satellite imaging, *Enemy of the State* insists that the political debates about national security versus individual rights come down to a question of how much one's domestic space can and should be put into relationship with national security practices and geopolitical systems. The increasing intrusion of the NSA into Dean's life also involves the revelation of his marital problems resulting from a prior affair, and the film moves frequently back and forth between his domestic space and his implication in the political conspiracy. The suggestions of marital difficulty are themselves heavily interspersed with clear visual and narrative representations of an upper-middle-class couple very much in love and happy in the domestic space that they share with their young son. As the surveillance is ratcheted up, the fallout from his infidelity is reactivated and his marriage and domestic life are destabilized; the plot thread in which he evades surveillance, clears his name, and manages to expose the government figures targeting him is joined with the plot thread in which he reconnects with his wife and reestablishes domestic propriety and happiness. In and of itself, this is unremarkable—surveillance films are certainly not the only Hollywood narratives in which the establishment or reestablishment of a heterosexual union is provided as the corollary resolution to a parallel or primary narrative thread. As has been argued in numerous contexts, this is the very lifeblood of classical Hollywood narrative. The particular insistence on this formula in this context is notable more for the significance that "intimate," domestic space comes to hold in a film that is on every other level concerned with presenting as broad an aesthetic and narrative as possible. Unlike the films of the 1970s and 1980s that Jameson discusses as conspiratorial narratives, which feature usually unmarried and often antisocial protagonists attempting to uncover a vast political system, the otherwise paranoid political vision of *Enemy of the State* returns to a more classical Hollywood formula. The film's structure and its reliance on heterosexual monogamy to define both discord and resolution imply that geopolitical stakes *are* in some ways reducible to the domestic stakes of the bourgeois household (another instance of Klaus Dodds's observation about the Bourne films: "The personal is geopolitical").[27]

To drive this point home (as it were), the film closes not with Dean's successful escape from surveillance, but instead with multiple formations of surveillant mediation "managed" within and by domesticity. The final scene presents Dean and his wife sitting on their couch watching television: they have exposed the "bad apples" in the U.S. government with the help of an ex-NSA operative now working as a surveillance expert, Edward Lyle (played by Gene Hackman, in what is one of this film's several references to the earlier canonical surveillance narrative, *The Conversation*). As they watch the political story from which they have now extricated themselves play out on their television, "resolution" here suggests a return to their proper roles as spectators. As Dean's wife (also an attorney) shouts her critiques of governmental surveillance at the screen, he playfully turns her comments into a sexual innuendo, and the connection between their position as media consumers, the liberal critique of government overreach, and the stability of their upper-middle-class existence becomes synonymous with narrative resolution.

The scene continues with Dean flipping through the channels until he sees a live video image of himself, sitting and watching TV. Realizing that this surveillance shot is a perversely playful greeting from his mysterious ally, he responds conversationally to the television as Lyle communicates a message through a series of televised images. Rather than respond with outrage that Lyle has invaded his home, Dean merely teases him—"You are one sick man"—and accepts this "friendly" invasion of his privacy as humorous. The film closes with Dean's television returning to its usual broadcast in the form of Larry King, who in 1998 was an iconic political talk show host, conducting a discussion about surveillance and national security, followed by a cut to the film's final imagery: satellite photography of the globe—the "Earth-shot" Lisa Parks cites as the emblematic image of idealized globalization. King's characteristic political narcissism provides the film's concluding dialogue in voiceover: "You've got no right to come into my home." The contiguity offered between domestic space and global imaging is announced here with little subtlety: a final political comment provided by a televised media figure on the sanctity of domestic space, accompanied by an image of the globe, sets the terms fairly clearly. Even while the media provides critiques of surveillance culture, it is that same mediating presence that provides the link between the "world system" and individual subjects within it. By establishing both a visual and narrative continuity between the personal and the political, the singular and the total, the house and the globe, all through devices of surveillance and mediation, the film indicates that it is in some ways proper domestic work—and the task of the media consumer—to establish one's place in the global system. The connection to legal and political debates about security versus privacy is clear, but what the film seems to suggest is that ultimately the privacy at stake is that of the liberal bourgeois subject who, even if his or her domestic life isn't perfect, ultimately has "nothing to hide" and must, like Dean, merely accept with begrudging good humor the pervasiveness of surveillance as part of the economy of mediation in upper-middle-class America.[28]

A reading of this film through its positioning of the ideal liberal bourgeois subject in a security state is bolstered by the casting of a black actor and celebrity, Will Smith, in the lead role. Beyond its function as a star vehicle for Smith, it is not inconsequential that a film about the unfair targeting of a black man by American surveillance and security operatives takes such pains to emphasize this targeting as an absolute, unequivocal coincidence. Both in the casting of Smith and the implicit reliance on his bankability as an action star, the film narrates the over-reach of state surveillance in the 1990s in a framework that completely ignores and even puts under erasure the racial projects of American surveillance (and cinema): the racializing and profiling central to the policing of black populations, the Islamophobic securitization characteristic of the 1990s on through today, and countless others that have rendered the histories of surveillance inseparable from the histories of race in the United States. Instead, Smith is cast in a role that in today's parlance would be referred to as "postracial" (in terms of both his upward career trajectory and his narrative function within the film), suggesting a significant disavowal at the heart of this critique of surveillance and an investment in the idea that this could happen to *anyone* (an idea that also has come to define contemporary forms of celebrity, especially as constructed by reality programming).[29]

Whatever critique of surveillance the film offers thus becomes firmly planted in the discourse of privacy protection and more concerned with the exposure of marital infidelities in the bourgeois home than with the exposure of subjects to the violence of a racist surveillant state. This disavowal is central to the wishful construction of the contemporary (neo) liberal subject, whose critique of surveillance as a universally invasive practice that might target anyone simply becomes part of the functioning of a security state that, like cinema, has built its structures on racial visibility while maintaining itself in the conceit of the neutrality of surveillant, technological vision. The liberal discourse of privacy protection that structures this narrative and continues to structure political debates on surveillance deflects attention from the historical and actual uses of surveillance; it also ignores how surveillance was involved in the construction of the (politicized) privacy of bourgeois domestic space using the same logic and practices that excluded racial difference from that formulation. Thus Robert Corber's claim in his essay about *Rear*

Window's representation of surveillance in the McCarthy era can be seen as equally, if not more, applicable to the narrative of *Enemy of the State* and the context of contemporary privacy versus security debates: "[T] he film suggests that the political identity of the liberal subject *should* wholly saturate its humanity, for if the subject's humanity did not coincide perfectly with its political identity, then it might make claims based on its identity as a gendered and/or racialized subject."[30]

If we consider the film's narrative formulation in relation to the stylistic constructions discussed earlier in this chapter, what emerges is that *Enemy of the State*'s narrative efforts to establish the individual subject in relation to a global system do *not* ultimately serve to highlight the political implications and context of an otherwise individualized subject. Rather, they serve to eclipse historically embodied political experience, particularly as defined by racial identity, in favor of a liberal subject defined in relation to an *aesthetic* of geopolitics, an aesthetic produced through the incorporation of global imaging and information systems into cinematic continuity devices and broader media culture. This aesthetic in turn serves to centralize and privilege the place of the bourgeois media consumer even as that consumer is shown to be endangered by the very technologies that enable his or her position, the implications of which become more clear later in this chapter.

Enemy of the State's more contemporary analogue, *Eagle Eye*, also proves revealing in terms of the way the lived political body (and the body politic) is erased from the consideration of Hollywood's contemporary surveillance action-thriller even in its very invocation: *Eagle Eye* follows a similar trajectory of the frame-up of an "ordinary," innocent American citizen, and offers a similarly superficial critique of the expansion of surveillance. This time, however, the surveillance system, though part of the U.S. government, turns out to be a computer system that has taken the surveillance and security directive upon itself and decided to have the executive branch of the U.S. government assassinated. This counterterrorist artificial intelligence has determined that the president and his administration are a threat to national security because they have made mistakes in military operations overseas, costing innocent lives and provoking retaliatory terrorist bombings targeting Americans. Though clearly less grounded in the realities of surveillance and security, the aesthetics of this film are very similar to the earlier *Enemy of the State* (though the intervening years have allowed the more recent film to produce even more elaborate surveillance and control fantasies). The targeting of a citizen by the government in the interest of security remains the same; in the later film, however, the politics of security, terrorism, and counterterrorism are reduced to a technology that has gotten out of hand. Thus, even as contemporary political issues are raised, they are repeatedly disembodied as the film reveals that the innocent hero is accidentally targeted because of the threat his (now dead) twin brother posed to the computer intelligence system, alongside the revelation that the surveillance/targeting is carried out independently of any actual human agents. In short, no-body surveils/targets any-body. *Eagle Eye* suggests that a totalizing system of surveillance is in many ways entirely technological, even as it is clearly a system that has been built upon and continues to build upon the production, management, and destruction of human bodies as markers in a geopolitical field.

Such a narrative, even or especially in its critique of technology, produces a representation of surveillance, terrorism, and war that is quite consistent—and even intersects—with the status of representation and mediation in U.S.-led military action since the Gulf War of 1991. Rhetorical theorist Barbara Biesecker's summary of the critiques of that heavily mediated war is extremely resonant:

> [Critics] argued that Operation Desert Storm delivered not a new kind of warfare but a new aesthetics of war whose strategically selected images and carefully crafted discourse together worked to literally "dehumanize" the cost of armed conflict. . . . For the general public whose perception of the war was given shape by what did and did not appear on their television screens, these scholars rightly insisted, the first Gulf War was a war without bodies—a technological exercise executed not by men but by machines whose "surgical" "smart bombs" took out "units," not enemy soldiers, a "Nintendo War" during which, as Paul Virilio put it, "the aesthetics of disappearance" (1989, 11) carried the day.[31]

Viewed as part of the same historical field of surveillance and violence, the variously erased bodies on which both *Enemy of the State* and *Eagle*

Eye build their narratives situate these films and their liberal critiques of a surveillance culture as operating within the same discursive logic of a hypermediated war.

*   *   *

However, this erasure of lived, political bodies is accompanied by a corresponding, seemingly contradictory, enlargement and extrapolation of those bodies as they are situated within a geopolitical context, as shown both in the cinematic narratives above and in contemporary surveillance and security practice. Michael Shapiro's book *Cinematic Geopolitics* emphasizes this expansion in relation to the logics of recent counterterrorist surveillance:

> In the contemporary period, in which we can observe an inter-articulation between pandemics and terrorism, the qualifications applied to bodies have achieved a high level of complexity. Thus, the secondary spatialization of terrorism (like that of disease), its location in the body, has resulted in a body that is expanded well beyond its corporeal existence. As A. R. Stone puts it, "[t]he socially apprehensible citizen . . . consists of a collection of both physical and discursive elements." It is a "legible body" whose "textually mediated physicality" extends to its paper [and electronic] trail. Hence, for example, the militarized, surveilling agencies connected with the war on terror treat the body's phone, email, credit card, and library borrowing records, and in some cases, phone conversations. Bodies inside and outside, citizen and non-citizen, thus have enlarged silhouettes, shapes that extend to their financial, communicational, and informational prostheses. Just as, in Foucault's terms, there are spatializations of diseases beyond the confines of the individual body to include "other distributions of illness," the location of a contemporary political pathology goes beyond directly implemented ideologies, beyond the desires and drives in the individual terrorist body, to networks and cells with a global distribution.[32]

Shapiro's account of the expansion of the body into the broad, global spatialization in geosurveillance demonstrates how globalizing surveillance technologies work to produce a circumstance in which there is no truly singular body—there is a body only in relation to the network it represents. And yet, it is the production of this body in relation to the system that in turn opens that individual, lived body up to a violent targeting.[33] In these action-thrillers, this expansion and spatialization is produced through the narrative incorporation of the individual into an explicitly visualized global system; it is a cinematic practice that demonstrates and even serves to produce an aesthetic model for how the parameters of a body targeted by surveillance expand exponentially.

*   *   *

The double bind of the geopolitical subjects in films such as *The Bourne Ultimatum*, *Eagle Eye*, and *Enemy of the State* and the structure connecting these films to the production of racialized, terrorist bodies in contemporary surveillance and politics are predicated on formations already at work in a surveillance film from the earlier 1990s, Philip Kaufman's *Rising Sun*. This film in many ways represents a prior era of surveillance narrative (pre-satellite, pre-GPS) but it sets a number of terms that are connected to the later films that deploy a more recognizably contemporary approach to the geopolitical aesthetic. *Rising Sun*, released in 1993 and based on a Michael Crichton novel, structures its "international" thriller around a murder caught on surveillance video: in fact a new global economy seems to become organized around the stakes of this single death. In its 1980s orientation, *Rising Sun's* vision of globalization gears itself toward the perceived threat posed by growing foreign economies to the culture of the United States. But as a film working with earlier, non-terrorism-centric tropes of surveillance narrative, newly digital technologies of surveillance, and conceptions of global systems, it represents the scaffolding of later geopolitical narratives of surveillance.

Rising Sun is remarkable largely for its historical specificity, as it demonstrates the hysteria of the 1980s and early 1990s organized simultaneously around the incursion of Japanese corporate power into the American economy and culture and the growth of surveillance culture, in this case represented by the transition of video surveillance systems into a digital medium. Globalization and the technologies of surveillance are hyperbolically orientalized in this film, which would seem to set it off markedly from later films that work to assume both surveillance and globalized subjectivity as part and parcel of American life. In addition to its economy-based, 1980s vision of a "world system," *Rising Sun's* generic formation as a traditional detective narrative rather than a political espionage thriller also sets it off from the other films addressed thus far in this chapter. However, this film, through its imagination of the intersection between international economies and surveillance practices, represents a structure that underlies both the narrative fantasies of contemporary geopolitical thrillers and the market concerns of the generic development and distribution of those films. The consistencies with as well as the shifts in the recent historical trajectory of the geopolitical thriller give insight into the shared logic between the global market economy, the production of global subjects, and the violence enacted on singular bodies in geopolitical warfare and contemporary discourses of security and counterterrorism.

The film's opening sets the tone immediately: a grainy image of a movie Western, from which the camera pulls back to reveal that the scene is actually a karaoke performance by a Japanese man singing the country classic "Don't Fence Me In." The terms are set right away, positing cross-cultural exchange as enabled by mediated imagery and performance and simultaneously highlighting the dissonance within this mediated exchange, which is presented first as comedic and then as leading to violence. The setting turns out to be Los Angeles, and the film goes on to trace the cultural, economic, and political implications of a young woman's murder caught on surveillance video at the Los Angeles headquarters of a Japanese corporation.

The film's protagonist, Lt. Webster Smith, played by Wesley Snipes, is a special services liaison officer for the Los Angeles police—it is his responsibility to communicate with non-Americans when the police are involved, though he is presented as either very new or very bad at this job. When called in by homicide detectives investigating the murder at the Nakamoto building during a giant corporate gala, he is also instructed to pick up Capt. John Connor, played by Sean Connery, whose presence has been requested by the Japanese executives. Connor is the man who truly performs the job of cultural liaison; in fact it is suggested that he is so deeply immersed in Japanese ways that he has perhaps "crossed over to the other side." As he patronizingly instructs Smith on what to do when they arrive, the very recognizable terms of this classic cop-partner narrative are also established: an at first combative relationship between the older, wiser, rogueish cop and the younger, naïve, earnest partner. The racial set-up here, separate from the consideration of the Japanese theme, is also highly recognizable in the context of detective/action films of the 1980s and 1990s: the tension/camaraderie between black and white cop duos is central in films ranging from *48 Hours* (1982) to the *Lethal Weapon* series, the *Beverly Hills Cop* series, and the *Men in Black* series, as well as the *Miami Vice* television series. In *Rising Sun*, unlike some of these other works, the race of its characters is explicitly addressed, and the more "traditional" racial tensions of the United States are presented against the backdrop and complicating factors of a Japanophilic white partner, a racist homicide detective (played by Harvey Keitel), a xenophobic white American senator critical of Japanese influence in the U.S., and a host of Japanese characters who are presented simultaneously as victims of xenophobia and dangerous, perverse, mysterious intruders who are themselves extremely racist. As such, the film already offers itself as a fertile field for analysis in terms of the construction of numerous subject positions, racialized and otherwise, in an increasingly globalized environment.

Added to this is the crux of the investigation—the sex and murder caught on in-house surveillance video—which eventually becomes the marker of both truth and manipulability. The film's plot takes numerous turns, marked in large part by changes in the video evidence, which shows different things when subjected to different forms of analysis. At first the video appears not to have captured the face of the murderer. Subjected to close, expert analysis, the murderer's reflection in a mirror is revealed: it is the Japanese lover of the woman, who was with her in the first scene as he sang "Don't Fence Me In," and then angrily chased her out of the bar. Still later, and upon further analysis by the detectives and their media experts, it is discovered that the video has been altered. The unaltered video appears to show that the murderer is actually the xenophobic Senator John Morton, who had intended to vote against Nakamoto's purchase of an American weapons company and who is now apparently being blackmailed with the video to change his vote. Later still, the film reveals that the video continues past the murder, and that Morton didn't kill her at all—he believed that he had mistakenly strangled her during consensual erotic asphyxiation, but in fact she had awoken after he ran off and *another* unidentified man came in and murdered her. Connor and Smith bring this unaltered, unedited video to the Nakamoto boardroom, where all the possible suspects are assembled, for a final confrontation that will force the killer to reveal himself (a wrap-up, again, in classic detective story style). The head of the corporation, Yoshida, appears surprised and disturbed by all of this, and as tension mounts among his employees, finally a character is fingered as the killer—the one white American working for the Japanese. He runs as the detectives give chase, and then either falls or is thrown by yakuza into a conveniently located giant vat of wet concrete. Mystery solved—until it is suggested to Smith by the half-Japanese video analyst, who turns out to be Connor's mysterious lover, that it is Japanese custom for underlings to take the fall for the boss, and that in fact Yoshida could have been aware of all this; Connor might even have been complicit in the whole elaborate set-up. The audience is left with Smith not knowing the real truth, which is hidden behind the maze of Japanese customs that are marked as powerfully sinister, and which, in the form of a surveillance narrative, manage to render even the certainty of death somewhat ambiguous.

As is apparent from the twists and turns in both the surveillance video and the plot (in a series of video-enabled misrecognitions and ambiguities that will be familiar from Chapter One), the incorporation of surveillance video and the production of racialized, political subjects appear here as mutually structuring narrative formations. The video holds the key to the "truth," but also testifies to its fundamental manipulability and, in this film, orientalized mystery. The video is coded as inflected by digital technological advancements that are also offered as representative of their Japanese origins: the American security guard operating the surveillance system at the Nakamoto corporation is clearly awed by the technology, telling the investigating detectives that it is all totally "next generation" as he demonstrates the pan-tilt-zoom (PTZ) function and the digital recording of the video onto disks.[34] Later, when the video is subjected to analysis, there is repeated reference to the pixels being "doctored," and thus some of the ambiguities and manipulability of video are only furthered by the digitization of the medium, as is now well evidenced by the discourse of digital cultures.[35]

However, it is the degree to which all of this is effectively orientalized in this film that is considerably more remarkable in this context than is the simple suggestion that video surveillance is a powerful technological tool in both its truth claims and its manipulability. Not only is the "next generation" technology of surveillance presented as a Japanese product but—absurdly—*Rising Sun* presents workplace surveillance itself as a Japanese cultural tradition, rather than as part and parcel of modern labor since industrialization. During the discussion with the security guard, Detective Connor states with authority, "I know in Japan they like to observe their workers, to help them improve their efficiency," effectively displacing over one hundred years of surveillance history in labor onto a cultural other that is seen as coming dangerously close to taking over the American economy, an economy presented as naïvely separate from anything so controlling as workplace surveillance.[36] Thus both the technology and the agenda of corporate surveillance are presented as coming to the United States from the East through the rise of a global market economy that is an essential threat to the ostensibly less ritualistic and controlling American way of life.

As mentioned above, the orientalization of surveillance practice is augmented by the orientalization of American racism. Detective Smith makes repeated and explicit references to his subjection to racist treatment, beginning with his suggestion that the mentoring relationship that Connor puts into place with him is a master/slave dynamic. When shortly thereafter he is mistaken for a valet, Smith yells, "Wrong guy, wrong century." Set against the backdrop of American xenophobia toward the Japanese, the references to domestic racial history in the U.S. gesture toward a more complex presentation of racial formation in the narrative (even as Smith's defensiveness is presented as vaguely hysterical and unfounded). However, the promise of incisive critique is undermined by the casting of Japan as more "backward" and insidiously racist than the United States. Among other instances, the beautiful, half-Japanese video analyst, named (ridiculously) Jingo, speaks of how badly she was treated in Japan because her father was a black American soldier. Ultimately, despite all the references to American histories of racism toward blacks, and the repeated representations of xenophobic, racist response toward the Japanese, the film manages to effectively place the role of racist xenophobes onto the Japanese. This is not to deny the historical existence of xenophobia and racism in Japan, merely to suggest that the film uses Japan, in a fascinating interweaving of representations of technological advancement and cultural traditionalism, as a convenient site of projection for both the development of more elaborate surveillance practice and the violent production of racialized subjects.

While this film as a single text means little, it should be placed in context with multiple other films of 1980s that build both narratives and aesthetics on the premise of a United States subject to the cultural and economic influence of both Japan and China. Ridley Scott's *Blade Runner* (1982) and *Black Rain* (1989), which also (in very different forms) construct the detective thriller as one with geopolitical tinges focused on an Asian market force, are clearly related. But even such works as *The Karate Kid* films (John G. Avildsen, 1984, 1986, and 1989), the comedy *Gung Ho* (Ron Howard, 1986), and other generically disparate films (such as the white American kung fu hero narrative best represented by the films of Chuck Norris) are indicative of the broad cinematic trend in the 1980s that set the terms of globalization in genre films as highly orientalized.[37] *Rising Sun* suggests a number of ways in which the more contemporary films' presentation of the complexity of geopolitics and new technology might be seen as predicated on an initial American orientalization of both the politics of surveillance and the violence constructed through globalization, which we see play out in the more contemporary era as a discourse of security against the terrorist Muslim other.[38]

* * *

This orientalization takes aesthetic form in the more recent explicitly geopolitical thrillers through the repetition of certain satellite-produced landscapes. In numerous cases, the Western, "global subject" of the action-thriller is idealized through his mastery of what are presented across the board as transnational urban spaces; the flipside of this mastery is the incomprehensible expanse of an orientalized desert. On the one hand, it is difficult to speak of the precise setting of any geopolitical action thriller, since the films are defined by the cinematically aided ability of scenes to unfold in multiple locations simultaneously and contingently. This sensation of spatial multiplicity produced through editing is augmented by the fact that the films move their protagonists from nation to nation, city to city with high-speed abandon: the settings are thus frequently aided by location (and often time) stamps alongside scene changes, adding to the sense of such films as piecing together a surveillant vision of the world. This globalized movement is characteristic of the mastery shown by the (Western, white, male) protagonists of the films, and often defines their geopolitical sophistication, especially when the spaces they move through are presented as exotically Other.[39] Such movement, as Caren Kaplan has shown, is characteristic of the romanticization of mobility underlying the construction of the modern Western subject: "Supported by numerous developing technologies of transportation and communication, the free subject of Western culture has been afforded an expansive consciousness of movement with accompanying discourses of sight, sound, and selfhood."[40] It is thus not surprising that surveillance technologies in geopolitical action-thrillers do not serve to undermine the mobility and mastery of the protagonists even if surveillance is presented as a threat, but instead provide them opportunities to perform their sophistication through evasion and reversal.

Both the more earnest geopolitical thrillers *Body of Lies* and *Syriana* and the more cartoonish action genre films *Mission: Impossible—Ghost Protocol* and *The Bourne Ultimatum* present protagonists moving expertly through the urban spaces of various cities of the "Middle East," but in most of these same films there are also scenes in which the otherwise masterful global subjects have become both visually and narratively isolated and abandoned to a desert. While the reasons and outcomes of this exposure are not uniform, the threat the desert poses is defined almost invariably by its association with the violently irrational power of political figures who narratively define the desert space (sheikhs, terrorists, arms traders, etc.).[41] The isolation and unrecognizability of these desert powers, as well as the threat to the Western protagonists now in their realm, is signified by the presentation of their figures via satellite image, rendering them as dots in a vast expanse of sandy nothingness.

Classical Hollywood established the mystique of the orient through the labyrinthine spaces of "Chinatown." While certainly this is still a common characterization (and has increasingly been reactivated in the form of the hectic mystery of a stereotyped "Middle Eastern city" more consistent with the Anglo-Orientalism that was the focus of Edward Said's defining work on the topic), these films have cast the contemporary version of "oriental inscrutability" in the mold of the hyperdistance

A figure isolated and targeted by satellite in the desert landscape: *Body of Lies* (2008).

of the satellite gaze and the expanse of a desert landscape. This element is opposed to the satellite chase scenes of *Enemy of the State* or *The Bourne Ultimatum*, which even as a threat to the protagonists served to show their capacity to use the city as a means of evasion, employing cosmopolitan ingenuity, physical stamina and grace, and video-game-style driving ability to show that their position was not, in the end, subject to the authoritative gaze of the paternal and ever watchful state. In the desert space, the protagonists generally function as little more than tiny figures to highlight the sheer power of the landscape to render them useless, and good driving and cleverness do little to help them.

The tension between the global subject in urban space and the threat of the orientalized desert, as well as the role geosurveillance plays in mediating that relation, are hyperbolically announced by the fourth film in the cinematic *Mission: Impossible* series and its construction of a battle scene between the desert and the city, with the action hero caught in the middle. In one of the many climactic scenes from *Mission: Impossible— Ghost Protocol* (Brad Bird, 2011), a sand storm envelops the urban and cinematic space that Tom Cruise (and I specifically mean the actor in his role) has just conquered: insistent on doing his own stunts, Cruise climbs out a window atop the Burj Khalifa in Dubai (the tallest building in the world) and scales several floors in a thrillingly vertiginous sequence.[42] Moments later, he must chase his suspect (a secondary villain) as he disappears into a wall of sand when the city of Dubai is overtaken by the desert in a paralyzing sand storm—it is his handheld GPS that allows the chase and the scene to continue and develop as spectacle, though ultimately the suspect escapes. There is no direct connection between the scene's twist ending, in which the suspect peels off an absurdly realistic mask to reveal himself as the film's arch-villain, and the sand storm; nevertheless, the escape and misidentification serve to further characterize the city consumed by the desert as impossibly slippery.[43] The fantasy that at any moment the desert could simply overtake this major city and produce a scenario of almost total unapprehensibility for a contemporary action hero (who is often defined by a generalized supercapacity and a genius for adaptability) is a pronounced one in the context of other narrative uses of the desert in geopolitical thrillers. The fact that the only possibility of recuperating visibility and control is offered here through geolocative technologies announces the triangulation between satellite-based surveillance, urban space, and what is an almost comedically orientalized desert space of violent invisibility and dissimulation.

Whether presented through the cartoonish excess of *Ghost Protocol*, or in the more "realist" dramatic treatment in *Syriana* or *Body of Lies*, the space of the desert, often visually defined by geosurveillance images, thus serves within the narrative as a foil or interruption of the characteristic authority and capability of the films' protagonists. Such cinematic uses of the satellite-envisioned desert, in combination with the very explicit political uses of satellite surveillance photos of Iraq to provide "evidence" of Saddam Hussein's now infamously nonexistent "weapons of mass destruction," paint a fairly uniform picture of the orientalist politics of satellite aesthetics. The unknowable, isolated figures in the desert are maintained as such through their (in)visible characterization in satellite imaging, and are also presented as simultaneously signifying a threat to the West by virtue of this same negative epistemology: the ambiguity of figures and structures from the distant, overhead shot is presented as an effort to conceal—the nothing becomes a signifier of a very deadly something.[44] Barbara Biesecker's analysis of Secretary of State Colin Powell's public performance of satellite image interpretation before the United Nations Security Council in 2003 shows how the case for war against Iraq built a rhetorical construct and ideological principle upon the opacity of an overhead shot of the Iraqi landscape. Powell's "explanation" of the evidence that these satellite images *show* but that one *cannot see* produces the viewer as "moved by exposure to our own blindness to believe that even—or especially—in circumstances in which we see nothing, something is likely taking place on the other side of a sign that *we* are incapable of reading on our own."[45]

This "hermeneutics of suspicion" is one that is in large part enabled not just by the lack of clarity of satellite surveillance photographs, but by those images' consistency with the historical and frequently *cinematic* production of orientalized space.[46] Film scholar Homay King's theoretical account of cinematic orientalism is useful here, as it departs from critiques based primarily in stereotyped characters and in its focus on mise-en-scène argues for a spatial understanding of the Orient's function as an "enigmatic signifier": a structuring unintelligibility upon which worlds of signification are built.[47] Viewed through the context and logic of King's framework, we might say that the contemporary political and cinematic uses of satellite imagery are predicated on the spatial premises of orientalism in order to function as part of an orientalizing spatial project, thus becoming perfectly reflexive, and, once again, building something out of nothing: "Every enigmatic signifier is a copy of an endless series of copies that has been passed down through the generations as in a game of telephone."[48]

Virilio's conception of an "aesthetics of disappearance," though it does not exactly refer to this formation, becomes an apt turn of phrase to describe how the configurations of the overhead, distant perspective and the imaging of figures offset by a desert expanse combine to serve a mystification of enemy power, which in turn both eclipses and rationalizes American military force that might otherwise be evident in that same image.[49] What Virilio has described as the representational effect of war—"Through its hyper-generation of movement, mixing the accomplishments of the means of destruction and the means of communicating destruction, war falsifies appearance by falsifying distance"—could equally be used to describe contemporary surveillance, in both political and cinematic form.[50] In her above analysis, Biesecker suggests that the shifts in rhetoric, form, and function between Operation Desert Storm in 1991 and the invasion of Iraq in 2003 as part of a broadly defined "war on terror" demand a reformulation of Virilio's ideas: "What was in one war an aesthetics of disappearance was transformed in the war on terror into an aesthetics of dematerialization—a stylization of war through which the specular was rendered spectral, uncertain, and indeterminate."[51] I would suggest, as Biesecker also implies with her focus on Secretary Powell's presentation of satellite images, that the shift toward indeterminacy both describes and in large part is effected by the uses of surveillance, which, as we saw with video in Chapter One, find greater effect in their uncertainty than in their evidentiary value. Satellites, utilized in war for "precision bombing," here are used in their imprecision to create reasons and targets to bomb. "Drones" or UAVs, remote controlled via satellite, are used both for aerial surveillance and to carry out many of the extralegal assassinations of the current iteration of the "war on terror." Once again, the boundaries between weaponry and surveillance evaporate, but we also see within the multiple uses of satellite technology—a centerpiece of military "interoperability"—a lack of distinction between precision and imprecision, even between target and civilian. It is in this space—the satellite-enabled zone of indistinction—that we might locate those killed by U.S. missile strikes in the current "war."[52] As this term becomes more and more abstractly representational, it becomes increasingly easy for Virilio's definition of war's representational effects to become reversed such that the representational effects serve to produce war; this reversibility appears to be one of the central functions of contemporary tactical surveillance. What I would emphasize in the current context is how the generic formations of geopolitical thrillers (even when critical of the politics they represent) provide a narrative structure that serves as a placeholder where one might otherwise find boundaries between surveillance, cinema, and contemporary war.

These relations are exemplified by the trajectory of *Syriana*, as its parallel narratives culminate in a violent intersection of virtually all the elements described above. Since the film is based both structurally and thematically on a consideration of the political and personal connectivity within a geopolitical tale of the oil economy, terrorism, and the arms trade, its general avoidance of a surveillant or hypermediated narrative style is notable. In the context of a decade in which the cinematic presentation of geopolitical relations has moved toward surveillance as the principle of connectivity (both within the story and in a continuity editing system using surveillance as a transition device between shots and narrative elements), *Syriana* defers explanation of connectivity, and thus defers surveillant narration. But the moment of climactic intersection that brings together the two central protagonists is also the moment when the film epitomizes the satellite-based geopolitical aesthetic, and thus highlights its narrative result: a scene envisioned by satellite images and the at-a-distance missile assassination of a geopolitical target (with those nearby becoming collateral damage). The satellite imagery and assassination is defined, unsurprisingly, by the desert landscape that provides the setting. The deferral of the narrative use of surveillance, a satellite-envisioned desert landscape, and political targeting and assassination, until the moment when the film seeks to *define the relations* between its narrative threads of diverse places and people, only foregrounds the degree to which all those elements overwhelmingly define geopolitical connectivity in cinema.

It is not simply a principle of connectivity that defines the narrative, surveillant, and weaponized uses of satellites in cinema and politics; it is also the fact that this connectivity is itself defined by indeterminacies and indistinctions. For instance, in the latest *Mission: Impossible, Ghost Protocol*, the relation between urban mastery and the destructive invisibility of the desert is offered through a sandstorm, in which the two separately defined spaces effectively become one. The film also produces a narrative fusion of the functions of satellites, which are now centralized in the plot with the black market purchase of a defunct Soviet satellite for use in transmitting stolen launch codes to nuclear missiles (which of course will themselves be guided to their targets by satellite technology). While still offering the recognizable aesthetic and narrative device of the satellite perspective, a globalized vision of tracking and detection, the satellite also becomes a clue in the hunt for the villain and thus an object in and of itself. In this case, the multiple uses of satellite technology as surveillance, targeting, weaponry, and communications (and the lack of distinction between these elements) are reflected in the increasing centrality of the satellite as the formal basis of surveillant narration as well as the content of the espionage story. The film is thus exemplary of a geopolitical thriller that emphasizes global relationality through the possibility of global destruction, enabled by that which has also defined the visual production of the world as globe.[53]

The collapsible relations between surveillance, targeting, and weaponry are also evident in the new arc of the Bourne franchise, which indicates that surveillance and assassination are increasingly synonymous. The original series starring Matt Damon concluded with the 2007 *Ultimatum* (which was also the most spectacularly surveillant of the original trilogy); the new cycle begun in 2012 with *The Bourne Legacy* (Tony Gilroy) updates its narrative with the use of a geosurveillant aesthetic for a drone assassination attempt against our new protagonist. The scene is structured in exactly the same way as a satellite surveillance scene (crosscutting between the drone/surveillance operators, the drone/surveillance point-of-view shot, and the action on the ground). While an obvious nod to contemporary military tactics and technologies, the ease with which a satellite surveillance scene is substituted (in terms of style, narrative positioning, outcome, effect, and so on) with a drone assassination indicates that the cinematic narration of these elements (which had always produced an equation between surveillance and death) finds virtually no distinction between the two.[54]

Both the narrative and historical uses of satellite technologies present a surveillant formation in which the processes and technologies through which figures are cast as dangerously unknowable have also served to provide evidence of their guilt, as well as to serve as the means of their targeting for death and even the means by which they are killed. This form of targeting provides a thread from the biopolitics of video surveillance discussed earlier in the book to the geopolitics of satellite images: not only is the desert produced as a crucial "zone of indistinction" in which the state power of the U.S. can locate its figures of "bare life," but in fact the entire geopolitical landscape is visualized in such a way that the whole world becomes such a zone. As Virilio has shown, there is a long history connecting cinematic and televisual representation with military engagement, in what he calls "the logistics of perception." The films discussed here suggest that rhetoric, technology, and aesthetic continue to develop these logistics as part of cinematic narrative space. It also seems evident that the technologies, geopolitics, and biopolitics of the Unites States "war on terror," though loudly insisting on their exceptional status, are in fact merely the current iteration/intersection by which modern surveillance, war, and representation serve to codefine visual fields and violent spatial politics.

* * *

Rising Sun, in its presentation of video as on the cusp of the digital age and its status as a surveillance thriller tinged by globalization and an orientalized threat, is both an ideological and stylistic precursor to the more recent GPS/satellite films. The film also serves as a type of middle ground between the use of video in the torture films discussed in Chapter One and the use of satellite and GPS in geopolitical thrillers, with both arenas exemplifying how (narratively and otherwise) surveillance manifests zones of indistinction. It is, however, the central position given the globalized economy in *Rising Sun* that indicates that the geopolitical violences discussed above are inconceivable without returning to Jameson's formulation of the geopolitical aesthetic, with which this chapter began, as a mapping of global capitalism. *Rising Sun*'s emphasis on the corporate market economy in its vision of globalization, and the implicit relation of this emphasis to the film's centerpiece—the murder caught on surveillance video—in some ways speaks as much to the shared logic of surveillance and military tactics as those films explicitly focusing on such uses. The rhetoric of "targeting," in particular, serves to define relations between surveillant and economic structures, and contextualizes the position of surveillance narratives within a globally defined media market.

In *Rising Sun*, both the narrative formations of surveillance and the formations of the global system the surveillance opens onto turn upon the death of an individual American subject who even in her specificity as a character and object of investigation seems to primarily represent the increasingly feminized and endangered position of the U.S. as its economic dominance is threatened. The women murdered on tape is implied to be a high-priced call girl, part of a group of white American women who cater to the sexual needs of the Japanese corporate executives. Even the psychosexual intrigue of the film is thus in large part defined by an economic relationship, adding to the manner in which this single murder, though sexualized and individualized, must be read as fundamentally indicative of an international economic structure. In this way, as in the later films, the violence upon a single body offered through surveillance is presented as central to an understanding of the global system—here a gendered system of exchange within the global economy. It is the explicitly economic frame of this film's narrative of surveillance and violence that shows how the construction of the de-racialized and in many ways dehistoricized bourgeois consumer that settles happily into his couch at the end of *Enemy of the State* is the systemic double to the subject targeted for death, even when those doubles are cinematically collapsed into one figure.

Central to Caren Kaplan's argument in "Precision Targets: GPS and the Militarization of U.S. Consumer Identity" (and as has been evidenced in other contexts) is the observation that consumption and militarization intersect in multiple ways, at levels that are at once technological, historical, structural, and discursive. In relation to the development of geographical information systems and GPS, Kaplan explores "the conditions that produce U.S. militarized consumer and citizen subjects in relation to technologies that link geography, demography, remote sensing, and contemporary identity politics (including geopolitics)":

> These subjects can be understood to be the "targets" of two seemingly distinct contexts and practices: the target of a weapon and the target of a marketing campaign. In both cases, something or somebody has to be identified, coordinates have to be determined with available technologies, and the target has to be clearly marked or recognized in time and space. GIS provides the model for databases as well as the representational logic for both warfare and marketing, while GPS offers enhanced precision in locating such targets through accurate positioning. Geographically based location technologies that draw on discourses of precision make possible the subjects of both consumption and war.[55]

In her analysis, Kaplan demonstrates how "the digital mingling of position and identity into target subjects underscores the martial and territorial aspect of mapping throughout the modern period."[56] This mingling can be found within all the individual narratives discussed in this chapter, but should also be considered in relation to the narrative shifts from the early 1990s to the late 1990s through today, from *Rising Sun*—which makes no mention of satellite or GPS but does conceive of a global market increasingly threatening to United States military and technological powers, economic supremacy, and, finally, social identity—to *Enemy of the State* and the *Bourne* films, which construct elaborate aesthetic and narrative relations between geopolitical subjects through the devices of GPS and satellite surveillance. Viewed as a generic arc, the orientalization of surveillance and globalization as presented in *Rising Sun* is reconfigured through the production of targets both in a market economy and in the imagination of a constant world warfare.

Clearly the connections between military rhetorics and marketing ones are neither new nor surprising—everything from the simple use of the term "campaign" to the construction of elaborate targeting strategies and the use of "psyops" connects the two in both discourse and method.[57] It is the specific way that geosurveillance aesthetics are exploited and consumers, as noted by Kaplan, become identified with those technologies and aesthetics that is of particular interest here. "Targeting" is one of the most quotidian of the militarized marketing terms, and it is related to surveillance in several clear ways: first, as was addressed in the preceding chapter, the accumulation and management of data that allows marketers to track the prior purchasing history of both individuals and groups, and more saliently for this context, the organization of "market segments" in order to target. Such market segmentation is based on socioeconomic "type" (ranging from the more traditional broad demographic categories of gender, age, and class to increasingly specific and precise target markets) and, importantly, location. Kaplan discusses in detail how location is used to identify target markets, and, more crucially, how consumers are asked to participate in this process by establishing themselves as active subjects in a global environment via locatability, represented by consumption in the growing market of GPS technologies: "The proliferation of ads, press releases, and media spots (such as coverage in tabloid TV and print media on celebrity use of GPS) throughout the 1990s and into the next century focused on location—where you are—but linked closely to that designation was almost always something existential: *where* you are reveals *who* you are."[58] This "where you are = who you are" formulation becomes an increasingly circular construction in marketing to the degree that if who you are is "revealed" to both consumers and marketers by locative technologies, then the ability to process such detailed information about consumers is in turn *producing* subject formations predicated on that information, which again, in turn, allows marketers to further target consumers with the kind of detailed precision offered by GPS systems (and perhaps even more so by internet tracking, which allows the targeting of movement and activity to form the very basis for online activity, as discussed in the preceding chapter), and so on.[59]

Kaplan goes on to connect and track the simultaneity of the consumer and marketing use of GPS with the technologies and discourse of the first Persian Gulf War, and ultimately proposes that one think of the United States "citizen/consumer subject" as "mobilized into militarized ways of being" through GPS and related systems, technologies used originally for defense purposes.[60] The 2013 film *The Call* goes so far as to build much of its narrative tension on the *danger* for a citizen-subject in using technology that *evades* surveillance: a young girl abducted by a serial killer is unable to be tracked by the authorities when she dials 911 from a car trunk because she is calling from a "disposable," prepaid cell phone that (according to the film) creates a life-threatening information delay in determining the phone's precise location. In this case, the security of a teenage girl going to the mall is directly threatened by the use of a technology that resists incorporation into the security and surveillance structure of the city of Los Angeles.[61] Stephen Graham has further developed the discussion of the militarization of the citizen in his analysis of the "new military urbanism," at the heart of which is the "unprecedented extent" to which such urbanism "fuses and blurs civilian and military applications of the technologies for control, surveillance, communications, simulation, and targeting."[62] The narratives that unfold in the *Bourne* films, *Enemy of the State*, *Eagle Eye*, and many others with similar structures represent the extreme of what this mobilization and fusion would look like as its protagonists increasingly resemble what Graham, similarly to Kaplan, dubs the "Citizen-Consumer-Soldier,"[63] and demonstrate how Jameson's allegories of totality have developed into a coalescence of market and military concerns in locative technologies.

As suggested by the narrative and technical formations of the satellite- and GPS-enabled action-thriller, the ability to precisely locate and target an individual body through surveillance technologies is absolutely tied to the production of that body as part of a broad geopolitical realm. Individual bodies are thus in many ways removed from their specificity and represented as of significance only in reference to a global system, which is itself in turn defined by its ability to surveil and target with (supposed) precision. The targeting of bodies through these technologies and aesthetics, as represented by films that repeatedly offer a narrative and vision of an individual subjected to the aggressive vision of geographical imaging, is thus an act of both extreme specificity and functional abstraction—a way to identify and accumulate bodies that primarily serves to rationalize the very system that produces these bodies as operative within a broader realm. When the personal and geopolitical thus become interrelated in these films, it serves to bolster surveillance by hailing the singular as evidence of the general, the node as indicative of the network, the consumer as evidence of the market, the terrorist as foundation for the "war on terror." Once again, lived experience is not of issue to the locative technology and its attendant cinematic forms; instead the "person" is used as a pin that helps to draw a map, and it is only the map that has consequence.

When considered as built upon the market concerns of *Rising Sun* and the militarization of consumers discussed by Kaplan and Graham, it becomes evident that this "map"—as with modern cartographical histories that demonstrate that global mapping, beginning with the voyages of Columbus and Magellan, has been inseparable from the economic expansion sustained by violent conquest and colonization—is really an *economy* sustained largely by the violences that attend the drawing of such a map.[64] Here we return to Jameson's original formulation of the geopolitical aesthetic as reflective primarily of modes of production that are not actually visualizable.

This geopolitical aesthetic and the modes of production it reflects or is mutually constitutive of move even further, from *within* the filmic frame into the realm of the production and marketing of the geopolitical thriller and other American blockbuster-level films on a global scale. As Klaus Dodds has noted in his abovementioned work, "Because action thrillers, including the *Bourne* trilogy, remain the most expensive films to make and market, circulating them beyond the traditional markets of the wider English-speaking world is crucial."[65] As production budgets rise, so does the necessity to increasingly target an overseas market; with the production budget essentially doubling between the first and third *Bourne* films, so did the overseas grosses, this time nearly equaling the domestic.[66] These figures are representative of a broader increase in the importance of foreign markets to rising costs of production in U.S. films, as Allen Scott has studied in detail: "Whereas the gross domestic box office for motion pictures increased (in constant dollar terms) by 40.9 percent from $5,970 [million] in 1986 to $8,413 million in 2001, exports of film and tape rentals over the same period increased by 452.8 percent from $1,683 million to $9,304 million."[67] This market growth is furthered by the fact that the major U.S. studios have multinational operations, and thus direct control over distribution in many of their foreign markets.[68] The result is, naturally, major foreign markets in which "American films garner never less than half and sometimes more than two-thirds of total box-office receipts."[69] It is, of course, nothing new that the United States has exported film globally, but the imbalance in export versus import has grown exponentially since the 1980s and reflects an increasing drive toward foreign market dominance.[70]

The "generic arc" of the action-thriller in terms of its narrative structure and content thus intersects with its financing and distribution. Another way to view this arc is as a mediated reterritorialization: as the genre develops, the U.S. distances itself from a position in which it is consumed *by* a broader global economy with a possible Asian dominance, as suggested by *Rising Sun*, into a situation in which the U.S. reconstitutes itself (at least within its cultural and political fantasies and the fabrications of the marketplace) as geopolitically enhanced through repeated cartographic and cinematic gestures that serve to identify and orientalize both markets and enemies (which are increasingly discursively related).

The global tensions that began as a market concern in *Rising Sun* are still definitively related to questions of dominance in a global marketplace. In this case the United States markets both the narrative centrality of its position in global surveillance and the larger media project of which that is part and parcel, selling both to the imaginations of foreign consumers. As Scott Olson has stated (to a very different, celebratory end), "Hollywood is an aesthetic, and is no longer just a place in California. . . . Hollywood is a global aesthetic."[71] Olson's intent here is to speak of Hollywood in less literal terms and to argue that the Hollywood aesthetic has become transnationally appealing, but the unintended implication is that to move toward the level of the global is actually to move *away* from a discussion of literal location and toward an aesthetic—that in fact the global can perhaps only be understood, as Jameson might agree, *as* an aesthetic, one that offers spatial form to its own modes of production. As the authors of *Global Hollywood 2* argue, "Hollywood's 'real' location lies in its division of labour": this labor, I would suggest, includes the spectatorship of a cinematic audience that identifies with itself as part of a "global system," in large part through the mediation of its own consumerism.[72]

While *Rising Sun*'s domestic grosses far exceeded its foreign, the later films, all planting surveillance more firmly in the action-thriller genre, are situated to profit enormously from the global market, with, for instance, *Enemy of the State*'s foreign grosses exceeding domestic by over 10 percent, and *Body of Lies*' foreign grosses nearly doubling its domestic. This is not to say that every geopolitical thriller is necessarily doing better overseas than at home (*Eagle Eye* maintained approximately the same percentages as *Rising Sun* in foreign versus domestic), but to point out the increasingly close relations between the intradiegetic establishment of the U.S. "citizen-subject" as a pivot point in the geopolitical aesthetic and the extradiegetic marketing of this aesthetic to a global market.[73] This relationship points to a simultaneously broader and more specific understanding of the intersections between the production of globalized and geopoliticized subjects through surveillance practices and the market concerns of a global economy—when viewed through the cinematic lens, both are dependent upon the media-enabled constitution of a world system in which any given subjects might participate in the double movement of watching and being watched through their targeting as either consumers, enemies, or both.

The fact that the continued economic and cultural impact of America cinema is directly bolstered by "strategic trade," the exertion of "governmental support of export activities in circumstances where national interests are at stake" makes the connection between the market and geopolitics in both cinematic and noncinematic realms even more explicit and underscores the relation of market concerns to the multiple modes of identification and identity produced through surveillance and mediation.[74] As Scott highlights, "The steady globalization of Hollywood as an expression of both market forces and US government action on the international trade front, has, of course, engendered numerous clashes and disputes . . . unlike wheat or coal, cultural products are also intimately bound up with matters of selfhood, identity, and consciousness."[75]

And it is certainly no surprise, given the coextensivity of the concerns mapped in this chapter, that it is the rise of electronic production and distribution technologies that threaten the global dominance of American cinema through more affordable production methods, digital media "piracy," and access to alternate forms of media, much of which has been characterized in the U.S. film industry as an orientalized threat.[76] Big-budget action-thrillers aestheticize and spectacularize the digital technologies that in different form might undermine Hollywood's dominance. Their incorporation into Hollywood narratives works to contain the threat and reassert technological mastery as a naturalized American domain, and, more significantly, regain market dominance through their status as blockbuster-level productions. The "global eye" offered by American cinema thematizing satellite, GPS, and other locative technologies, initially presented as a removed and omniscient perspective capable of seeing any given point in the whole world, is thus also the eye of the cinematic spectator, who is simultaneously situated and targeted in relation to the film's characters, the film's presentation of global surveillance, and the global reach of the media market.

This market formation is bolstered by and serves to bolster the historical and growing connections between military and consumer concerns in the media and beyond. Such connections are another way that surveillant formations are increasingly blurring lines in the service of U.S. geopolitical power. As is evident from the generic arc of the action-thriller, the market structure—within these filmic narratives, in the consumption of the narratives, and in more general global systems—is what recent counterterrorist narratives are built upon. The supposedly "post-9/11" geopolitical world is predicated not just on earlier cultural hysteria about decentralization of the United States by the East in a global economy, but on the geographical imagination and re-orientation of locative technologies that, in their dual usages as both market tools and weapons, insist on an increasingly inevitable link between death and consumption in the geopolitical aesthetic.

4

Temporality and Surveillance I

Terrorism Narratives and the Melancholic Security State

The politics of the films discussed in the preceding chapter were characterized largely in spatial terms. But the politics of surveillance are also structured by considerations of time. The temporal logic of surveillance is one that cinematic narrative production accesses in pronounced ways, insofar as narrative itself is based upon the ordering of events, and thus a number of surveillance films point to the temporal aspects of broader surveillance structures. Temporality, as was already clear in Chapter One's discussion of the temporality of video surveillance and its function as a narrative "zone of indistinction," is integral to a number of the political and representational systems already explored. Both this and the next chapter explore how temporal formations occupy much of the space between representational mediation and surveillance practice, and also often serve to define the relations between representation, mediation, and surveillance. Though perhaps the most ineffable aspect of surveillance, I would also suggest that "time is of the essence" for political action (whether reactionary or radical) within surveillance cultures.

The temporal conceits of cinematic surveillance narratives have been put front and center by Thomas Levin in his discussion of "real time," which, he argues, is essential to an understanding of how cinematic narration has been structured and restructured around "rhetorics of surveillance."[1] Arguing that "[b]y the late 1990s . . . cinematic narration could be said, in many cases, to have effectively become synonymous with surveillant enunciation as such," Levin examines how the claims to indexical realism of photography, are, in a digital era, replaced by what he calls the "temporal indexicality of the real-time surveillant image."[2] The truth value of the moving image, no longer based in the photographic principles of indexical imprinting, has, according to Levin, been replaced by the "real-time" possibilities of closed-circuit television and other forms of video surveillance. His seminal essay points to films of the 1990s ranging from *Sliver* to *The Truman Show* to demonstrate that at the same time that digital culture was undermining the primacy of photographic imagery and revolutionizing information, cinema began to incorporate real-time surveillance as narrative. This use of surveillance, even in its reflexive interrogation of the practices of representation, creates "a spectatorial position that is in large part identical to that of the surveillance operator."[3] And though my discussion in Chapter One implies that ultimately these diegetic invocations of video surveillance technologies reveal how ambiguous and even unstable a "temporal index" becomes within surveillance, it is quite evident that the cinematic narration of surveillance practice is in large part defined by and as a temporal relationship. Beyond the temporal ambiguities produced by the use of video in torture porn, in Chapter Two of this book it becomes clear that the widespread use of video as reality representation is in part defined by its claims of immediacy. It is not only with video that we see surveillant narration operating on the basis of a temporal logic; the cinematic incorporation of satellite and GPS discussed in the preceding chapter emphasized their usage within elaborate chase scenes that serve to establish broad, geopolitical relations. Such scenes are defined by crosscutting, which is the cinematic language of simultaneity: a principle of editing that communicates a narrative relationship of "meanwhile." The incorporation of a satellite surveillance operation into a parallel action sequence to connect disparate people and places, in "real time," restructures the otherwise largely associative principle of parallel editing as a function of surveillant mediation. Levin's account of video surveillance in the 1998 thriller *Snake Eyes* (Brian De Palma) suggests how widespread this redefinition is: "[W]hat we see here is the degree to which the stylistics of surveillance has enabled contemporary cinema to displace the highly 'artificial' (i.e., foregrounded) classical structures of omniscient narration *into the diegesis itself* in the form of a now increasingly plausible surveillant omniscience."[4] A scene of satellite surveillance similarly "displaces" the crosscutting structure (a specific form of "omniscient narration") onto the satellite technology, turning a surveillant device into a narrative one. In doing so, the globalizing vision of satellite surveillance establishes the different figures in a scene as operating contingently at the level of global politics. Thus rather than the "rhetoric of surveillance" here representing a shift from a "spatial to a temporal indexicality," what we see in this instance is the use of simultaneity—the temporal principle of crosscutting—to *subject* cinematic space to politicized space through geosurveillance. That the narrative relationships produced in such a scene are also defined temporally demonstrates just some of the ways that *time* becomes the logic through which surveillance and cinema integrate and become a political formation.

Although "real time," as suggested by its multiple cinematic incarnations above, is absolutely central to surveillance culture, surveillance narratives also point to the many other logics of temporality involved in the political investments in surveillance practices, particularly as defined by counterterrorist security policy. Some vicissitudes of surveillant temporality have been examined by Gary Senosko and Scott Thompson in their essay "Tense Theory," which argues that surveillance and theories of surveillance can be characterized—at least in part—by three modes of time: a (troubled) past, a (fragmented) present, and a (future) past.[5] All three of these modes are instructive in understanding the role that narrative plays in organizing the stakes and practices of surveillance, but it is this "(future) past," or the future perfect tense, to which contemporary surveillance cinema finds itself compulsively returning. The assumption or invocation of the future as a past event has clear resonance in any discussion of surveillance, which is based in logics of both prevention and, increasingly, preemption, and for Senosko and Thompson is "one of the most important dimensions of post-panoptic theory."[6] In another essay from the same volume, Greg Elmer and Andy Opel suggest that the logic of preemption has replaced the "what if" logic of surveillance with "when, then," and go on to argue that "through the pre-emptive lens the future becomes an inevitable series of events, elevating 'fate' to an agent of historical evolution."[7] In a related move, Joseba Zulaika has argued that the discourse of counterterrorism has become a self-fulfilling prophecy, which "substitutes the spectacle of a constant 'waiting for terror' for actual historical temporality."[8] All of these theorists indicate how current surveillance and security practices, with their anticipatory nature, invest in the future to a degree that they have come to construct the facticity of the present and past in relation to a future that has not yet happened.

As Senosko and Thompson indicate when they interweave their tenses to show the interaction and ambiguity emerging between the times of surveillance, so do surveillance films inevitably seem to not just project into the future, but also to render the past as the future that has not yet happened. In doing so, these narratives fragment their present visions by means of thematizing surveillance technologies that define themselves by assuming, in several senses of the word, both the past and the future. Whether the resulting temporal relations serve to concoct a proleptic and reactionary political formula or a discourse that acknowledges historical dynamics and representational ambiguities is what many of these narratives, intentionally or not, explore.

Two films, *Déjà vu* and *Vantage Point*, are of particular use as introduction to what surveillance cinema offers as constructions of surveillant temporality. Both are "post-9/11" films, both are focused on terrorist attacks, and both use narrative to reconstruct time in a manner that suggests that surveillance has the capacity to prevent terrorist events that have already occurred. As discussed in Chapter One, narratives organized through surveillance have often pivoted around time—much of the ambiguity introduced into a narrative by incorporating video is produced by the possibility that something could either be a live feed or prerecorded. This possibility is exploited by and figures within the narrative to blur the line between surveillance and representation, and thus manipulate understanding of and response to events within the narrative on the part of both characters and the film's audience. That fundamental ambiguity and corollary manipulability is one possible basis for broader fantasies around temporal reorganization that we find in such films as *Déjà vu* and *Vantage Point*. However, while *Déjà vu* uses cinematic narrative to construct a fantasy technology that is capable of actually seeing into the future and thus changing the past, *Vantage Point* uses cinematic narration *as* the technology that accomplishes this feat.

Déjà vu, directed by Tony Scott and released in 2006, is, in and of itself, largely (and ironically) forgettable, except insofar as it exists in relation to broader cinematic constructions of surveillance, the "war on terror," and a number of intersecting political concerns of its time. Set in New Orleans, but presenting its cinematic disaster there as the result of a terrorist bombing of a ferry rather than a "natural disaster," the film conflates, perhaps purposefully, the defining political events of the second Bush administration: the response to terrorism and the disastrous nonresponse to the devastation of Hurricane Katrina in 2005. The narrative premise that violence visited upon New Orleans would be the result of a single terrorist attack rather than the result of long-term and suddenly, shockingly obvious structural neglect is a strong enough implication of a connection between the "war on terror" and the devastation in New Orleans. However, the film, whether as an excuse for its own symptomatic appearance at that historical moment or as a direct announcement of the implicit connections between the politics of the war on terror and the violent and often racist neglect of impoverished Americans, makes the terms explicit as the end credits roll: "This film is dedicated to the strength and enduring spirit of the people of New Orleans." Clearly its production had begun before Hurricane Katrina hit in 2005, and thus the dedication, like the film's own fantasy technology, is retroactive. Reading more like an apology than a firm statement of support, the producers indicate to the audience an awareness that there is something perverse about a cinematic narrative staging a terrorist attack in the city of New Orleans little more than a year after the hurricane hit. But questions of intent aside, what the film offers is a set of fantasies that demonstrate how key surveillance is in formulating a political agenda that goes beyond conservatism and into a temporality that must, I believe, be characterized as problematically melancholic.[9]

The film opens as it will end, in what will become in these types of films a formulaic circular narrative. Dockside in scenic New Orleans, happy sailors and their families board a ferry headed to a party—the credits, and the opening sequence, end with an explosion destroying the ferry and everyone on it. A fairly traditional detective narrative begins as ATF agent Doug Carlin (Denzel Washington) arrives and begins his investigation with the collection of trace evidence and a review of available surveillance. Obviously this, as with all investigation narratives, involves a reconstruction of the past—narrative structure and criminal investigation become one and the same (and this formula is of course the basis for the *CSI* television boom of the same era). But this film takes it one step, and then several steps, further. Agent Carlin is approached by the FBI to review a highly advanced, secret surveillance operation that provides him with what appears to be an almost three-dimensional recreation of events four days prior. Presented as a collage of digital screens with one screen dominating at any given time as they focus in on an action, Carlin is told by a team of agents and scientists that he is looking at a "digital recreation, combining all the data they have into one fluid shot, any angle, any view within the target area." Satellite imagery, CCTV recordings, and thermal imaging are all evident in this single representation through which they can visually maneuver with controls not dissimilar to the pan-tilt-zoom of more quotidian closed-circuit television cameras. Such fluid imaging is far-fetched, but still theoretically possible and certainly consistent with principles of computer imaging and assemblage theories of surveillance. However, the film builds upon the restaging of the past using surveillance data in order to construct a fantasy of actual time travel. After noticing strange elements of this digital re-creation (including the presence of audio), Carlin forces the science/law enforcement team to disclose that they are looking into the *actual* past, in fact have "found a way to fold space back on itself"; they have, they claim, created a wormhole using "concentrated bursts of energy." Through the use of this technology they do even more than just reconstruct the crime and capture the culprit as in a traditional investigation narrative. The film follows Agent Carlin as he first surveils the past and then physically travels into it to prevent the bombing of the ferry.

It is not my concern to determine the degree to which the laws of physics are broken by this cinematic construction of time travel. What is striking is the narrative fantasy that in attempting to "enhance the sensitivity of optical telescopes," a team of U.S. government operatives and scientists has had a "breakthrough" and managed to manipulate the fabric of time and space in order to prevent a terrorist attack that had already killed hundreds: in short, surveillance has prevented not only a future terrorist bombing, but a past one. The movie, while implausible, nevertheless reflects almost directly the temporal fantasies of existing surveillance and security practices, which, even in their projection into the future, function as pathologically attached to undoing past events and circumventing loss. This temporal logic of surveillance is inseparable from the political logic that is coincident and contiguous with it, and suggests that surveillance formations and political formulations have become so mutually reinforcing that they are completely inseparable.

Barbara Biesecker has argued that the discursive form of the "war on terror" is primarily a "carefully crafted and meticulously managed melancholic rhetoric," one of the main features of which is "the discursive transfiguration of a historic and political catastrophe into the harbinger of an epochal Act 'to come' and, hence, the ubiquitous deployment of the future anterior."[10] Through analysis of the speeches of George W. Bush and members of his administration in the aftermath of September 11, 2001, as well as the handling of the political discourse in the news media, Biesecker demonstrates that these discourses, "whose aim is to persuade us to act *as if* a certain loss had occurred even though it has in fact *not yet* been lost," treat the attacks of September 11 as things still to come and yet which can be prevented.[11] Bush's assertion in his address to Congress following the attacks that "[o]ur nation has been put on notice" serves to structure not just the rhetorical character of his administration, but the preemptive logic of military action, surveillance, and security practices that have become a matter of course.

Bush's speech goes on to symptomatize a triumphant refusal to grieve in favor of taking up the task of defense against loss: "Our nation—this generation—will lift a dark threat of violence from our people and our future. We will rally the world to this cause by our efforts, by our courage. We will not tire, we will not falter, and we will not fail."[12] Biesecker argues that this rhetoric structures a national mission to disavow actual, historical loss: "Instead, the events of 9/11 must be deciphered as the sign, indeed omen, of an incomparable, Absolute loss that will have been ours were we to refuse to answer it."[13] The architectures of surveillance and security that derived from this national mission statement follow its structural elements accordingly, and serve to produce America as an idealized object that can now be claimed because it has been (not yet) lost: "What melancholy stages, in other words, is the loss of an impossible object, ideal, or relation that the subject has never had."[14] As discussed in the preceding chapter, Biesecker's essay goes on to show how this politics manifested in such forms as the presentation of satellite surveillance imaging as a rationale for the invasion of Iraq. Correspondingly, the visual and spatial logic of the satellite imaging used in geopolitical thrillers is shown by a film like *Déjà vu* to be bolstered by a temporal logic. The narrative functions of satellite and GPS that structure geopolitical relations within a single action sequence are already predicated on simultaneity, as mentioned above; in *Déjà vu* such simultaneity is part of a broader scaffolding upon which the construction of a rich and action-filled present is invested with the full affective force of a disavowed past recast as a preventable future.

Thus, despite the fact that *Déjà vu* is a film one is unlikely to want to see twice, it produces an explicit rendering of the implicit function of the reactionary melancholic politics at the heart of the Bush Doctrine. In its representation of a number of surveillance practices organized around temporal manipulation, retroactivity, and projection, the film structures its surveillance narrative around the possibility of literal time travel, and thus introduces a science-fictional element that testifies to the fantasy embedded within the logic of surveillance and its surrounding politics.

The film's joint narrative and investigatory threads demand that its surveillance fantasies be read alongside a romance, and it is the particularity of this romance that connects its politics to the desire and pathology that Biesecker describes as characteristic of the post-9/11 rhetoric of the Bush administration. For Agent Carlin, the drive to solve and ultimately prevent the ferry bombing is constructed as a morbid fascination with a dead woman, with whom he falls in love. After the bombing, the burnt body of a young woman washes up downriver, and she is assumed to be a bombing victim. However, because of the time the discovery of the body was called in, and its purposely severed fingers, Carlin surmises that she was killed before the bombing, but manipulated to look like she was a victim of it. The issue of *timing* thus presents itself before we even enter into science-fictional time travel: Carlin's first clue in the case is about a disjunction in timing—the woman was a murder victim before the explosion, but placed to appear as a victim of the bombing, and thus Carlin correctly assumes that whoever killed her knew the bombing was going to occur. The terrorist attack is distilled into the murder of one woman onto whom both Carlin and the spectators project their fantasies, and in no uncertain terms: as Carlin puts it, "Solve her case, you solve this case [the bombing]."

The fetishization of the woman's murder and the woman herself develops quickly. Since she is Carlin's hook into the investigation, when he is introduced to the surveillance equipment and told by its operators that they simply need to be told where to look four days ago in order to investigate the bombing, he points them immediately to the home of the woman.

He stares enraptured and amazed as she is resurrected by the surveillance equipment before his eyes: he watches her move through her apartment, the surveillance equipment zooms in on her face, and her giant image overtakes the screen as Carlin stands in front of it, almost appearing to occupy the same space as her as his bodily frame is superimposed onto her image. When asked if he knows her, he responds morbidly in reference to her corpse: "We held hands once, but I didn't know her." His creepy attachment to a dead woman he never knew is thus established with little time lost and without the narrative build-up offered by Hitchcock's *Vertigo*, the paradigmatic example of this form of cinematic romance.

As predicted both by Carlin and the formulaic narrative, the investigation into the bombing and the investigation of this woman's murder, in its singularity, become one and the same, and thus the fantasy around the catastrophic explosion and the structure of the narrative of desire are also mutually inflecting. In the end, Carlin is able to physically travel back through time, save Claire, his newly loved and lost object, from being burned alive by the bomber (who, somewhat improbably, can place the bomb on the ferry only by stealing this particular woman's truck, which apparently also requires killing her), and drive the bomb inside the truck off the ferry. Carlin dies but saves the girl, and then, also defying explanation, reappears as the temporal version of himself that comes to investigate the now *attempted* bombing, meeting anew the woman we know he will love/has already loved. He has no memory of any of the events that are *past* in the narrative we have followed, and now futural (but never to actually occur) in the story. In short, our protagonist prevents the bombing, prevents the woman's death, *and* "gets the girl," and furthermore doesn't even have to remember that there ever was a loss, because in fact it now has never happened. Thus, as Carlin had predicted, to solve the case that reflects his own pathological investment in a lost object (which he never even had) is also to not only "solve" a terrorist attack, but to allow surveillance and counterterrorist security to emerge as so triumphant that no attack will have ever occurred.

Because of this, it is striking to note that while the film does situate itself historically in terms of real-world terrorism (and also refers both within the narrative and extradiegetically to the real-world trauma of Hurricane Katrina), it completely eclipses the events of September 11, 2001, in favor of reference to the Oklahoma City bombing of 1995. The

The surveillance operation of *Déjà vu* (2006): fixation and melancholia as strategies of counterterrorism.

character of the bomber in *Déjà vu*—a white, American, far-right extremist—is clearly a Timothy McVeigh–like figure, and Oklahoma City is explicitly referenced when Agent Carlin is introduced as one of the investigators of that bombing. There is no mention of the more contemporary context of the film, and one must wonder what to make of a film released five years after 9/11 that situates surveillance and counterterrorism solely in relation to an earlier bombing. On one level (and I return to this further below), the film appears to disavow the current conditions of its production in order to avoid entering into the racial and civil rights politics of the post-9/11 security state. But even if *Déjà vu* is engaging in what is a rather routine avoidance of direct political commentary by metaphorizing through an earlier and relatively uncontentious event now safely consigned to "history," the *effect* is to multiply the denial of trauma and loss that is suggested by the time travel narrative.[15] While the film's refusal to be a "9/11 movie" might be admirable in terms of reminding us that "terrorism" is also produced in the form of white American "patriotism," that same gesture also symptomatically redoubles the fantasy of the film and produces a space where not only did the ferry bombing never happen, neither did the attacks of September 11, 2001.

This narrative thus represents an absolute refusal of loss *and* the reaction formations around that loss—what is ultimately a highly political fantasy around undoing American trauma that follows the logic of melancholia and shows how narratives of surveillance are participating in the production of a political sphere in which there is no actual engagement with the progression of time, or, crucially, the *movement* of history (rather than historical events as static facts). As Wendy Brown has written, "The irony of melancholia, of course, is that attachment to the object of one's sorrowful loss supersedes any desire to recover from this loss, to live free of it in the present, to be unburdened by it. This is what renders melancholia a persistent condition, a state, indeed, a structure of desire, rather than a transient response to death or loss."[16] This structure, of course, suggests that the fetishistic attachment to the object of loss becomes an attachment to the loss itself—it is that loss that renders the object so stable as an attachment. Translated from the terms of an individual loss to an event such as the bombing in this film, or the events of September 11, 2001, to which such narratives implicitly refer (even if they refuse to explicitly address them), we are confronted with a politics that, in seeking to prevent future attacks, fantasizes the prevention of past attacks, but in order to do so must install the attack itself as the object of desire.[17] Though we can see this structure playing out in a number of forms of "security" practice—preemptive wars, airport security, and detention practice—it is striking that it is in the realm of surveillance that the grounding fantasy announces itself in such exaggerated form.

Nevertheless, it is worth noting, as does Biesecker, that a number of political theorists have been troubled by any sweeping critique of melancholic politics and suggested that "the injunction to pass from melancholia to mourning is to be read as normalizing and, thus, disempowering for those of us threatened by racism, Eurocentrism, sexism, and homophobia."[18] My own critique of the melancholic imaginary of surveillance films should not be read as an assertion that all melancholic engagement is reactionary (as I will discuss in some detail in the following chapter), but that the uses of surveillance and security within the national (and here cinematic) imaginary build upon a melancholic structure for their rationale, and do so in a way that often continues to rationalize the manipulation of past and future in order to cement a regime of power in the present.

*   *   *

This manipulation of past and future continues in the 2008 film *Vantage Point* (Pete Travis), which does not simply reiterate the melancholic fantasies of the earlier film, but demonstrates how the fantasy power that surveillance has to prevent terrorism is presented not just in the content of cinematic narratives, but in the use of narrative as itself a technology that might produce a temporality of retroaction. There is no literal "time travel" in the film, but like *Déjà vu*, it follows a circular path in which it ends where it begins and prevents a central traumatic event that is given as a fait accompli at the beginning of the film.

Vantage Point addresses the issue of a "post-9/11 world" far more directly. There are two central traumatic events in the film (the assassination of the American president and a series of coordinated bombings in public spaces), both the related actions of the same terrorist campaign, this time undertaken by ambiguously Muslim terrorists in Spain. The film opens with a montage of a major public event as it is broadcast by an American news team: the U.S. president is in Spain to hold a summit between the West and Arab nations, presenting a *post*-post-9/11 future in which that event has occurred, but is now the impetus for a historic accord between "West" and "East" in which, as the voiceover of a news anchor sets the stage, state interests "from over 150 countries meet to sign onto [the U.S. president's] bold new counterterrorism strategy." Thus, like *Déjà vu*'s reference to Carlin's previous work on the Oklahoma City bombing, there is reference here to a foundational trauma, but that trauma serves as the ground for a utopian future in which not only loss but even political difference can be prevented.

Also like *Déjà vu*, within minutes of the film's opening, the terrorist attack occurs: as the U.S. president (played by William Hurt) begins to speak, he is gunned down. Shortly thereafter, several bombs explode, killing hundreds in the plaza in which the president has spoken. All of this is presented through elaborate crosscutting between the actual events and the news production of those events in a nearby mobile production van. The wall of monitors involved in the video production of a live event for the news strongly resembles the operation of the multiple monitors of a CCTV surveillance station, and immediately presents the events as both highly mediated and closely surveilled. As the smoke begins to clear in the plaza, the film stops and rewinds (as if it were itself a piece of the news production we have just been witnessing, and not dissimilarly from the fast-forwarding and rewinding of *Caché*'s opening scene discussed in Chapter One) and begins again with the caption "23 minutes earlier." The same events replay, this time loosely following the perspective of Secret Service agent Thomas Barnes (Dennis Quaid).

The film follows this pattern repeatedly, restarting the sequence of events that include the assassination, explosions, and then the aftermath and resolution of the crimes a total of six times. Each time the film focuses on a different character (or, in one case, a group of characters) who has witnessed or played a part in the events—hence the name *Vantage Point*. Clearly not a new narrative device, the move to replay events from multiple perspectives does not here function to highlight the subjective nature of narrative, as it has been used before (most famously in Akira Kurosawa's *Rashomon* [1950]), but instead serves to uncover the "truth" of these crimes, and even undo something that appears to have already happened. Midway through the repetitions we are offered the perspective of the president, and come to understand that the president who will be/has been shot at the beginning of the film is in fact a double and the actual president is being subjected not to an assassination, but instead to a kidnapping—a kidnapping from which he can and will be rescued. Unlike *Déjà vu*, the bombing cannot be prevented through this narrative device, but the symbolic center of American power—the U.S. president—is narratively "saved" from an assassination that has already occurred, and goes on to wage a post-9/11 peace that the terrorists are unable to destroy, as had been their intent.

Notably, though again less definitively than in *Déjà vu*, it is the technologies of surveillance and mediation that facilitate and motivate the multiple reframings of the story, the same reframings that allow the pivotal narrative event to be undone. As mentioned above, the first rewinding quite explicitly emerges in the mobile news production facility following the second bomb blast, as the scene is being closely monitored and constructed by and as media. The film's repeated plotting continues to get to its truth (and its undoing of the assassination) by assembling a series of mediated representations as evidence. The second iteration of the events, this time from Agent Barnes's perspective, shows him attempting to collect the footage of an American tourist (Forrest Whitaker) who has videotaped the events, and then finally running into the news production van to look at the footage shot by the media. As he sees something crucial on one of the monitors (at this point we don't know what), the film rewinds for the second time, and the next iteration starts, which pivots around the tourist's videotaped images and involvement in figuring out what happened. The third iteration begins with the real president safe in his hotel room, as he then watches the events unfold on television. The "truth" is all finally constructed out of these multiple perspectives, which are overwhelmingly grounded not just in acts of witnessing, but in technologically surveilled and replayable mediations. It is thus the surveillance and representation of the events that allows the narrative to turn the way it does, and piece its resolution out of that "surveillant assemblage."[19] Ultimately, the compiled multiple perspectives allow the film and its characters to undo what we have already witnessed, and use the logic of surveillance technologies (replayability and multiplicity of perspective) to prevent actions with which the narrative began. Many detective stories are predicated on the reconstruction of events—the surveillance sleuthing of films such as this take that a step further into actual un/re-doing of crimes with different outcomes.

The film thus uses temporal manipulation to melancholically install certain foundational losses, and simultaneously undo loss, such that an idealized image can emerge—this time the image of America as the just and wise leader seeking to unite the nations of the world against the threat of terrorism. The narrative *about* time travel of *Déjà vu* becomes simply time travel *through* narrative in *Vantage Point*, but both are significantly devoted to the service of building a romantic national identity atop a refusal of the facticity of time's passing—it is of considerable consequence here that this refusal is enabled by the cinematic incorporation of surveillance technologies and practices.

This temporal formation, like the satellite and GPS aesthetics discussed in the preceding chapter, also appears in serial narrative on television. CBS's *Person of Interest* (2011–present) imagines a computer program designed to predict terrorist attacks and thus prevent them from ever happening—it turns out the computer can predict other crimes as well, and thus the counterterrorist technology is used by its creator to try to prevent more quotidian murders unrelated to terrorism (with the assistance of an ex-CIA agent who is, totally unsurprisingly, in a state of devastation following the death of the woman he loves). The counterterrorist logic of preemption is now cast as a foundation for a crime drama. When *Los Angeles Times* television reviewer Mary McNamara states about *Person of Interest* that "the notion of preventing crimes rather than solving them is an appealing twist, although the crime in the pilot is fairly boring. At least the surveillance graphics are very cool," what she misses is that such a plot is less and less of a "twist" and that both the aesthetics and logics of surveillance are central to that now highly recognizable fantasy.[20]

The Fox network's 24 (2001–2010, 2014) remains the privileged example of the action-thriller aesthetics of surveillance as they have made their way into television, and the show's conceit of "real-time" narration would seem to dispute the manner in which counterterrorist thematics are accompanied by melancholic circularities rather than the passing of time.[21] However, the show is committed within its real-time structure to similar kinds of temporal acrobatics, here with a race-against-the-clock structure distilling an absurd amount of significant geopolitical events into always overdetermined moments. Each season represents a single day, each episode an hour of that day, and terrorist threats, attacks, and their prevention and/or punishment are always contained within that single day. Thus one could say that the performance of "real time" in 24 provides as much of a fetishistic emphasis on the singularity of traumatic loss as those texts discussed above that disavow loss entirely, and all of them attest to the manner in which contemporary discourses of counterterrorism rely on a single date—"9/11"—as a logic unto itself, a logic inevitably tied to surveillance practice.

This characterization of contemporary American politics as one deeply invested in temporal management through surveillance and media formations has also been noted by Richard Grusin in another context. Grusin (building on his earlier work with Jay Bolter on "remediation"— the process of new media refashioning old media—which forms the basis of my analysis in the next chapter) has argued that the characteristic logic of media in the "post-9/11" United States culture and media is one of "premediation," which points to some of the same political stakes outlined above that have developed in the media's handling of trauma, security, and war: "The logic of remediation insists that there was never a past prior to mediation: all mediations are remediations, in that mediation of the real is always a mediation of another mediation. The logic of premediation, on the other hand, insists that the future itself is already mediated, and that with the right technologies . . . the future can be remediated before it happens."[22] Grusin writes of "9/11" as "in some sense the paradigmatic global remediation event," in which the experiential immediacy of the disaster was broadcast via television but simultaneously remediated via split screens, rolling headlines, the web, cell phones, and so on. He goes on to show how the war in Iraq and the response to other post–September 11 perceived attacks of terror (such as the anthrax scare) were increasingly covered by the news media not in terms of "reporting what has already happened but of premediating what may happen next."[23] In this way Grusin shows how media technologies and practices are deployed to enforce (and even produce) the logic of preemption, which here takes even stronger form in the politics of retroactive prevention.

Grusin's account of the manner in which the events of September 11, 2001, consolidated a news and entertainment media culture that seeks to contain the future by "premediating" it is extremely apposite for understanding surveillant media both *within* the narrative fantasy of *Déjà vu* and in the use of narrative *as* surveillance and security in *Vantage Point*. While Grusin suggests that "the United States seeks to try to make sure that it never experiences live a catastrophic event like this that has not already been premediated," I would add that the incorporation of surveillance technology within cinematic narrative is central to this process of premediation (is in fact precisely what Grusin refers to as both remediation and premediation), and further demands that we see the mediated reprocessing (within narrative fantasy or otherwise) of surveillance technologies and practices as central to the politics of national security. In other words, without the functions of both remediation and premediation that Grusin describes, which serve to fashion the past and future of our relations to media technologies, the circular logics of projection into the future and retroaction discussed here would not adhere so easily to surveillance technologies. While premediation and the disavowal and retroaction of melancholia are certainly not the same formal structure, projection and retroaction, particularly within cinematic narrative, find a strong structural basis when considered as part of the remediation/premediation nexus of contemporary media that Grusin outlines.

Both the fantasy and critique of the time/surveillance model are addressed probably most directly (and in one of Grusin's privileged examples of cinematic premediation) in the science-fictional account *Minority Report* (Steven Spielberg), based on the Philip K. Dick short story from 1956, but not rendered cinematically until 2002, when the temporal logic of surveillance was emerging as a trend in film and television narrative. In this film's dystopic vision, human subjects known as "pre-cogs" are used to psychically envision murders before they happen, and those who will have been responsible are arrested before an act of violence is committed. Here the fantasy of retroaction central to the war on terror films becomes a fantasy of anticipation and prevention that is the more explicit goal of surveillance practice. The film raises the obvious ethical questions of prosecuting a criminal for a crime that has not yet been committed, or even outwardly intended (some "criminals" in the film have not even *conceived* of the crime they are supposed to commit in the future), and thus serves as a critique of the preventative project central to surveillance. The film's "pre-crime" office is presented as just one part of a futuristic surveillance society, complete with eye scans in public transit areas and personalized advertisements addressing consumers by name as they pass by (this latter seems increasingly realistic given the rise of consumer tracking). *Minority Report* shows any number of ethical and functional problems with the pre-crime system, but ultimately its failure is presented as the result of corruption: manipulation by the system's creator so that he can get away with a murder. The critique is also forwarded that in order for the surveillance to function, human beings (the pre-cogs) must be turned into slaves—technologies of surveillance. The titular "minority report" refers to the fact that occasionally the group of three pre-cogs disagree, and one sees an alternate future in which the crime does not happen. Thus it is not the case that these people are fallible as surveillance technologies—in fact, they are incredibly accurate about the fact that alternate possibilities exist. It is the system's refusal to acknowledge ambiguity of data that makes the pre-crime unit "wrong." The film ends up having it both ways about surveillance: you really can access the truth through using people as tools of surveillance culture, but that truth may well be unclear.

*　*　*

More recent, and speaking more directly to the reactionary narrative formation around terrorism presented in *Déjà vu*, is the 2011 film *Source Code* (Duncan Jones), another film that imagines a surveillance technology that allows time travel (of a sort) and the prevention of a terrorist attack that has already taken place. But rather than the merely symptomatic fulfillment of a melancholic fantasy, *Source Code* intriguingly exposes the fantasy as a narrative (and politics) that has a deep investment in the occurrence (and recurrence) of the traumatic event. The film thus shows how such a fantasy produces a temporal loop that traps one endlessly in nothing less (or more) than a dying moment.

Source Code would not appear at first glance to be an explicit surveillance narrative, but instead one that imagines a technology that allows (through what the film vaguely refers to as "quantum physics") soldier Colter Stevens (Jake Gyllenhall) to enter the body of a man during the last eight minutes of his life—a man who dies, along with hundreds of others, on a Chicago commuter train blown up by a domestic terrorist. The program engineering this system, a government operation composed of both military personnel and civilian scientists, sends Stevens into these eight minutes repeatedly, instructing him to track down the bomb and identify the bomber. The film's narrative is thus one of compulsive repetition: Stevens is asked to return and die over and over again until he retrieves the information required to locate the bomber and stop the next attack. While it might appear to be more of a time travel narrative than a surveillance narrative, as with *Déjà vu* they become one and the same. The scientist in charge of the source code project, Dr. Rutledge (Jeffrey Wright), employs a metaphor of a video surveillance camera in order to explain to Stevens what his task is, comparing the technology to a video that records only the last eight minutes of the day. But it also becomes clear that, beyond the metaphor, the purpose of the time travel (or, as Rutledge calls it, "time reassignment") is exactly that of a surveillance recording: something to be played over and over again and analyzed closely in order to find significant details that will lead to a suspect. The difference here is that Stevens enters into the recording as a participant, and can affect events, at least within those eight minutes. Stevens is told that nothing that happens when he goes back into these last eight minutes of the man's life has any permanent effect on the present reality. The eight minutes—the source code—is presented as its own self-contained alternate reality, referred to at one point as a mere computer program, though crucially differentiated from any sort of simulation.

From this different science-fictional basis, the movie would appear to follow exactly the same trajectory as *Déjà vu*: Stevens latches romantically on to a woman in the train and becomes obsessed with saving her;

this romantic attachment leads to the protagonist's desire to not only "solve" the crime but to actually prevent it from ever happening; and, just as in *Déjà vu*, though the protagonist is initially told that the technology does not allow them to change the course of events, he does end up preventing the bombing, saving and winning the girl, and leading the narrative full circle to a terrorist attack that has now been foiled. The similarities in narrative structure are striking. However, as striking as the similarities are, the differences are equally compelling, and the nuances of *Source Code* access and repeat the logic of *Déjà vu* only to indict it and reveal some of its deeply problematic investments.

One of the most notable and significant departures concerns the subject positions of the two films' respective protagonists. While both are masculinized heroes representing a desire to undo trauma via a fetishistic attachment to a lost object, there is one crucial difference: as is revealed to both us and him before the film has progressed even halfway, Colter Stevens of *Source Code* is himself also a lost object—an as-good-as-dead helicopter pilot who has suffered critical injuries in Afghanistan and is now being kept in a completely liminal state so that his brain can be used to access another liminal location, the source code. The "capsule" he returns to after each eight-minute segment on the train, and from which he speaks via video monitor to his contact from the source code operation, Goodwin (Vera Farmiga), is explained as a fabrication, a way for him to make sense of his situation. His actual body is not what the spectators see—we don't know where he really is any more than he does (until slightly later in the film)—and he is used merely as a tool of the government operation, a part of the technology. As a military casualty from Afghanistan, the hero of this film is thus himself a victim of the American "war on terror."

But even further, he is a man whose fetishistic desire around the exploding train and the dead woman are indicative not of his wish to *outrun* death, but to be allowed to gain access to it; he wants nothing more than to be released from his "service" and allowed to die, insisting that dying for his country one time was enough. When he goes back to the train's last eight minutes a final time, it is characterized as his dying wish. He is repeatedly told he cannot change the past events in reality—but he convinces his sympathetic "operator," Goodwin, to not only send him back one more time, but to terminate his barely alive existence at the end of those eight minutes. This action simultaneously allows him to save the train, and to die, and to also be forced to live forever in order to save the train over and over again. In other words, if Colter Stevens can be characterized as melancholic in his refusal to accept the loss of the train and the woman, it is only because he is himself trapped within a moment of endless death: a dead man who is not allowed to die, a dead man who dies over and over, a dead man who must live over and over in a repeated moment of life that has become his death, and a death that has become its own new life.

The politics that such a shift in subject positions implies are significant: the film makes it clear that the "heroic" impulse to save the (already lost) day, and the surveillance technology that allows it, function only to the extent that they operate within the field of a constant death; it is necropolitical to the core, inhabiting and reproducing death and dying in order to sustain the system of reality that has been constructed on top of that death.[24]

Source Code drives this point home with the narrative management of the retroaction: the undoing of the train explosion. While Stevens appears to have succeeded in preventing the bomb from going off, in fact *has* succeeded, the film's subtle and confusing conclusion suggests that preventing the terrorist attack was actually the production of a temporal loop, rather than a real undoing. Or, put another way, the fantasy of undoing shows that all that it does is produce an inescapable loop. The ending unfolds as follows: Stevens, without providing a clear explanation of why, firmly believes that he *can* stop the explosion—he begs Goodwin and Rutledge to let him try and while Rutledge refuses and plans to wipe his memory and start him over for the next source code operation, Goodwin bonds with him and defies her superior. When he returns for his final attempt, he successfully dismantles the bomb and captures the bomber. As the eight minutes expire, he kisses the woman, the activity on the train freezes in frame, and the film cuts to Goodwin terminating his life on the other end (implying that he has stopped the attack, but only within the alternate reality). But remarkably, the action continues as we cut back to the "source code": the train arrives safely in Chicago, and Stevens leads his love object into a romantic future (staring at their reflection in the Cloud Gate sculpture at Millennium Park) that implies the eight minutes of death has been surpassed.

But once again the movie refutes its own logic—we are again sent backward in time, but this time considerably beyond those eight minutes. We see Goodwin arriving at work that morning; the train attack has now been prevented, and she watches news coverage describing how it was foiled. Apparently, this reality has been changed as well. Goodwin then receives a text message sent from Stevens *within* the source code, explaining what has happened, and telling her that the source code operation works better than anyone could have possibly imagined. But here, in this reality, in this past, Stevens is still (marginally) alive waiting to participate in an operation, and Rutledge is still waiting for a terrorist attack to happen so that his technology can be tested. Goodwin says nothing to Rutledge, and it appears that the film has presented the absolute triumph of this form of temporal surveillance: a surveillance that works so well that its operators won't even know they have used it to prevent terrorism. Thus, at first glance, the film's "happy ending" supports the reactionary politics of *Déjà vu*. But the happy ending is confusing and unsatisfying, given that Stevens had merely wanted to die, an option that is now denied him, and the audience is left with a vision of his broken body in a hyperbaric chamber rather than an image of him walking through Chicago with his new love, as had been offered moments before.

Ultimately the dissatisfaction of the conclusion makes sense only when we begin to realize that, in fact, the film's open-ended closure implies *not* that we have returned to an earlier time in the "original" cinematic reality, but instead that we are now endlessly trapped within the disjuncture of the source code that is *Stevens's* last eight minutes of life—an eight minutes in which he has saved the girl and stopped the terrorist attack, and thus prevented himself from ever being sent back to find the bomber. The confusion of this ending thus does not reside only in the paradoxes that attend the "resolutions" of many time travel narratives; it also firmly establishes the logic of retroactive surveillance that is merely hinted at by the elements of the film discussed earlier: the surveillance can function as a preventative measure only if one becomes trapped within an endlessly repeating circuit of death. *Source Code* highlights that the circumvention of the traumatic moment of loss becomes a compulsive circling around it that brings one back to the beginning, waiting (hoping) for the next disaster to emerge so that the prevention can take place. This is announced most explicitly by Dr. Rutledge's disappointment in the prevention of the train bombing: as we see Goodwin go in to tell Rutledge of the text message she has received from Colter Stevens, Rutledge and another colleague discuss their hope that soon an attack will actually occur, so that they can put their technology to use. It is, simply put, a system of prevention that relies on the production of disaster and death in order for the fantasy of prevention to work. While the earlier films clearly support such a politics as the fulfillment of national security and even national identity, *Source Code* provides a more studious critique of such narrative production. In many ways it is the culmination of the fantasies of the earlier films, and, as such, cannot help but establish the degree to which such fantasies of preventative surveillance and security are enmeshed in a nationalist project predicated on establishing—in several senses—a time of death.

* * *

Though the films discussed in this chapter are all "post-9/11" examples, the analysis offered here of the temporal imagination of these films suggests that it would be deeply problematic to participate in the fetishistic idealization of that event and insist that these narratives and politics are an exclusively posttraumatic structure. In fact, rather than similarly circling back to the idea of a single event, the temporal formations of these narratives demand that we revisit the temporal structures of the surveillance cinema that precedes them, and how that cinema addressed the melancholic imagination of surveillance. The films discussed above, though insistently focusing their surveillance practices around terrorism, also largely disavow any racial project—both *Déjà vu* and *Source Code* critique racial profiling and cast their terrorists as domestic and white (modeled after the Timothy McVeigh "radical patriot" figure, as though there were no other possible configuration imaginable for a domestic white terrorist). And *Vantage Point* suggests that even in the more recognizable post-9/11 rendering of terrorists, that it is a white American Secret Service man masterminding the plot. In the above films, race is a signifying absence in the context of a postmillennial "war on terror" so explicitly focused on the threat of a Muslim other.

The next chapter asks that we view these films in the light of an earlier film that plays similar temporal games, but that uses its temporal formation as a cinematic point of entry to the intersections of surveillance and race. The analysis offers a necessary historicization of the science-fictional production of time-based surveillance narratives. Simultaneously, and at the risk of collapsing into circularity, it offers *cinema as a mediating history of surveillant mediation*, and the possible function of mediated history as intervention in the use of surveillance as a racial project.

5

Temporality and Surveillance II

Surveillance, Remediation, and Social Memory in Strange Days

Thomas Levin has suggested that the surveillance cinema of the 1990s represents a kind of technological and rhetorical flashpoint in which cinematic narration becomes increasingly intertwined with surveillant narration.[1] Technologically—and this is central to both cinema and surveillance—the 1990s served as a theoretical and practical transition between analog and digital modes. Within film and media studies, the phenomenological, aesthetic, and philosophical assessment of this transition has dominated theoretical circles since that time, prompting a return to (and myriad reformulations of) critic and theorist André Bazin's still pivotal question: "What is cinema?"[2] On the surveillance front, the exponential expansion of digital models of surveillance helped push the study of surveillance into a dynamic interdisciplinary field: dataveillance has been a frequent reference point for arguments that the framework of panopticism cannot account for the coding, communication, aggregation, and variation that has broadened the definition of surveillance into multiple formations and functions, and simultaneously taken multiple formations and functions and subjected them to an informational paradigm. These discussions in both film and surveillance studies have been just one aspect of the diverse social, cultural, scientific, and philosophical analyses that have posited the digital turn as having enormous implications for everything from the nature of identity and subjectivity to constitutional and intellectual property law, definitions and divisions of labor, political activism, systems theory, the future of capitalism, and so on.

Within this context, director Kathryn Bigelow's 1995 film *Strange Days* emerges as a compelling, multichanneled intersection of subjectivity and surveillance as understood among cinematic, televisual, and digital media. The film has served as a crucial instance of *remediation* for Jay

Bolter and Richard Grusin: its narrative premise is their book's introductory and defining example of "our culture's contradictory imperatives for immediacy and hypermediacy."[3] For Grusin, the film also exemplifies the logic of *premediation*: his essay, discussed in the preceding chapter, provides a framework through which to view the incorporation of surveillance into cinema as a politics in which remediation is used as premediation.[4] *Strange Days* focuses on a (mostly) imaginary technology that is functionally analog in both its pseudo-scientific makeup and its cinematic presentation, but that invokes the digital in its references to virtual experience and millennial anxiety; the film thus serves as a nexus for changing configurations of technology in relation to narrative formation. *Strange Days* also ties together several of the functions of surveillance covered in the prior chapters: the circuits and circularities of time, the production of individualized and racialized bodies, and the relations of those bodies to broader politics and social organization within a surveillance culture. Accessing the many institutions, dispersals, and reorientations of surveillance practices and technologies through the fantasy of a "new media," *Strange Days* sets the stakes of surveillance narratives in a number of ways that play out (often through disavowal) in the more contemporary films. And, much as Grusin makes it clear that the "premediation" of the "post-9/11" United States was already emerging in the 1990s, it is important to show yet again that while September 11, 2001, may have provided a shift in the degree and form of surveillant temporality, many of the structural elements of this function preexist and define their post-9/11 usage. An in-depth analysis of *Strange Days* is thus a way to historicize and contextualize the next decade's surveillance cinema, especially its temporal trends, with a film from the recent past—a film itself organized around its own near future.

Made in 1995 but set in 1999 Los Angeles on the eve of the new millennium, the film anticipates a cultural moment defined by crisis, in large part a fear of a total systems breakdown based in digital dependency: and yet the "Y2K" or "millennium bug" that described the possibility of widespread computer crashes with the date rollover to "oo" is never referenced in the film, and the looming threat of apocalyptic failure develops through other multiply mediated registers. Somewhat less explicitly, though with clear visual and narrative resonance, *Strange Days* also reflects events from Los Angeles's recent past, in particular the events surrounding the video recording of the police assault on Rodney King in 1991. Despite its bids for historical referentiality, the film has not stood out as particularly influential nor does it fit as neatly within a trend or generic structure as do most of the films under discussion in this book. Considering that director Kathryn Bigelow went on to win an Oscar in 2009 for *The Hurt Locker* (and to receive a nomination for the also historical and also surveillance-related *Zero Dark Thirty* in 2012), the film might be notable as part of the early oeuvre of the first woman to win an Academy Award for directing. However, it is generally eclipsed by her action-surf thriller *Point Break* (1991), which achieved cult status soon after its release.[5] But even, or especially, because one would be hard pressed to make a strong case for this film's historical import, it represents a diffuse mediation of technological, stylistic, and social histories that exemplifies how surveillance and politics emerge as cultural memory in cinematic form.

Strange Days presents the possible reproduction of exact sensory experience through a technology called a superconducting quantum interference device: SQUID. Under the auspices of this premise, the film engages in a possibly symptomatic, but often incisive, analysis of the relations between subject position, representational mediation, and political actions. It suggests a series of levels at which identity is structured and restructured by a series of mediations. This is perhaps another reason that the film is of significance to Bolter and Grusin, who foreground mediation, and thus also remediation, in the definition of both personal and cultural identity: "As these media become simultaneously technical analogs and social expressions of our identity, we become simultaneously both the subject and object of contemporary media."[6] However, as has been made amply clear by the prior chapters, technologies and practices of mediation are also functions of *power*—particularly as they are increasingly defined (or remediated) through surveillant formations. It is thus also not surprising that the focus on mediated subjectivities in *Strange Days* is joined with a narrative that turns upon the use of those subjective structures as both forms and effects of surveillance. As such, the film draws attention to a crux in the theorization of surveillance, as well as cinematic representations of surveillance: that surveillance both defines and is defined by the technologies and subjects it incorporates. Kevin Haggerty and Richard Ericson state, "The politics of identity as it pertains to surveillance has at least two dimensions. The first concerns the monitoring of pre-constituted social groupings; the second involves establishing new forms of identity"[7] While the production of new social subjects is a significant function of surveillance, underlying this formulation is the corollary point that surveillance (as either technology or practice) is not itself stable, but is also formed, reformed, and deformed through the productions and resistances of subjects within surveillance culture. *Strange Days* serves as a critical meditation on this seemingly circular action of surveillance, manifesting a number of both narrative and technological formations that have become central to the concerns of postmillennial surveillance cinema, and also showing where those formations might be configured to different political ends.

The film's treatment of the SQUID as a technology of immediacy navigates interrelated problematics of surveillance, representation, memory, and politics by establishing the circularity of the medium itself. This circularity is deployed as a form of temporal intervention—intervention that is pivotal in any framework in which the political exceptionalism of the "war on terror" insists on the unique specificity of the present historical moment while, as argued in the preceding chapter, the future is hailed as a past that can be prevented.

Strange Days' central premise is the science-fictional possibility of recording an individual's perceptual experience "straight from the cerebral cortex" with the SQUID technology. These sensations are then replayed with the same technology, allowing the recordings to emerge as "raw" first-person experience for the wearer, presented cinematically as a first-person point-of-view shot similar to the first-person-camera films discussed in Chapter Two (though here shot with a 35mm Steadicam rather than handheld video). The film proceeds from this science-fictional basis to multiple real-historical references; at the intersection of science fiction, history, and cinematic narrative style, it establishes connectivity between absolute subjective experience and the use of representational media in surveillance and racial formations. In doing so, the film also traces the possible intersections of individually, historically embodied experience and systematic intervention in technologies of surveillant mediation and social politics—precisely the elements that a film like *Enemy of the State* avoids even as it appears to present a critique of surveillance culture. Alongside and through this, the film demonstrates how the melancholic and reactionary temporality discussed in the preceding chapter might be reconfigured as radical, historical *memory* through a different approach to the narrative incorporation of surveillance.

* * *

Strange Days focuses its story, at least initially, around Lenny Nero (Ralph Fiennes), an ex-cop who now peddles SQUID "clips" on a black market presented as comparable to a drug trade. As an ex–police officer turned dealer, Lenny embodies the trajectory of the SQUID technology, which we are told was initially developed for the FBI for surveillance purposes before it was outlawed and used for illicit purposes. Both Lenny and the SQUID have now transgressed their law enforcement functions and are presented as conduits for "underground" technological perversion. Lenny is also characterized as a "user" (problematically so) of his own SQUID clips: his unhealthy attachment to his ex-girlfriend Faith (Juliette Lewis) is highlighted by his ecstatically melancholic review of his recorded first-person experiences with Faith. Lenny's narrative of overattachment to his lost objects (strongly reminiscent of the guiding pathologies of the protagonists from the time travel films discussed in the preceding chapter) is woven together with two interrelated murder mysteries—notably murders that are, respectively, racialized and sexualized—also "played out" on, through, and against the SQUID technology. These plotlines all unfold against the pivotal background of the impending millennial New Year's Eve celebration, which is presented as a looming disaster. The film proposes both the SQUID and its embodied users as mechanisms of surveillance, while also thematizing the production and erasure of both personal and historical memory as functions of surveillance.

The narrative production of Lenny's melancholia in relation to historical and political violences constitutes representational and surveillant technologies as ones that manage and even technologize time itself, as we see in the "millennial" setting of the film. Film scholar Mark Berrettini aptly summarizes the milieu:

> *Strange Days* portrays an apocalyptic future that centers on LA's public sphere, as shown in Lenny's tour of LA and in the televisual representation of New Year's Eve preparations. Such visual "rumors" of war, unrest,

and impending doom circulate throughout most of the film within various representations from visual-media technologies—television, the film camera's depiction of the diegetic world, and the film's recurring special effect representation of the fictional Superconducting Quantum Interference Device (SQUID).[8]

This background becomes the foreground, while the film's personal narratives become wider social narratives, and vice versa. Given the film's emphasis on technologized systems of memory it is striking that the possibility of computer systems breakdown with the date switch from 1999 to 2000 is not more central to the film's envisioning of a "Y2K" disaster. But significantly, and symptomatically, the concerns of Y2K and computer memory are refocalized through a nondigital technology (the SQUID). Even the SQUID experience is presented visually through a first-person point-of-view shot, cinema's most recognizable, and insistently analog, representation of subjective experience. The SQUID point-of-view shots are not associated with a diegetic video camera as are the first-person-camera films discussed in Chapter Three, but instead are supposed to represent "direct" subjective experience (which is to say, experience mediated by a technology that is paradoxically defined by its ability to record unmediated, "raw" experience). However, the similarity in form connects this film's science-fictional presentation of recorded experience with the explicitly mediated first-person-camera films, in which the video gaze and subjective reality are coded almost identically.

The film's millennial anxieties are played out through the lens of the "racial tensions" of the 1990s, which, represented most obviously by the videotaped assault of Rodney King, the televised slow-speed chase of O. J. Simpson, and the televised trial that followed, were in many ways characterized by a visibility mediated through surveillance technologies and problematized representations. It is thus not surprising that the concerns around the remediation of subjective experience in *Strange Days* become implicated in the visual discourse of racial politics and social histories. The technologizing of subjectivity, memory, history, and ultimately *time* emerge as key to understanding how surveillance (especially in its intersection with racial formations, and its remediation in cinematic narrative) has become part of social memory and political history, and thus a central aspect of what is increasingly referred to as a "surveillance culture."

The film's treatment of memory as both purpose and effect of surveillance technology is thematized as three "mysteries" in the filmic plot. Each one provides a link in the narrative chain binding together individual subjectivity, surveillance technologies, and racialized political violence. The first mystery that initially draws Lenny into and through this immanent background begins when he is left a "blackjack" clip: the SQUID version of snuff.[9] Blackjack consists of a SQUID subject dying while recording; Lenny has already emphatically stated that he doesn't deal in such clips. This blackjack clip represents a woman's rape and murder, from the perspective of her attacker. The victim, Iris, is a woman we recognize from an earlier scene in which she is chased by two Los Angeles police officers in what appears to be a violent assault rather than a "legitimate" police procedure. Her rape and murder are presented to Lenny and to the audience as the limit case of SQUID violence and perversity: the rapist/killer wearing the SQUID mechanism forces his victim to wear a connected mechanism during the assault and murder, thus presumably experiencing the attacker's sensations at the same time as her own.

This first mystery becomes part and parcel of the second mystery: Iris was running from the police because, while making a SQUID recording for another purpose, she had recorded those same policemen murdering Jeriko One, an African American political icon and recording artist. Both Iris's murder and the murder of Jeriko One eventually circle back to Lenny's personal investment in reclaiming/rescuing his ex-girlfriend from her new lover, music industry mogul Philo Gant, what might be understood as the third and final "mystery" of the plot. In this third mystery, we learn that the two other mysteries, murders that in different forms have broad social implications, are in fact joined through the subject formation, the desires and memories, of one individual: Lenny. Lenny's investigations reveal that it was Philo who asked Iris to wear the SQUID while with his star recording artist, Jeriko One, in a fit of paranoia about Jeriko's possible disloyalty. Philo then hired Max, who Lenny believed was his friend, to murder Iris and reclaim the SQUID clip so he would not be exposed as a paranoiac surveilling his own artists.

The other connective thread between these three plotlines is chauffer/ bodyguard Mace (Angela Bassett), Lenny's best friend. Throughout this entire circle of violence and political and psychosexual intrigue, Mace grudgingly aids, protects, and berates Lenny for his involvement with the SQUID, his obsession with his former girlfriend, and his general lack of motivation and judgment. As a black woman surrounded by violence coded as white, male, and pathological, Mace is presented as the explicit moral compass of the film, a positioning that is neither unusual nor un- problematic in the history of racial representation in cinema.[10] Tellingly, and despite her externality to the circuit of violence and her rejection of the SQUID, her position also produces her as the representational nexus of the violence in the film, the cinematic fiction of the SQUID technol- ogy, and the historicality of surveillance and/as racial violence.

Specifically, Mace is the narrative figure who largely refuses the logic of technologized memory that Lenny represents: she finds the use of the SQUID both perverse and irresponsible, right up until she wrests it from Lenny's pathological pursuits and returns it to the realm of social in- tervention in the form of evidence against the LAPD officers.[11] *Strange Days* culminates as Mace forces Lenny to realize that while he wants to trade the SQUID clip of Jeriko's murder for Faith's safety, the clip must be handed over to the authorities so that justice can be served. In doing so, she clearly presents a choice of the political over the personal, but also an insistence on the use of the SQUID as the production of a his- torical "now" that rejects both the compulsive repetition of a "then" rep- resented by Lenny's melancholic relation to his personal past, and the fear of a projected future of upheaval and racial violence resulting from the revelation that Jeriko has been murdered by white cops.

The SQUID, thus initially used in the film for personal satisfaction, moves through a circuit of violence represented in intertwined narra- tive threads, until all those threads join together and the technology re- emerges as evidence against the institution for which it was originally developed. Through examination of this narrative arc, several critics have drawn attention to the political/theoretical stakes of the mediations narrated in this film. Berrettini traces how the film uses intranarrative technological mediation (not just the SQUID, but television and radio as well) to weave together the threads of the plot, ultimately eschewing this mediation in favor of what he calls a "resounding endorsement of the individual over the politicized social realm."[12] Brian Carr, in a not unrelated move, has shown how a theoretical view of politically productive identification—both technological and otherwise—is effectively and importantly critiqued in this film. Carr's examination of cinematic identification in conjunction with what he considers a problematic celebration of the "mobile" urban subject is a significant account of the politics of representational media in *Strange Days*.[13]

The present analysis builds upon but departs from such discussions to take up the film's questions concerning technology in the light of the SQUID's dual and intersecting uses as surveillance and representation. The relations between these uses, especially as defined by the circularity of *Strange Days*' narrative, become the film's point of access to racial formations in the 1990s. As a film that I would characterize neither as entirely symptomatic nor critical, *Strange Days* nevertheless positions itself as *historical*—in the context of surveillance cinema but also within the broader, mutually reinforcing histories of surveillance and racial formation in the United States. The film's remediation of video and television, in conjunction with its science-fictional vision of surveilled/ surveilling subjectivity reproduced for consumption, shows how these elements interpenetrate and circle back through mediation to become history, memory, and culture. This remediation—as part of its narrative representation of racial violence—serves to inform but also productively *deform* the way this violence is staged by surveillance and reframed as historical and social memory. In this way *Strange Days*—again neither symptomatically nor actively—provides a narrative intervention in how surveillance technologies function in relation to racial projects, which Omi and Winant argue do the "ideological 'work'" of making a "linkage between structure and representation" that is a significant basis of racial formations.[14] Ultimately, technologized memory itself becomes its own peculiar racial project in the film, pointing to how time-based surveillance technologies (e.g., video recordings) have established a historical circularity between individual and social bodies in racial formations. The film also suggests how the temporal manipulations and refabrications at the heart of the reactionary politics of films such as *Déjà vu* and *Vantage Point* (films that eclipse the racial politics of their own surveillance narratives in order to construct their idealized nationalist visions), might be deployed toward opposite effects. *Strange Days* ultimately demonstrates that while some surveillance cinema intersects with surveillance practice as a consolidation of power, other forms of it suggest that cinematic remediation might serve to redefine the powers of surveillance.

*　　*　　*

In order to trace the politics of the circularity in *Strange Days*' approach to time, it is helpful to begin at the end: while Berrettini and Carr have gestured toward the climactic scene and its aftermath as either a resolution or a "coda" to the issues of mediation raised by the SQUID narrative, questions remain as to how it relates to the politics of representational technology that are so explicitly addressed by the rest of the film. In the closing scenes there appears to be an abandonment of the SQUID narrative, and its mediations, in favor of direct interpersonal relations. However, a number of visual and narrative signifiers suggest not a move *away* from the technological mediation of subjective memory (as the storyline more superficially suggests), but instead a layered representation that exposes the racial projects at the intersection of mediated memory and surveillance practice.

The climactic episode shows Mace, having given the SQUID clip of Jeriko's murder to the police commissioner, as she flees from the two policemen who murdered Jeriko and are now firing at her (and accidentally hitting numerous others) as they pursue. After they lose her amid the New Year's Eve crowd, Mace attacks, subdues, and restrains the two with their own cuffs, nightsticks, and guns. Several riot police, in place for the Y2K celebration (which is about to hit a crescendo as midnight approaches), witness her restraining the other officers at gunpoint, and "naturally" assume that the black woman has attacked two innocent members of the LAPD. Even as she lays down her weapon and tries to explain, the police encircle her and begin to attack her with their nightsticks, in what becomes a striking visual quotation of the Rodney King beating that, in 1995, had yet to fade as an afterimage in the collective mind's eye—a social memory constructed and reconstructed through the remediation of surveillance and representation. Recorded on consumer home video by a nearby resident (in one of the earliest and most famous reversals of traditional surveillance dynamics), the violence of the police attack on King was widely disseminated and viewed on television news outlets, described by a media pundit as recently as 2012 as arguably "the most famous home video of all time."[15] After we see Mace suffering these recognizable blows, the police are attacked by the encircling crowd, which, by virtue of the few individual faces and figures that are shown, is clearly defined as black. The film's reference to the King video is thus immediately followed with (and in fact partially identified by) a reference to the reaction to the video (also widely viewed on television) that in reality came much later: a response not to the beating itself but to the exoneration of the police involved. As Berrettini describes, the film's direct move from the police assault to the violence of the outraged crowd eliminates the "calm before the storm" preceding the actual Los Angeles uprising, a period of time in which the trial of the policemen took place, since here the crowds "see Mace as she is beaten and react violently against the police without waiting for a trial or verdict."[16] More precisely, we might say that this scene collapses the major events of the Rodney King narrative into a visual and narrative immediacy: the riot immediately follows the beating, but also included is the interpretation of Mace as the hostile party and the policemen as innocent—the implied inclusion, in other words, of the Simi Valley trial verdict that exonerated the policemen, a verdict based on the interpretation and recoding of the video by the policemen's legal team.

To the degree that the film effectively ignores the legal process that acquitted the officers in the King assault, which was what ultimately precipitated a violent uprising, the film is sorely lacking as a critique of the systemic racism out of which such police brutality emerged. This is especially true given the following scenes that show that order will be restored by "the system." However, what the story lacks in its critique the film somewhat makes up for through the process and effect of its *mediation. Strange Days'* climactic scene replays the drawn out video/televisual events of the beating/trial/uprising as a single "clip": a single continuous visual and narrative experience for both Mace and the film's viewer. Thus even as the film has presented a rejection of the SQUID mediation, the film has itself become invested in playing out a series of temporally discrete events into a single *cinematic* experience, embodied this time most fully by the film's viewers as we survey the scene from within, above, and around the unfolding circumstances. This highly media-referential scene, a scene that can be fully understood only in

Police surround and beat Mace with nightsticks in *Strange Days* (1995).

relation to images and historical events the audience is already familiar with, signals the circularity with which we must come to understand the film's relation to the technologies and practices it highlights, and how this circular logic is organized around the body and character of Mace.

Having repeatedly chastised Lenny for his involvement with the SQUID, Mace has stated that "memories were meant to fade"; she also later demands that Lenny turn over the clip of Jeriko's murder to her so that justice can be served. Both despite and because of her overdetermined embodiment of the film's responsibilities and ethics, Mace is also the figure that serves as the focal point of the film's quotation of the highly mediated images of the King beating and the L.A. uprising. Her figure, as both action hero and object of violence, is subjected to the central position in the film's final scenario because throughout the film she has been at the center of the historical thinking that here becomes the basis for choosing a political/ethical use of surveillance over Lenny's personal use—the disturbing but revealing result is the *cinematic* and personalized rendering of an assault historically identified with video and televisual mediation.[17] The video beating of Rodney King, the narrative of the film, and the singularly embodied experience offered by SQUID technology all coincide with Mace (despite the ostensible centrality of Lenny's character).[18]

The narrative intersections of video, cinema, and the fictional SQUID technology are, on the most basic level, organized by similarities between the King video and the SQUID as surveillance technologies. The

The resulting riot: the shot from directly above echoes news helicopter footage of the 1992 civil unrest in Los Angeles.

King video reversed traditional surveillance structures insofar as it was a citizen surveilling police. The "video" as phenomenon also includes the televisual mediation and dissemination of the recording, and thus consumer video surveillance became simultaneously evidentiary, narrative, and spectacular. This mediated release of the surveillance resulted in widespread public outrage, in many ways for the first time allowing non-racialized subjects a "view" of the brutality of American police activity, even if the events on the video were often regarded by the white media and public as an aberration rather than routine.[19] The use of home video and televisual spectacle against the police became the catalyst for the events that followed, and arguably an ongoing threat to one-sided surveillance culture, especially with the increasing economic availability of digital video and the increased possibilities of distribution provided by online user-generated video-sharing sites such as YouTube.

In a film that visually and thematically centralizes the events surrounding the Rodney King assault, it is more than incidental that the narrative of SQUID usage follows the same trajectory: as the film explains, the SQUID was initially developed by the government for surveillance (a very advanced form of "wearing a wire"); it then hit an underground market, akin to both a drug and pornography trade.[20] Finally, the SQUID is again used for (incidental) surveillance by the "public" within the film, accidentally capturing a clip of the racially/politically motivated murder of Jeriko One. As a structural and functional double for video within cinema, and the pivot point upon which both the personal and political narratives turn, the SQUID fantasy in *Strange Days* becomes a multiply mediated and layered representation of surveillance that highlights how such a formation is integrated with individual, subjective experience, representations of racial and political subject positions, and the construction of social memory.[21] Precisely because of this extensive and layered remediation, *Strange Days* is an exemplary and instructive instance of surveillance cinema, even as it is a less direct representation of surveillance than some of the films discussed in the prior chapters.

In order to more easily understand the relations between surveillance, mediation, and subjectivity, and the political implications of those relations for surveillance cinema, it is of use to review the narrative aspects of *Strange Days* discussed above:

a) The film introduces the SQUID technology as one that provides an exact record of human perceptual experience, for the pleasurable use of its wearer.

b) Dialogue reveals that this technology was originally developed for governmental surveillance use.

c) The technology, now privatized and criminalized, is used by a corrupt white music industry mogul, Philo, to track his political and politicized black rap star, Jeriko One, whom he fears has become an out-of-control commodity.

d) Accidentally, the SQUID instead records Jeriko's murder by two white police officers.

e) The SQUID, in a parallel narrative thread, is used as a weapon in the rape and murder of the young woman who recorded the Jeriko murder.

f) After a tug of war between Mace and Lenny as to whether the clip of Jeriko's murder should be used for personal or wider social purposes, Mace delivers the clip to the apparently ethical police commissioner to expose the murder and see justice done.

g) Mace goes after the two corrupt policemen herself, and is severely beaten in a visual-historical reference to a prior (ostensibly) extradiegetic phenomenon: the Rodney King video, itself a surveillance recording of police produced by a citizen and disseminated by television news.

The above account highlights the seemingly circular logic of the surveillance technologies addressed by the film both explicitly and implicitly. Simply put, *Strange Days* presents a series of events in which the SQUID technology is deployed in the service and as a function of violence and power, and every time there seems to be a recuperation of the technology for use against those dominant powers, it is reintroduced as a weapon against those who have undermined its original uses.

However, the circularity in the use of SQUID technology is complicated when, after the SQUID-defined narrative is effectively ended with the clip turned over to the police commissioner, Mace is surrounded by the police and beaten with nightsticks. The film here *removes* the power of surveillance and its effects from the internal narrative at hand and it reemerges through the mediated social memory of the film's audience as we are positioned to "recognize" the beating of Mace from and as the beating of Rodney King. Thus, even as this sequence seems to be outside of the logic of the SQUID technology, we are returned to the question of mediation and surveillance through the broader mediation of a historically situated spectatorship—a spectatorship, originally surveillant, here redefined cinematically. Unlike both the single-shot, first-person Steadicam sequences that characterize the SQUID representations and the videotaped beating of King, the audience is presented with this attack as an edited spectacle from a number of perspectives, ranging from a low-to-the-ground shot that places the spectator close to Mace's position while offering a close-up of her pain, to a wide shot from above and at a distance, and including many reaction shots of the crowd watching in horror. The editing of this sequence, as opposed to the subjective perspective of the SQUID recording and the perspective of the King video and video surveillance more generally, is almost routinely cinematic, presenting a structured narration of the event and its multiple affects and effects. Such a narrativized and aestheticized representation of violence has frequently been the ground of critiques of cinema that supposedly desensitizes audiences to violence through these "aestheticized" renderings. But it is clear here that the multiplicity of perspectives, and their commingling, render the experience of the violence against Mace not less, but *more*, extreme by virtue of their resonance with the larger social, juridical, and racial violence surrounding the Rodney King video. In other words, the first-person extremity of experience represented by the SQUID is indeed rejected at the end of the film—not however, as Berrittini suggests, in favor of unmediated experience, but in favor of a kind of referential abstraction, a move away from "pure" or literal personal experience, that situates first-person experience as legible and exchangeable primarily through both technological and social mediation and sociohistorical memory formations, all of which come together under a now very broadly defined cinematic structure.

As noted in the beginning of this chapter, Bolter and Grusin have privileged *Strange Days* in their definition of new media as a process of remediation, describing the film as one that "captures the ambivalent and contradictory ways in which new digital media function for our culture today." They argue that *Strange Days* "demonstrates what we call a double logic of *remediation*. Our culture wants both to multiply its media and to erase all traces of mediation: ideally, it wants to erase its media in the very act of multiplying them."[22] What Bolter and Grusin describe as the logic of the SQUID technology within the film—a mediating technology designed to produce immediacy—is something I would extend to the narrative as well. While both the technology and the narrative surrounding that technology offer the conceit of reducing mediation, they ultimately function only through reference to multiple forms of mediation and representation, and also serve to define cinematic discourse through such reference.[23] And though a hypermediated field of reference might now seem to be an indisputable conclusion to reach about the constitution of "experience" in the postmillennial United States, a mediated and relational subjectivity is less clear in terms of what that might actually *mean* for the uses of technologies and mediations. In this context more specifically, it also poses the question of how we are to understand the continued production of the cinematic mediation of surveillance, and its involvement in the politics of racial representation, beyond the largely ideological formations discussed in many of the prior chapters.

This issue is perhaps best addressed through an examination of the relations between Mace's assault and what follows: the film's bizarre conclusion, a scene that seems to undo much of the already weak critique of systemic racism and violence that the film has centralized. The plot wraps itself up a little too neatly in the face of the personal and social mess it has spent two hours creating. At first the city appears to be swallowed up by the uprising after Mace's beating—a scene the enormity of which we are offered by a shot from far above, an aerial shot that introduces the riot as also highly mediated by news and police helicopters. In fact, this very brief shot structures the also very brief riot as much through the mediated memory of the audience as the beating that preceded it: though the film does not quote the actual event, the aerial shot is enough to reference the attack on truck driver Reginald Denny, who was severely beaten during the Los Angeles uprising in another attack caught on video, this time by a television news helicopter. The referentiality here is thus further multiplied by the introduction of another recorded and televised act of violence, once again rendered as a cinematic construction of spectacle. But rather than an escalation of violence and further references to the mediated recent history of Los Angeles, this cinematic "race riot" is averted by the intervention of the tuxedoed, paternalistic police commissioner, to whom Mace had earlier delivered the clip of Jeriko's murder. He commands that Mace be freed and the cops who murdered Jeriko be arrested. The crowd is appeased (though there is no visible consequence for the riot police who delivered such a severe and unnecessary beating in full view of the crowd) and Mace and Lenny are free to share a kiss that seems to seal a future of interracial harmony. Given the tensions built, and the sheer magnitude of the crowd presented in Los Angeles, one's suspension of disbelief is sorely tested at this point. Following from the more complex and even cynical representations of the rest of the film, this tidy conclusion is dumbfounding.

It is tempting, and frankly necessary, to read the film's closing at least in part as a disavowal of all that preceded—a renewal of trust in the "proper authorities" to handle technologies of surveillance, and thus, apparently, racial justice properly. This fantasy resolution is not inconsistent with the types of wishful undoing of trauma characteristic of the time travel films discussed in the preceding chapter. Berrettini sees the final note of the film as simply utopian: "Interracial and social relations will improve and succeed because technology (SQUID) has been used for the right purpose."[24] But a reading of the conclusion as a straightforwardly utopian turn (even if intended to be just that) requires that we ignore the complexity of the entire preceding film, as well as the curious affect of this closing scene. Brian Carr's analysis of the film's mediated temporalities provides a starting point to address the narrative and affective implications of the film's conclusion: "In the end, their love—if it is that, yet—emerges not out of the imagistic access to the other but out of what Mace, in an earlier scene, calls 'real time.' This real time is not, as it may seem to be, Mace's reference to an unmediated 'reality,' but a reference to the mediation and limits we all suffer paradoxically as a condition of our relation to others."[25] Much as I suggest that the scenes of Mace's beating and resulting crowd violence are the most highly mediated moments of the film, despite their existence outside of the realm of SQUID recording and thus outside of the intradiegetic mediation, Carr also shows that we must understand the ending in relation to mediation, this time that of intersubjectivity. Taken together, these points show why the end of the film seems simultaneously "unrealistic" and "unsatisfactory" (in opposition to cinematic closures where the lack of realism is counterbalanced by affective satisfaction in romantic resolution). What Carr highlights is the mediation, the unsuccessful habitation of any moment of "personal satisfaction" in this kind of image—for the characters maybe, but certainly for the viewers as well.

But the lack of satisfaction or believability in the ultimate avoidance of a massive riot and the final romantic joining of Mace and Lenny must be tied to one other crucial point: on several levels, the riot following Mace's attack *should have happened*. Because the film's audience is accessed here through visual and narrative reference to the mediated events surrounding the assault on Rodney King, the logic of representation and repetition will emerge as a desire for the memory/media narrative to repeat itself fully. That desire is thwarted when the riot is averted and we are left with the frustration associated with an incomplete or failed repetition.[26] On this level, this film's resolution is a strange mirror of that of *Source Code*, discussed in the previous chapter, in which the prevention of a traumatic bombing is coupled with a romantic conclusion (all of which also register as confounding at both narrative and affective levels); in that case, the resolution was revealed as *predicated* on a possibly infinite repetition. Both films, in different forms, implicitly present the "resolution" of their narratives as an intervention in a temporality defined by repetition, as a refusal to repeat. *Source Code*, I have argued, uses the time travel paradox to reveal that such a refusal is the (violent, failed) production of the circular space of repetition. *Strange*

Days, on the other hand, in beginning to play out a repetition via the remediation of the audience's (mediated) social references, produces violence through a *refused* repetition.

In other words, it is no accident that the "riot"/defense of Mace is averted by the appearance of the white patriarch, the representative of the law. While the (white) law in the film restores the colorblind and just legal standards that allow "peace" to also be restored, it was in fact the law, more particularly the video in the hands of the legal process, that produced the most profoundly violent act of the series of events in the King case. As Crenshaw and Peller suggest, we must look at the acquittal of the policeman in the King case not as an aberration of the American legal system, as an extraordinary moment, but as *typical*.[27] This is why it produced the response it did despite every effort on the part of liberals and conservatives alike to read the beating and trial as anomalies. Similarly, when the commissioner, the "good cop"—whom Lenny refers to as the "only honest cop in L.A."—arrests the policemen who attacked Mace and calms the crowd, the sense of dissatisfaction at the end is less interesting if read as an unrealistic, utopian moment found only in Hollywood narrative denouements.

In order to locate the profound frustration of that conclusion—and the continuing interest of the film and its treatment of surveillance, media, and mediated surveillance—one must see the restoration of the rule of law in the film as a typical reproduction of representational and institutional repression of violent response in the United States. These instances range from the "calming" of the outrage over the King verdict to the installation in 2000 of George W. Bush in the U.S. presidency even in the midst of mounting evidence of voter disenfranchisement, to a more recent repetition of 2013: the acquittal of neighborhood watch vigilante George Zimmerman in the murder of teenager Trayvon Martin. Notably, in this last instance the memory of the Rodney King assault and the resulting uprising was hailed as a projected future by media and pundits through calls for "calm" before the verdict was even reached.

Thus the "hypermediacy" of the climax of *Strange Days*—the violent representation of Mace's beating, and the quite explicit reference therein to the videotaped beating of Rodney King—is tied to the implicit violence of the *lack* of representation that follows it. This is not the "immediacy" of the SQUID, the other side of the coin in Bolter and

Grusin's account of the "double logic" of remediation: it is a nonmediation, a produced invisibility that suggests that there are outside terms in remediation, and that they are produced by and as a politics that refuses to represent its own forms of violence, in fact *can't* represent those violences, because they are in part defined by this erasure—in Virilio's terms, once again, and in yet another form, "an aesthetics of disappearance."

More straightforwardly: seen against the context of the instances/remediations of violence that precede the "peaceful resolution" of the film, the foreclosure of the widespread violence that has been building throughout the film *becomes itself an act of violence*. In her analysis of race relations in 1990s disaster films, film scholar Despina Kakoudaki summarizes how deeply unresolved the resolution of *Strange Days* is: "[T]he first policeman kills himself, the other is killed (by the armed crowd-control forces), and nobody is tried or convicted. The murder of Jeriko One thus remains a politically invisible event."[28]

Whether or not one believes that violence is a necessary or satisfactory response to widespread and institutionalized social violences, its absence, particularly the representational absence of that response in a film so defined by remediation, constitutes an additional act of violence—a policing of response in the form of a repressed social memory, a refused counterhistory of surveillance, and a "calmed" outrage. The melancholic temporalities of the films explored in the preceding chapter enacted—through repetition—a fantasy of retroactive prevention as a politics of preemptive security. In distinction, the narrative movements of *Strange Days* create a circuit of mediation and history that ends up in the laps of the spectator and offers insight into how a melancholic narration might serve a different politics of radical memorializing. Davids Eng and Kazanjian have stated in the introduction to their volume *Loss* that "we find in Freud's conception of melancholia's persistent struggle with its lost objects not simply a 'grasping' and 'holding' on to a fixed notion of the past but rather a continuous engagement with loss and its remains. This engagement generates sites for memory and history, for the rewriting of the past as well as the reimagining of the future."[29] In the present context, we see how such engagement operates on multiple levels of form and content, function and effect—how surveillance, *remediated*, might serve as a repetition that *avows* trauma, *remembers* loss, and *deforms* the use of surveillance. Though somewhat removed from the real politics and practices of surveillance, it also brings us closer to an understanding of the possibilities of *surveillance cinema*, even within the confines of the logic of surveillance.

Strange Days is ultimately less a call for the elimination of forms of media in order to restore authentic relations and caring for others than it is an instance of mediation as a means to open individual experience and memory to social forms of reference and interventions. Or put another way, the film's (likely unintentional) affective work opens onto a politics whose task is not to "reduce" violence by containing it within a singularly embodied experience but to *extend* the violence through representation and time, to abstract it from an individual moment, and to refer it to, through, and against other subjective scenarios and mediations. This suggests how contemporary subject formations might be thought of in relation to a proliferation of surveillant technologies and mediations, and serve to construct a politics within the cinematic remediation of surveillance.

This extension and referral of violence could be thought of in several ways: first, there is the proliferation of imagery that allows us to view the institutionalized violence that is often seeing but unseen. Much as both the Rodney King video and *Strange Days* suggest, surveillance can be turned against the power structure from which it emerged. However, despite occasional instances of this kind of reversal, it remains largely an ineffectual mode of resistance, primarily because the logic of reversal implicitly bolsters the initial use of surveillance technologies, visual and otherwise. As Mary Ann Doane has pointed out in the context of gendered looking relations, "The male striptease, the gigolo—both inevitably signify the mechanism of reversal itself, constituting themselves as aberrations whose acknowledgement simply reinforces the dominant system of aligning sexual difference with a subject/object dichotomy."[30] Similarly, reversing the look of surveillance, focusing a video camera or the SQUID technology on police or government, still implies that such technologies can be used to provide legitimate evidence within the existing power structure of the law. Both the King verdict (and the restoration of "law and order" after the ensuing unrest) and the reemergence of the white patriarch of *Strange Days* point to the manner in which the reverse deployment of surveillance technologies ultimately upholds the structure that insists that those technologies can reveal the truth, even as many of the other films discussed in this book undermine the truth claims of surveillance repeatedly.

Instead we might examine the implications of refusing the very logic of these surveillance mechanisms as they are institutionally deployed, and doing so via the mediations of time and memory that *Strange Days* both avows and represses. In *Cinema 2: The Time-Image*, Gilles Deleuze introduced the notion of the "powers of the false" in the creation of political cinema.[31] Deleuze uses the concept of falsification not only to illuminate how time "crystallizes" in post–World War II cinema but, crucially, to suggest how "time has always put the notion of truth into crisis."[32] In describing a "crystalline" image emerging out of experimental cinema such as Resnais's *Last Year at Marienbad*, Deleuze's ideas on the time-image are distinct from a discussion of a Hollywood action film, in which both form and content are so focused on bodily experience. Such a film would seem far more logically, even hyperbolically, aligned with Deleuze's "movement-image."[33] But his characterization of the time-image's "irreducibility" as consisting of the "indivisible unity of an actual image and 'its' virtual image" becomes extremely salient in accessing the multiple diegetic and extradiegetic (even paradiegetic) ways that *Strange Days* accesses surveillant imagery in a multiply mediated formation also understood as "history."[34]

Deleuze states that with the crystal-image, "the image has to be present and past, still present and already past, at once and at the same time."[35] While this is an apt account of the way the fantasy of the SQUID technology operates within the film as well as the way video surveillance functions in many of the films discussed in Chapter One, it also—and with more significance—describes what happens when the SQUID experience is "abandoned" for the ostensibly unmediated experience at the end of the film, and we are confronted with the "crystallized" moment of Mace's beating. The film's reference in this scene to the Rodney King video proposes a cinematic narrative of the present only through images completely saturated by not just the past, but a past itself most fully represented by video images. Thus Deleuze's assertion that "the present is the actual image, and *its* contemporaneous past is the virtual image, the image in a mirror" is clearer if one defines the virtuality of the time-image as that which extends and refers beyond the cinema—and beyond the subject of cinema—into the apparatus of the mediated world, a substantial portion of which is increasingly defined as surveillant.[36]

Pointing out that we live in a highly mediated social environment is not earth-shattering: what is more pertinent in this temporal account of mediation is the way cinematic narrative interacts with the truth claims so central to surveillance culture. In this context, technological and narrative analyses of the relations between the image representing reality and the image representing fantasy are crucial. For, as Deleuze puts it, "The indiscernibility of the real and the imaginary, or of the present and the past, of the actual and the virtual, is definitely not produced in the head or the mind, it is the objective characteristic of certain existing images which are by nature double."[37] While arguably *all* cinematic images (like video) are both present (we are watching them now), and past (they are records of past events), real and imaginary, actual and virtual, what is highlighted here is that certain cinematic images, in this case in the form of remediation, *utilize* this doubling to achieve political effects.

In this light, and while this book's emphasis has been on mainstream films and generic structures, it is worth turning to the low-budget, feminist, and hyperbolically political film *Born in Flames* (Lizzie Borden, 1983), to which *Strange Days* clearly owes a great deal. *Born in Flames*, which perhaps not coincidentally features *Strange Days* director Kathryn Bigelow in a minor acting role, includes a number of structural and thematic elements that *Strange Days* (among others) recasts as big-budget action spectacle in the context of 1990s politics and technologies. Employing a pseudo-documentary aesthetic, *Born in Flames* presents a near-futural or alternate-reality New York City through an assemblage narrative composed of surveillance and mediation, including the investigatory gaze of the FBI, staged radio and television broadcasts, and stock television and film footage. Though it is classified as "science fiction," only its presentation of an alternate or future reality and its emphasis on mediation register that type of generic constitution; while *Strange Days* presents a hypermediated mise-en-scène and a science-fictional technology through which politics are filtered, *Born in Flames* uses the surveillant and hypermediated narration to present what would more

accurately be described as "political fiction," where the political formations of a postrevolutionary United States take the place of the SQUID
as the central organizing premise. The surveillance/media assemblage
structure of narration functions explicitly to explore politicized subjects
and social subject positions (that go far beyond the black/white racial
formation of *Strange Days* and demand attention to the intersections of
gender, sexuality, race, class, and nationality), and perhaps more significantly, to layer and interpenetrate discourses of political activism and
representations of direct political actions.

Born in Flame's use of hypermediacy as both science/political fiction
and (fictionalized) documentary in a narrative that self-consciously
and insistently demands a consideration of subject position in relation to political action and social justice demonstrates in clear terms
what *Strange Days* leaves implicit, undeveloped, or repressed.[38] But it
also provides a compelling instance of where surveillance cinema and
political cinema intersect at the level of narration, and thus shows the
political immanence in the otherwise often symptomatic *Strange Days*.
In advocating cinema that deploys "realist" techniques in the service
of producing *both* fiction and documentary films, Deleuze points to
the notions of falsifying, not only or necessarily narratively, but also
stylistically, and—I would add—technologically and functionally.
His focus on films that highlight how the seemingly indexical reality of cinematic devices is combined with—in fact become contiguous
with—narration from a series of interpenetrating (though not "merely
subjective") locales implicitly suggests that it is through a creative refusal of the truth claims of the cinematic technology itself that radical
politics emerge. And now, with not just forms of cinema but multiple
technologies (cinema, video, digital media) functioning through contiguity and remediation of one another, the possibilities of perversions
of intended uses increase exponentially. In other words, mediating and
mediated, remediating and remediated images are uniquely poised to
avoid the dichotomous logic of truth/fiction through a series of both
technological and narrative interpenetrations that render that duality
nonfunctional.

Thus, though in some ways we must think of "surveillance cinema"—
films that narrate and often spectacularize surveillance technologies—as
often legitimizing, or in John Turner's words, even "celebrating" a sur-

veillance society, I think this approach at times ignores how narrative and technology function in these films as interpenetrations and re-mediations.[39] Narratives of surveillance also often function—even if unintentionally and symptomatically—to destabilize the forensic and disciplinary practices of surveillance. While this destabilization is often followed by a recoding and restabilization, nevertheless the great major-ity of these films, as shown in Chapter One in particular, cannot help but highlight how the incorporation of multiple surveillance technologies into cinematic narrative almost always includes a series of misrecogni-tions, abstractions, displacements, and falsifications around technology, representation, and subject position. As I have argued, it is in this way that surveillance formations have functioned in both narrative and in politics as "zones of indistinction" through which power manifests as violent bio- and geopolitics; however, it is also precisely these aspects that make surveillance difficult to contain and control representation-ally, functionally, and politically.

The concrete implications of this in terms of the cinematic repre-sentation of surveillance and its relation to "real world" uses begin to emerge if we note that for Deleuze the chronological temporal relations undermined by the powers of the false are inherently connected to is-sues of legality: "Truthful narration is developed organically, according to legal connections in space and chronological relations in time. . . . Falsifying narration, by contrast, frees itself from this system: it shat-ters the system of judgment because the power of the false (not error or doubt) affects the investigator and the witness as much as the person presumed guilty."[40] This is to say the power of the false disrupts the logic of legality that is the basis of many of the systemic uses of surveillance, and which is both invested in and rendered spurious by virtually every film discussed in this text.

In the context of *Strange Days* and its explicit references to the legal uses of surveillance, it is important to distinguish between the kinds of temporal "crystallization" that Deleuze discusses in relation to the powers of the false, and what Crenshaw and Peller critique as a "disag-gregation" and "narration" of the King video in the hands of the de-fense attorneys at the trial of his attackers. As Crenshaw and Peller note, the video was slowed, divided into frames, and reconstructed via their narration as a representation of King's supposed aggression and the policemen's necessary and proper procedure. This disaggregation and repurposing still presupposed, however, the chronological *truth* of the video as evidence. Rather than the crisis of chronology suggested by Deleuze, this instance of disaggregation (much like the Bush administration's presentation of the satellite images of Iraq discussed in Chapter Three) is a reification of the ideology that posits that video and other visual surveillance imagery, even or especially as broken down into abstraction and interpreted by "experts," holds the status of visible, verifying, and verifiable evidence of physical reality. On the contrary, Deleuze's formulation speaks of a falsification of such an agenda—without necessarily rejecting the notion that either a personal or a political reality can be accessed through representation.

"What is opposed to fiction is not the real; it is not the truth which is always that of the masters or colonizers; it is the story-telling function of the power, in so far as it gives the false the power which makes it into a memory, a legend, a monster."[41] Deleuze's formulation of a story-telling function of power is not simply a reference to ideological constructs, since these are the very constructs that claim the value of the real, that "truth" that Deleuze locates on the side of "the masters or colonizers." Rather, it is a gesture that highlights those images "which are by nature double," and manifest the remediation of history in representational structures—in this case the racial formations of 1990s Los Angeles as mediated and remediated by video surveillance, broadcast media, and cinema. It is in this context that I find it to be not just of interest, but also a political project, to add analysis of narrative cinema to any discussion of surveillance practices and technologies.

*   *   *

The focus on a single film in this final chapter is not necessarily meant to suggest that it is to be treated with some significance not granted to any other. However, especially since it could itself be seen as a remediation of the earlier political fiction *Born in Flames*, it is of use to detail the forms by which *Strange Days* layers many of the narrative structures of surveillance explored in this book—retroactive temporality, visualized violence, consumer surveillance, technologized perception, narcissistic self-reference, political intervention, media convergence, realist representation, documentation and evidence, and so on—in the form of a hypermediated fantasy of social and racial justice that is simultaneously dystopian and utopian. Such layering is emblematic of the degree to which cinematic narrative functions in both associative and structural relationships to surveillance. But even in such an overdetermined form, or perhaps because of such overdetermination, the multiplicity of function delivers this and many other surveillance narratives over to an almost campy absurdity that could be said to define the contradictions and confusion of something like *Strange Days*. Cinematic narrative becomes the leaky container that doesn't quite hold the ideological and technological excesses of surveillance culture, and exposes the power of both surveillance and representation, especially in their intersecting formations, as a practice and a *performance*—and, almost inevitably, a failed one. This failed performance might also be understood as repetition with a difference.

Viewing cinematic narrative as a technology of surveillance renders the cinema deeply suspect on a political level, and yet it is difficult to escape the awareness that even in the most extreme narrative of surveillant power, the very demands of narrative introduce failure, excess, ambiguity, and reversibility. If cinematic narrative is thus a functional element of a surveillance culture, it is one that, in order to succeed as narrative, *depends* on the dysfunction of surveillance. From the slapstick misrecognitions of early cinema to the paradoxes of time travel and the contradictory drives of remediation, so much in the narration of surveillance *requires the failure* of the conceits of surveillant power: visible evidence, verifiable facts, identity and identification, provable guilt, immediacy and historicity. Thus despite how frequently such films appear as functions or symptoms of the ideologies of surveillance, these narratives also often manifest as betrayals of their own premises.

The cinematic remediation of existing, emerging, and imaginary surveillance technologies and practices, though easily and rightly subject to the various ideological critiques offered throughout this book, are also in some ways inherently resistant to many political simplifications. What "surveillance cinema" often attests to is the unavoidability of processing mediation through mediation—whether as convergence, remediation, or referentiality. The results of this tend to be cinematic texts that reflect a surveillance culture that is unstable, contradictory, and unclear in its effects. While this does not diminish the fact of historically real subjects who have suffered and continue to suffer violence at the hands of regimes or systems utilizing powers of surveillance, it does suggest that whether it is the panopticon, the society of the spectacle, global capitalism, or another force of the seemingly insurmountable hypermediated "world system" of surveillance and power, the very multiplicity of mediation provides a space in which the *always* flawed practices of power can be accessed.

Conclusion

In the spirit of the temporalities outlined in the preceding two chapters, it seems appropriate to follow up with a few words about chronology and retroaction that, summed up with a certain crude extremity, might simply be this: I take it back. The concluding chapter on *Strange Days* was actually one of the first to have been written, in somewhat different form.[1] Though I am still invested in the political and theoretical arguments offered therein, my impulse to end the book with a bit of optimism and "possibility" should not be read as either my most recent thoughts or my sense of the direction things are headed. I continue to have little doubt that cinematic surveillance narratives exemplify the defining ambiguities of surveillance practice and politics. Unfortunately, these elements have increasingly been exploited as the basis and structure of state and corporate power rather than as an avenue for undermining that power. What was already a meager note of optimism has become even more dubious in the light of a recent history that includes revelations about the extent of the Obama administration's sweeping surveillance operations and continued illicit drone strikes in Pakistan and Afghanistan; the exoneration of "neighborhood watch" vigilante George Zimmerman in the murder of unarmed, seventeen-year-old Trayvon Martin; and a continued economic depression in which more and more people contribute information (with and without their knowledge) to vast caches of computer data, and fewer and fewer people stand to profit from it. Such circumstances, rather than offering any sense of possibility, have instead made more obvious the centrality of surveillance in the seemingly interminable, Islamophobic, and deadly state of exception dubbed the "war on terror"; the violence of the pretense that the law, politics, and culture of the United States (let alone its surveillance formations) function as "postracial"; and the absurdity of investing in a digital economy based on the unpaid labor and content production of consumers who are told to revel in the power of interactivity and the freedom of information even as their personal data and online activity is commodified, exchanged, and sold back to them as a "customized" product.

Zero Dark Thirty and *Homeland*: Feminized National Security and Islamophobia

Within this context, the cinematic and televisual narration of surveillance and its politics has simultaneously become more ubiquitous and less creatively engaged with "possibility." It is thus perhaps not surprising that after *Strange Days*, a film I presented as one that—however symptomatically—showed cinematic narration to be a site for the potentially radical remediation of surveillance, politics, and history, director Kathryn Bigelow went on to helm the production of *Zero Dark Thirty*—a disturbing example of cinematic engagement with surveillance in the form of historical narrative. This Oscar-nominated film from 2012 about the tracking and assassination of Osama bin Laden represents, like *Strange Days*, a fictionalized recent history of United States politics, and, also similarly, does so through extensive use of surveillant aesthetics and historical revisionism. This is where the similarities end. Even while touting itself hyperbolically as the story of "the greatest manhunt in history," the film denies the narrative and stylistic excesses of Bigelow's earlier work and maintains a conceit of historical neutrality— the remediation of surveillance thus reified as a passionless procedural. While *Zero Dark Thirty* might be admirable in its attempt to expose how torture was employed with regularity by the U.S. in the "war on terror," the factually inaccurate suggestion that such torture was pivotal in the discovery of bin Laden belies the ideological neutrality of the film's realist pretense, and cements a relationship between surveillance and torture in the guise of "history."[2] As Bigelow's first film released after her Academy Award for *The Hurt Locker* in 2008, the treatment of surveillance is mirrored by an increasingly "serious" career trajectory that suggests that at least in Hollywood, surveillant narration is "important" to the degree it is unquestioned as a tool of realism.

Unsurprisingly, given the way feminism has been cynically marshaled as part of the discourse of the "war on terror," Bigelow's journey to critical success and the disturbing earnestness of her more recent

The marketing of *Zero Dark Thirty* (2012).

films' "historical realism" (and the always overvalued "moral ambiguity" that seems to largely define such realism) have also been attended by the narrative of her position as the first (and still only) woman to win an Academy Award for directing. The political relationship between Bigelow's career success and the content of the films that have come to define that success is mirrored and evidenced by the centralized position of female characters in both *Zero Dark Thirty* and the Showtime television series *Homeland* (2011–present), the other recent surveillance narrative to earn widespread critical repute. Remarkably, Bigelow's career history also includes a move from her minor acting role in the 1983 radical feminist film *Born in Flames*, which (as noted in the preceding chapter) concludes with feminist terrorists/revolutionaries destroying the World Trade Center towers, to her being hailed as a beacon of feminism in Hollywood as the female director of a film about a woman who hunts down the terrorist responsible for the destruction of the World Trade Center towers. The image of the towers in flames that constitutes the final shot of *Born in Flames* is precisely the image that Bigelow refuses to include in the opening of *Zero Dark Thirty*—instead it becomes the structuring absence behind that film's opening shot: a black screen and the sound of an actual 911 call made by a woman trapped in one of the towers on 9/11. This Bigelow trivia is incidental perhaps, but in the context of this book it's also a rather mind-boggling cinematic and metacinematic arc of narrative, representation, and politics, especially as they concern the historical/narrative construction of feminism in relation to terrorism and counterterrorism.

Both *Homeland* and *ZDT* have won multiple awards and have been some of the very few American surveillance/investigation-based productions to be regarded as "serious" or "quality" since the 1970s. The gravity attributed to these productions has come alongside suggestions that they offer more complex accounts of the "war on terror" than something like the Fox network's *24*, and even offer useful critique. Such evaluations seem outrageous especially in regard to *Homeland*, which though it might provide moments of sympathy and identification with the "terrorist" position, is one of the most patently Islamophobic productions in recent memory—in the first two seasons virtually every Muslim character on the show (including Americans) is proven to be a terrorist. The show makes special efforts to define terrorism through repeated narrative and visual reference to Islamic religious life, with the male lead Brody's conversion to Islam presented as synonymous with his recruitment into an anti-U.S. terrorist plot. Even *24*, in its endless paranoia and delight in the powers of surveillance, takes pains to include multiple instances in which Muslims are mistakenly profiled, scapegoated, and framed.[3]

This critical regard for *Homeland* and *ZDT* has also come with what has been considered the complex and sensitive exploration of the pathology of their female lead characters (particularly in the case of *Homeland*), a psychological depth that also defined a great deal of the acclaim given *The Conversation* in 1973 (or *Caché* more recently, for that matter). It thus seems worth remarking upon the fact that the same highly valued films that are defined by the centrality of women are also defined by the elements that made earlier surveillance narratives "nuanced" and thus reputable (i.e., more than mere spectacle and suspense): an investment in their characters, evidenced by the presentation of those characters, to various degrees, as pathological in their pursuits. However, now that surveillance narratives are no longer defined as male, this pathology is no longer defined as voyeuristic (one might/should reverse this formation easily and repeatedly, since I am not claiming a cause/effect here but simply a contingent relationship). In the classical forms defined by Jeff in *Rear Window* or Harry in *The Conversation*, it was clear the male domain of pathological surveillance was characterized by desire and paranoia; female pathological surveillance is similarly obsessive, but now such obsession, in terms of its narrative significance, appears purely self-referential—it is both means and end, cause and effect. For Carrie in *Homeland* this is a function of an explicitly thematized bipolar disorder; for Maya in *Zero Dark Thirty*, no such explanation is offered because it need not be: obsession for a female CIA operative is as easily naturalized within surveillance narrative as voyeurism had been in prior iterations. And despite claims that these recent narratives offer complex and compelling representations of "real" women, frankly one could find more nuance in the characterization of Tess McGill in *Working Girl* (1988).[4] But it is clear that similarly to the function of voyeurism for a masculinity/power/surveillance formation that (literally) characterized the politics of many other surveillance narratives, the alignment of surveillant practice and female subjectivity in these contemporary counterterrorism narratives has similarly served to reify surveillance practice through gender. Here we are also offered an additional element with which gender can serve this project: the politics filtered through pathology can easily also be defined as beginning and ending with gender. For instance, the pathologically single-minded investigatory figure of *Rear Window* or *The Conversation* is still the one who solves the crime, but that protagonist's epistemological drive is no longer filtered through the fetishistic stunted sexuality of the masculine ego. Here we are provided instead with a perverse triangulated relationship between counterterrorism, the feminization of subjectivity, and gender equality: hence the unexplained obsessive investment of the investigation narrative in *Zero Dark Thirty* that seems to make no distinction between patriotism, an object of desire, and a need to break the glass ceiling.

The ease with which the irrational force of feminine subjectivity is naturalized serves the obsessive and unquestioned needs of security in the "war on terror" quite well. It is hard to tell at any given moment in either *ZDT* or *Homeland* if Maya or Carrie is interested in national security or in simply being heard. Such are even today the rhetorical and narrative powers afforded to women—they will win an argument not because they *are* right, but because they *must be* right. Insofar as these narratives are resituating the powers of surveillance, intelligence, and security as gendered, they have also reinvested in narrating such mysterious/hysterical powers of women as intuition and a refusal to let anything go. Once again, hailing these productions as "complex," "progressive," or "realist" seems bizarre given the forms these characters take and the purpose they serve in defining and legitimizing effective intelligence and security practices as irrationally single-minded. "Join *Zero Dark Thirty* in celebrating the crucial role women play in America's national security": this call for mass synchronized tweets as part of the film's social media promotional campaign could not make it more obvious how the supposedly neutral, realist representation of the bin Laden pursuit is inseparable from a discourse that joins and *celebrates* the now codefining projects of women's professional achievement and nationalist security practice. The reactionary and Islamophobic politics of the "war on terror," traditionally pathologized female subjectivities, and the banality of pop feminism all come together in a surveillance narrative such that each of those elements serves to distract from the other, and critics can hail it all as "morally ambiguous."

"Well, Welcome to My Life, Mr. War Criminal"

This is certainly not to say that there is a general movement toward female-centered narratives or critical glory for surveillance cinema. The broad and popular uses of surveillance as narrative style within action, horror, and science fiction film and television outlined in the prior chapters are increasingly so recognizable that they have become unremarkable. Numerous structural and thematic elements, merely within the time of the writing of this book, have gone from being a trend to a generic fact: it would be more difficult to find a big-budget action film that didn't utilize satellite and GPS imagery than one that did. When Tom Levin suggested in his 2002 essay that cinematic narration had "effectively become synonymous with surveillant enunciation" it was still not quite apparent how widespread and multilayered this would become, and that it would become an increasingly reversible and circular formulation.

Perhaps most exemplary of the almost absurd overdeterminations of the cinema-surveillance complex is the Satellite Sentinel Project— spearheaded by actor/"activist" George Clooney—that has contracted with satellite surveillance company DigitalGlobe to monitor, expose, and publicize war crimes in Sudan. Clooney, the star of *Syriana* (whose character in that film fell victim to U.S. satellite surveillance and satellite-

guided missile attack), has *personally* engaged satellite surveillance as political activism—activism that literalizes in many ways the links in what
James Der Derian calls the "military-industrial-media-entertainment
network."[5] In all fairness, Clooney does introduce a reasonable critique
that as a celebrity he is subjected to an intense scrutiny that might more
properly be focused on the atrocities of war and war criminals. However,
his leap from this argument to the use of his personal fortune to hire
satellites to monitor Sudan and South Sudan is an astonishing and literal investment in a surveillant political economy that marshals virtually
every ideological, technological, and structural aspect of modern imperial power from colonialism through the "war on terror." Media accounts
of Clooney's crusade and his organization's website speak for themselves.

From the Satellite Sentinel Project website:

On a trip to southern Sudan in October 2010, George Clooney and
Enough Project Co-founder John Prendergast had an idea. What if we
could watch the warlords? Monitor them just like the paparazzi spies on
Clooney? "Why can't I be a guy with a 400-mile lens, a tourist, taking
pictures and sticking them on the Internet?"[6]

From the *Guardian*:

Nathaniel Raymond is the first to admit that he has an unusual job description. "I count tanks from space for George Clooney," said the tall,
easygoing Massachusetts native as he sat in a conference room in front of
a map of the Sudanese region of South Kordofan. Close by, pins and ink
scrawlings on the map detail the positions of Sudanese army forces and
refugee populations in the troubled oil-producing province, where the
Sudanese army is carrying out a brutal crackdown.[7]

From Yahoo omg!:

Many stars pocket their ridiculously large paychecks, but George—who
appears in commercials for Nespresso—said he's spending the cash on a
satellite aimed at Sudan.

"Most of the money I make on the [Nespresso] commercials I spend
keeping a satellite over the border of North and South Sudan to keep an

eye on Omar al-Bashir [the Sudanese dictator charged with war crimes at The Hague]," the Oscar winner said in Paris on Tuesday. "Then [Omar al-Bashir] puts out a statement saying that I'm spying on him and how would I like it if a camera was following me everywhere I went and I go 'Well, welcome to my life Mr. War Criminal.' I want the war criminal to have the same amount of attention that I get. I think that's fair."[8]

Clooney, star of at least three films that are structured in part by surveillant narration, with his personalized use of the logic and finance of celebrity to in effect further U.S.-led global surveillance projects, global policing, and privatized surveillance and security, serves as an embodiment of the systemic integration of cinema and surveillance, along with the multiple forms of mediation that both of those terms now include.[9]

The Snowden Ultimatum

Narrative structures have also been central to an increasing seamlessness between surveillance in cinematic texts, practical instantiation, and media accounts. The assemblage narrative of the 2008 film *Vantage Point* makes reality into an uncanny double when the structure reemerges in the televised bombing and crowdsourced investigation of the 2013 Boston Marathon. The massive and unauthorized NSA surveillance program in *Enemy of the State*, though hopefully not enabled by the secret murder of resistant congresspeople, reappears, also in 2013, in the revelation of the NSA's PRISM program, a massive data-collection effort begun during the Bush administration, and maintained and possibly expanded during the Obama administration. The counterterrorist rationale of the corrupt officials in the 1998 film is reiterated by the contemporary administration, as is the refusal to be held accountable or to provide any transparency; such arguments are justified by the unspecified terrorist plots that the public is told have been foiled by the PRISM program—further information naturally cannot be provided since it would compromise security.[10] And while Larry King is no longer the media figurehead to articulate the privacy versus security debate that closed the 1998 film, the debate has remained unchanged, and its universality still ignores the issue of the discriminatory targeting that continues to structure American surveillance practice.

The importance of the form of narration taken in the media-constituted processing of the politics of surveillance is apparent in the above example of the privacy versus security debates, but also, and perhaps more significantly, in another aspect of the recent PRISM revelations. It is at this juncture far more likely that any given person in the U.S. (or possibly the world) will be more familiar with the name of Edward Snowden, the whistleblower that revealed the surveillance program, than PRISM, the name of the program itself, largely due to the structure of the media narration of the issue. As Matt Taibbi argued in a prescient web article about Bradley (now Chelsea) Manning's trial just days before the PRISM story emerged, the press was "missing the point" in its construction of the story about this previous iconic whistle blower, and in doing so was serving the interests of the government prosecution.[11] The numerous variations of the "Hero or Traitor?" framework (that with Snowden have become even more widespread and amplified) are, Taibbi argues, detracting attention from what these characters revealed. Thus even accounts that support Manning or Snowden are keeping the focus on the whistleblower rather than the foul.

With Snowden, a former NSA contractor, on the run from the U.S. government, and bouncing from Hong Kong to Moscow while requesting asylum in South America, we are provided a narrative that, even in its noncinematic presentation in written journalism, assumes the structure of a Bourne-like global escapade, with numerous articles making the reference explicit.[12] While unlike the always resourceful Jason Bourne, Snowden has had to now stay put and wait for assistance from a foreign government, even his sojourn in the liminal space of the "transit zone" at the Moscow airport is also filtered through a cinematically defined narrative: Steven Spielberg's 2004 *The Terminal* (which presented an interesting reversal of the current scenario in which an Eastern European man, played by Tom Hanks, is trapped at a U.S. airport)—accordingly, this comparison also frames a number of journalistic accounts.[13] The constitution of these narratives as "cinematic" appears so circularly defining that even Taibbi's critique is trapped within this cycle of referentiality: he begins his article by noting that "the government couldn't have scripted the headlines any better," and turns immediately thereafter to a scene from a television show that provides the framework for his analysis. Months later, a fake news story about American reality television star "Dog the Bounty Hunter" promising to hunt down Snowden in Russia and bring him to justice was mistaken for a real one and widely circulated as the latest development in the Snowden "story."

To be clear, the point here is most definitely not that "life imitates art," nor even to further evidence the hypermediated cross-referentiality of contemporary culture and politics. What I want to foreground here is how *the demands of narrative* as currently defined (in these cases largely by cinema) *assure* that Snowden becomes the focus of the story. Much like the Will Smith/Robert Dean configuration of *Enemy of the State*, or as Klaus Dodds describes Jason Bourne, the political implications of surveillance and geopolitics become reduced to the personal narrative of an individual subject who—rather than suggesting the implications of politics for a lived reality—functions as a character that *reduces* politics to personal narrative. As Taibbi suggests in his real-world examples, the effect of this is to make sure that the *politics* do not become the story, and it is thus on some level immaterial whether one believes Manning or Snowden to be a "hero" or a "traitor."

A broader problem that emerges here is that despite the fact that the political formations of surveillance are increasingly evident in narrative structure and the cinematic system of signification, we seem to have fewer narrative models that critically engage politics at the systemic and/or structural level. It becomes that much more important to produce narratives of surveillance that don't simply thematize politics, but work to creatively integrate politics into the narrative form such that they *work through* and reframe recognizable elements of narrative: character, causality, desire, effect, resolution. Here again we see the use value of films such as *Caché* or *Strange Days* that demand in different structural and systemic ways that we understand character positioning, visual signification, and plot organization—and their parts in the cinematic remediation of surveillance—as functional elements of historical and political contexts.

"I Am (Not) Trayvon Martin"

If the stakes of the imagery in *Strange Days* had not been clear before, they were brought home by the "not guilty" verdict that exonerated George Zimmerman in the murder of seventeen-year-old Trayvon

Martin. The verdict came out of a self-defense strategy by Zimmerman's defense team that took an unarmed boy's murder and—like the defense lawyers of the police officers in the Rodney King assault, like the riot police who took their nightsticks to Mace in *Strange Days*, and in the continued functioning of American legal process—turned it into the familiar narrative of black aggression. That this story is still so compelling that in 2013 a man with a gun who stalked a boy and shot him at close range is able to even *introduce* a defense that he did so because he was afraid for his life—let alone be set free and *handed back his gun*—is reason enough to refuse to end this book with *Strange Days*, a largely forgotten film about memory, when the narrative and imagery surrounding the Rodney King assault refract yet again as anything but "possibility."

But it is also reason to continue to demand more and different stories, as well as make sense of the varied forms of repetition. *Strange Days*' re-presentation of the Rodney King video alongside a science-fictional surveillance technology offering total subjective identification finds yet another echo in the rhetoric of the angry and horrified responses to this more recent instance of racial profiling and violence: "I am Trayvon Martin." This defining rhetoric—reiterated widely in multiple forms (visual iconography, video messages, speeches, songs, tweets), from multiple subject positions and diverse platforms (from President Obama's press conferences to videos on YouTube and teens on Tumblr), as well as through its negative construction ("I am not Trayvon Martin")—frames, for better or worse, racism and social justice through identity and identification. Whether science fiction spectacle or social activism, these mediations and remediations of racialized violence seem to both demand and offer negotiation between mobile identifications and embodied identities. Arguably, it is this very negotiation that I have described in varying forms as central to the formations of most surveillance narratives. Framed in this context, surveillance serves to define the stakes of that negotiation largely through power and violence, while also constituting the terms of renegotiation and, in its more common usage, remediation.

Thus, while surveillance is just one aspect or description of the legal-political-economic systems that produce a continued history of violence, it is clearly a significant part of the narratives emerging from and forming those systems, and has been a defining element of cinematic remediation. As there appears to be growing convergence between surveillance in political formations, cinematic, televisual and journalistic discourse, fiction and reality programming, technological innovation and political aesthetics—a convergence with very real consequences—I would again stress the import of continuing to explore methods that allow us to attend, very closely, to every aspect of how these stories are constructed.

NOTES

INTRODUCTION

1. I use the term "racial projects" as developed by Michael Omi and Howard Winant in *Racial Formation in the United States: From the 1960s to the 1990s*. Omi and Winant's theory of racial formation argues that a "vast web of racial projects mediates between the discursive or representational means in which race is identified and signified on the one hand, and the institutional forms in which it is routinized and standardized on the other" (60). Surveillance, as both representational and institutional in a variety of instances and definitions, functions both routinely and in shifting forms as a racial project. (Michael Omi and Howard Winant, *Racial Formation in the United States: From the 1960s to the 1990s*, 2nd edition [New York: Routledge, 1994].)

2. Cf. Alan Sekula, "The Body and the Archive," in *October* 39 (Winter 1986); John Tagg, *The Burden of Representation: Essays on Photographies and Histories* (Minneapolis and London: University of Minnesota Press, 1993); and Suren Lalvani, *Photography, Vision, and the Production of Modern Bodies* (Albany: State University of New York Press, 1996).

3. Christian Parenti, *The Soft Cage: Surveillance in America from Slavery to the War on Terror* (New York: Basic Books, 2003), 37.

4. Linda Williams, *Hard Core: Power, Pleasure, and the "Frenzy of the Visible"* (Berkeley and Los Angeles: University of California Press, 1989), 36.

5. Lisa Cartwright, *Screening the Body: Tracing Medicine's Visual Culture* (Minneapolis and London: Minnesota University Press, 1995), 3. See also Norman Denzin, *The Cinematic Society: The Voyeur's Gaze* (London: SAGE Publications, 1995), which posits cinema as one of the many visual, epistemological projects of the late-nineteenth and twentieth centuries. More recently, in relation specifically to surveillance and cinema, Dietmar Kammerer has also pointed to these series photographs as foundational evidence that the cinema's prehistory is defined by its relation to nineteenth-century scientific pursuit and to the "self-control of human motions through image technology." (Dietmar Kammerer, "Video Surveillance in Hollywood Movies," in *Surveillance and Society* CCTV special issue [eds. Norris, McCahill, and Wood] vol. 2 no. 2/3 [2004]: 464–473; 466.)

6. Comolli's most famous essays were originally published as a series, "Technique et Idéologie," in the French journal *Cahiers du Cinema* (1971–1972) and have since been widely translated and reprinted. Baudry's seminal essay "Ideological Effects

of the Basic Cinematographic Apparatus" was originally published in *Cinéthique* nos. 7–8 in 1970.

7. Jean-Louis Comolli, "Technique et Idéologie" and "Machines of the Visible," in *The Cinematic Apparatus*, ed. Teresa de Lauretis and Stephen Heath (New York: St. Martin's Press, 1980), 121–142.

8. Thomas Levin, "Rhetoric of the Temporal Index: Surveillant Narration and the Cinema of 'Real Time,'" in *CTRL[SPACE]: Rhetorics of Surveillance from Bentham to Big Brother*, ed. Thomas Levin, Ursula Frohne, and Peter Weibel (Cambridge, MA: MIT Press, 2002), 578–593; 581.

9. "Inside an American Factory: Films of the Westinghouse Works, 1904," 15 April 1999, on *Library of Congress: American Memory*, available at http://lcweb2.loc.gov/papr/west/westhome.html (accessed 7/23/2009).

10. Tom Gunning, "Tracing the Individual Body: Photography, Detectives, and Early Cinema," in *Cinema and the Invention of Modern Life*, ed. Leo Charney and Vanessa R. Schwartz (Berkeley and Los Angeles: University of California Press, 1995), 35.

11. Ibid.

12. Kammerer, "Video Surveillance," 473.

13. See John S. Turner, "Collapsing the Interior/Exterior Distinction: Surveillance, Spectacle, and Suspense in Popular Cinema," in *Wide Angle* vol. 20 no. 4 (October 1998): 93–123; 101.

14. Kammerer, "Video Surveillance," 473.

15. Noël Burch, *Life to Those Shadows* (Berkeley and Los Angeles: University of California Press, 1990), 149.

16. The gender politics of the fact that it is the female image that seems to particularly trouble these technologies is also clearly worth further discussion.

17. Some notable discussions of this film include Susan Courtney's work in *Hollywood Fantasies of Miscegenation: Spectacular Narratives of Gender and Race, 1903–1967* (Princeton, NJ: Princeton University Press, 2005) and Jacqueline Najuma Stewart's *Migrating to the Movies: Cinema and Black Urban Modernity* (Berkeley: University of California Press (2005).

18. Stewart, *Migrating to the Movies*, 39.

19. Parenti, *The Soft Cage*, 14.

20. Ibid, 15.

21. Levin, "Rhetoric of the Temporal Index," 581.

22. Ibid., 582.

23. Ibid., 592.

24. Sébastien Lefait, *Surveillance on Screen: Monitoring Contemporary Films and Television* (Lanham, MD: Scarecrow Press, 2012): xviii.

25. Turner, "Collapsing the Interior/Exterior Distinction," 96. Film scholar Wheeler Winston Dixon's book *It Looks at You*, particularly the chapter "Surveillance in the Cinema," also introduces some significant intersections of surveillance and cinema, though he discusses few surveillance narratives such as those focused on here. The

book examines the manner in which actors gaze at the camera and thus the film appears to return the gaze of the spectator, and Dixon makes a number of salient points about the reciprocity of the cinematic look, ultimately making the absolutely necessary observation that so much attention has been paid to the spectator's gaze at the film that little attention has been paid to the way that the film is structured to incorporate the viewer through its own kind of gaze. The discussion, for instance, of surveillance of the audience in movie theaters by surveillance cameras, smoke detectors, and trailers reminding moviegoers of the rules of spectatorship reminds us that "every aspect of the reception experience in the cinema is monitored, seen by the unseen, a space of fabulation that masquerades as semiprivate, when it is, in fact, part of the public sphere," and thus is suggestive of a number of extratextual ways that cinema and surveillance intersect. (Wheeler Winston Dixon, *It Looks at You: The Returned Gaze of the Cinema* [Albany: SUNY Press, 1995]: 17.)

26. Of course, when voyeurism is not the guiding principle of discussions of cinematic surveillance, it is inevitably the panopticon that takes its place, so it is fair to say that the discussion of cinematic surveillance struggles with the ubiquity of that model also.

27. Norman Denzin, *The Cinematic Society: The Voyeur's Gaze* (London: Sage Publications, 1995), 9.

28. Parenti, *The Soft Cage*, 185.

29. This second phrase refers to work by David Lyon, a central figure in surveillance studies, who has shown the value of considering film and media scholarship on voyeurism in relation to surveillance. He has gestured toward the historical and cultural specificity of both voyeurism and scopophilia; however at times he too has deployed these concepts as explanatory paradigms that in some ways seem to exceed or exist in a separate political context: "It is not too much of a stretch to suggest that part of the enthusiasm for adopting new surveillance technologies, especially after 9/11, relates to the fact that in the global north (and possibly elsewhere too) the *voyeur gaze* is a commonplace aspect of contemporary culture." (David Lyon, "9/11, Synopticon, and Scopophilia," in *The New Politics of Surveillance and Visibility*, ed. Kevin D. Haggerty and Richard V. Ericson [Toronto, Buffalo, and London: University of Toronto Press, 2006], 35–54; 49.)

30. Robert Corber's analysis of the epitomic voyeur narrative *Rear Window* (Alfred Hitchcock, 1954), "Resisting History: *Rear Window* and the Limits of the Postwar Settlement," is a significant precursor of Denzin's analysis. Through his reading of the film, Corber insists that we must account for the pathological *and* the political, as "the psychologizing of political behavior . . . enabled . . . the establishment of the postwar settlement known as the liberal consensus" (128). Corber examines the film's construction of voyeurism not in addition to or alongside the film's political context, but as intersecting and even mutually dependent formations. The film's thematic and formal attention to voyeurism must be considered as a historically specific construction that intersects with political formations of surveillance, in which the "abuse of voyeuristic pleasure is directly related to a set

of specific social conditions in which privacy had become politicized" (139). This analysis makes clear that voyeurism is a *political project* that seeks to define and redefine the relations between individual desire, the security state, and the emergence of liberal culture through surveillant formations. Corber's work highlights the extensive political disavowals involved in the naturalization of voyeurism that I have been discussing, and also provides evidence that the feminist critique of the gendered power relations of cinematic voyeurism (in its original Mulveyan iteration, now widely considered to be oversimplified and presumptive of whiteness, heterosexuality, and same-sex identification, among other things) might actually be reinvigorated by a historical account of the place of voyeurism in the political landscape. (Robert J. Corber, "Resisting History: *Rear Window* and the Limits of the Postwar Settlement," in *boundary* 2 vol. 19 no. 1 [Spring 1992]: 121–148.)

31. Kevin D. Haggerty and Richard V. Ericson, eds., *The New Politics of Surveillance and Visibility* (Toronto: University of Toronto Press, 2006), 4.

32. See Haggerty and Ericson's earlier essay, "The Surveillant Assemblage," in *British Journal of Sociology* vol. 51 (2000): 605–622, and Bogard's essay, "Surveillance Assemblages and Lines of Flight," in *Theorizing Surveillance: The Panopticon and Beyond*, ed. David Lyon (Devon, UK, and Portland, OR: Willan Publishing, 2006), 97–122.

33. For some early accounts, see David Denby, "Stolen Privacy: Coppola's *The Conversation*," in *Sight and Sound* vol. 43 no. 3 (Summer 1974): 131–133, and Lawrence Shaffer, "*The Conversation*," in *Film Quarterly* vol. 28 no. 1 (Autumn 1974): 54–60. More recently the film's historical themes have been revisited by W. Russel Gray with "Tuning in to *The Conversation*: Twenty-Five Years Later," in *Journal of Popular Culture* vol. 33 no. 2 (Fall 1999): 123–130.

34. Carolyn Anderson, "*The Conversation* as Exemplar and Critique of Sound Technology," in *Post Script* vol. 6 no. 3 (Spring/Summer 1987): 13–30; 15.

35. See Rick Altman, "The Evolution of Sound Technology" in *Film Sound*, ed. Elisabeth Weis and John Belton (New York: Columbia University Press, 1985), 44–53.

36. Mary Ann Doane, "Ideology and the Practice of Sound Editing," in *Film Sound*, ed. Weis and Belton, 54.

37. Dortë Zbikowski, "The Listening Ear: Phenomena of Acoustic Surveillance" in *CTRL[SPACE]*, ed. Levin, Frohne, and Weibel: 33–41; 41.

38. Bringing sound "into the mix" here offers a more materially and historically grounded understanding of the coincidences between surveillance practice and narrative film production in such a way that not just the specific technologies but the logic of these modes seem mutually defining as well as mutually problematizing. Arguably, it is the film's focus on sound technologies that has lent it to more historicized readings than a film such as *Rear Window*, which has lent itself to the broader assumption of a voyeuristic gaze that is presented as a given that structures all film. The attention paid to sound as a structuring

device of cinema has been relatively little, even if for over seventy years eavesdropping on conversations has been as much of the experience of cinematic spectatorship as watching, and thus sound surveillance narratives seem much more likely to be read in terms of historical context, whether in the context of their making, such as with *The Conversation*, or the context of their setting, such as with the Oscar-winning *The Lives of Others* (Florian Henckel von Donnersmarck, 2006), which is viewed primarily as documentation of life under the Stasi in the DDR.

39. Dennis Turner, "The Subject of *The Conversation*," in *Cinema Journal* vol. 24 no. 4 (Summer 1985): 4–22; 5.

40. Lefait's account of surveillance in cinema also points out the degree to which such films serve as reflexive texts. Reflexive films and surveillance films have had frequent crossover for some time, as made clear by Robert Stam's reference to *Rear Window*, another canonical surveillance film, as "the paradigmatic instance" of an "allegory of spectatorship" in his book *Reflexivity in Film and Literature: From Don Quixote to Jean-Luc Godard* (New York: Columbia University Press): 43.

41. Turner, "The Subject of *The Conversation*," 9.

42. Ibid., 17.

43. Levin, "Rhetoric of the Temporal Index," 583.

44. Denzin, *The Cinematic Society*, 15.

45. Andrew Sarris, *Politics and Cinema* (New York: Columbia University Press: 1978), 47.

46. Zbikowski, "The Listening Ear," 34.

47. Giorgio Agamben, *Homo Sacer: Sovereign Power and Bare Life*, trans. Daniel Heller-Roazen (Stanford, CA: Stanford University Press, 1998).

48. Fredric Jameson, *The Geopolitical Aesthetic: Cinema and Space in the World System* (Bloomington and Indianapolis: Indiana University Press, 1992), 4.

49. Gary Genosko and Scott Thompson, "Tense Theory: The Temporalities of Surveillance," in *Theorizing Surveillance*, ed. Lyon.

50. Achille Mbembe, "Necropolitics," in *Public Culture* vol. 15 no. 1 (Winter 2003): 11–40.

51. Jay David Bolter and Richard Grusin, *Remediation: Understanding New Media* (Cambridge, MA: MIT Press, 1999).

CHAPTER 1. VIDEO SURVEILLANCE, TORTURE PORN, AND ZONES OF INDISTINCTION

1. David Edelstein, "Now Playing at Your Local Multiplex: Torture Porn," in *New York*, 6 February 2006, available at http://nymag.com/movies/features/15622/ (accessed 5/2/2013).

2 While many argue against this latest exercise in gore being a true generic mutation, the sheer marketability of the concept has garnered much attention in both production and reception contexts and effectively established it as such. See for

instance, Claude Brodesser, "Why 'Torture Porn' Is the Hottest (and Most Hated) Thing in Hollywood," in *Advertising Age* vol. 78 no. 21 (21 May 2007): 3. My analysis of surveillance within the genre will also suggest a certain degree of subgeneric specificity.

3. Though there are certainly compelling international instances of films focused on torture scenarios, often preceding and influencing the American films, such as Takashi Miike's 1999 *Audition*. Edelstein's account of these films in his oft-cited essay, and many others, have designated torture porn as an American phenomenon. However, Edelstein himself cites the Australian *Wolf Creek* (Greg McLean, 2005) as one of the defining examples of the trend ("Now Playing").

4. *Saw III* (Darren Lynn Bousman, 2006) is somewhat of an exception, as has been noted by Evangelos Tziallas, who persuasively argues that the film's liberal use of biblical and religious references can be seen as a reference and critique of the Christian right-wing's support for torture in post-9/11 politics. I would add, however, that the use of broad religious allegory also functions as a way to *avoid* addressing more specific historical and political discourses around torture that would highlight the film's contemporary context. See Tziallas, "Torture Porn and Surveillance Culture," in *Jump Cut: A Review of Contemporary Media* no. 52 (Summer 2010), available at http://www.ejumpcut.org/archive/jc52.2010/evangelosTorturePorn/text.html (accessed 6/12/2013).

5. In somewhat different terms, Dean Lockwood's Deleuzian analysis of the film similarly suggests that despite the films' intriguing gesture towards a liberatory *affect* offered by extreme bodily experience, the films end up not fully engaging that possibility, and "[t]he *effect* becomes all." See Lockwood, "All Stripped Down: The Spectacle of Torture Porn," in *Popular Communication* no. 7 (January 2009): 40–48; 47.

6. The 2012 film *Zero Dark Thirty* (Kathryn Bigelow), which tells (with ostensible historical realism) the story of the search for and assassination of Osama bin Laden, is a notable exception, and in fact for the first time produced a situation in which the stakes of showing torture onscreen became part of the discourse around the film. In suggesting that CIA interrogations that included torture such as waterboarding yielded the information that led to the discovery of bin Laden's location, *Zero Dark Thirty* ends up centralizing torture by betraying historical accuracy, since none of the information that led to the assassination was garnered through torture. See this book's conclusion for more on this film, as well as my essay "Zero Point Breaky" on the culture blog *Avidly* (7 February 2013), available at http://www.avidly.org/2013/02/07/zero-point-breaky/ (accessed 6/18/2013).

7. In particular, see Tziallas, "Torture Porn," and Lockwood, "All Stripped Down."

8. David Lyon, "The Search for Surveillance Theories," in *Theorizing Surveillance*, ed. Lyon, 11.

9. It is of some note in this context that the science fiction film *District 9* (Neill Blomkamp, 2009), which, along with the earlier *Children of Men* (Alfonso

Cuarón, 2006), foregrounds the status of refugees and the space of the refugee camp in its political thematics, uses the video surveillance and documentary aesthetic as a central mode of narration. Though surveillance technology is in no way the centerpiece of the film (in fact the film is deeply invested in the "primitive" space of the camp), the punctuation of the narrative with shots from surveillance cameras at various locations suggests a kind of intuitive interplay between the "wild" space of the camp and the surrounding environs that are marked incessantly by surveillance aesthetics.

10. See, respectively, Bülent Diken and Carsten Bagge Laustsen, "Zones of Indistinction: Security, Terror, and Bare Life," in *Space and Culture* vol. 5 no. 3 (August 2002): 290–307; and Derek Gregory, *The Colonial Present: Afghanistan, Palestine, Iraq* (Malden, MA, and Oxford: Blackwell Publishing, 2004).

11. To name just a few essays with varied approaches: Didier Bigo, "Security, Exception, Ban and Surveillance," in *Theorizing Surveillance*, ed. Lyon, 46–68; Jeremy Douglas, "Disappearing Citizenship: Surveillance and the State of Exception," in *Surveillance and Society* vol. 6 no. 1 (2009): 32–42; and Daniel Palmer and Jessica Whyte, "'No Credible Photographic Interest': Photography Restrictions and Surveillance in a Time of Terror," in *Philosophy of Photography* vol. 1 no. 2 (2010): 177–195.

12. Cultural theorist Benjamin Noys, in his 2005 book *The Culture of Death* (Oxford and New York: Berg, 2005), has also noted the consistency between recent cultural representations of extremity and death and Agamben's figure of "bare life," though he does not address torture porn in particular.

13. Dean Lockwood's account of the *Saw* series, "All Stripped Down: The Spectacle of Torture Porn," also introduces Agamben's concepts (also through reference to Noys's above book) as a possible analytical framework only to reject it. Lockwood views the films instead as allegorizing a Deleuzian "becoming" through extreme experience, arguing that the films work toward (though don't quite achieve) a kind of radical masochism and that viewing them through a "logic of affect rather than effect shows that challenging and transgressing the limits of the acceptable can be a valid, revitalizing, and life-intensifying aesthetic strategy" (47).

14. Giorgio Agamben, *Homo Sacer: Sovereign Power and Bare Life*, trans. Daniel Heller-Roazan (Stanford, CA: Stanford University Press, 1998).

15. Anthony Downey, "Zones of Indistinction: Giorgio Agamben's 'Bare Life' and the Politics of Aesthetics," in *Third Text* vol. 23 no. 2 (March 2009): 109–125; 111.

16. Agamben, *Means without Ends: Notes on Politics*, trans. Cesare Casarino and Vincenzo Binetti (Minneapolis: University of Minnesota Press, 2000), 41.

17. Agamben, *Homo Sacer*, 166.

18. Catherine Mills, *The Philosophy of Agamben* (Stocksfield, UK: Acumen Publishing, 2008), 85.

19. The complex phenomenon of cinematic space has occupied film theory from its inception and has taken numerous forms for both cinema scholars and others. (Cf. André Bazin, *What Is Cinema? Vol. 1*, trans. Hugh Gray [Berkeley and Los

Angeles: University of California Press, 1967]; Stephen Heath, "Narrative Space," in *Questions of Cinema* [Bloomington and Indianapolis: University of Indiana Press, 1981]; Chris Lukinbeal, "Cinematic Landscapes," in *Journal of Cultural Geography* vol. 23 no. 1 [Fall/Winter 2005]: 3–22.) As is made clear by the analysis of *The Conversation* in this book's introduction, the effect of surveillance on the coherence of the narrative space of cinema is considerable in a number of contexts.

20. Jasbir K. Puar, "On Torture: Abu Ghraib," in *Radical History Review* no. 93 (Fall 2005): 13–38; 31. See also Judith Butler, *Frames of War: When Is Life Grievable?* (London: Verso, 2009).

21. Puar, "On Torture," 18.

22. See my earlier essay, "The Eye of Horror: *Peeping Tom* and Technological Perversion," in *Horror Film: Creating and Marketing Film*, ed. Steffen Hantke (Jackson,: University of Mississippi Press, 2004).

23. This is similar to the use of video monitors in the torture scenarios in *Saw*, though here we are presented with flat screens for a more contemporary look than the square monitors of the *Saw* films, which are clearly meant to evoke a kind of violent primitivism even in the use of technology.

24. This type of film based on faux "reality" footage and video point-of-view shots will be the focus of the following chapter on consumer-level surveillance as narrative structure.

25. Umberto Eco, *The Role of the Reader: Explorations in the Semiotics of Texts* (Bloomington and Indianapolis: Indiana University Press, 1984).

26. Kammerer, "Video Surveillance in Hollywood Movies," 473.

27. The temporality of video will be discussed further in the following chapter.

28. Given these more straightforward examples of the temporal ambiguities of video surveillance, it is not surprising that David Lynch uses video surveillance as the narrative crux that opens up the complexity of space/time in his highly destabilizing *Lost Highway* (1997).

29. Turner, "Collapsing the Interior/Exterior Distinction," 94.

30. Jo Becker and Scott Shane, "Secret 'Kill List' Proves a Test of Obama's Principles and Will," in *New York Times*, 29 May 2012, available at http://www.nytimes.com/2012/05/29/world/obamas-leadership-in-war-on-al-qaeda.html (accessed 7/3/2013). Emphasis mine.

31. Agamben, *State of Exception*, trans. Kevin Attell (Chicago: University of Chicago Press, 2005), 2.

32. Ibid., 4.

33. Agamben, *Homo Sacer*, 86.

34. Ibid., 89.

35. Elaine Scarry, *The Body in Pain: The Making and Unmaking of the World* (New York and Oxford: Oxford University Press, 1985), 27.

36. Sean Hier, "Risky Spaces and Dangerous Faces: Urban Surveillance, Social Disorder, and CCTV," in *Social Legal Studies* vol. 13 no. 4 (2004): 541–554; 550.

37. Ibid., 542.

38. Agamben, *Homo Sacer*, 11.

39. Thomas Y. Levin, "Five Tapes, Four Halls, Two Dreams: Vicissitudes of Surveillant Narration in Michael Haneke's *Caché*," in *A Companion to Michael Haneke*, ed. Roy Grundmann (West Sussex, UK: Wiley-Blackwell, 2010), 75–90; 75.

40. Ara Osterweil, "*Caché* (Review)," in *Film Quarterly* vol. 59 no. 4 (Summer 2006): 35–39; 35.

41. D. I. Grossvogel, "Haneke: The Coercing of Vision," *Film Quarterly* vol. 60 no. 4 (Summer 2007): 36–43; 36.

42. Levin, "Five Tapes," 76.

43. As film scholar Catherine Wheatley points out, this technological confusion is significantly produced by the use of high-resolution digital video. While earlier video images within film are often marked off as low-res, and thus stamped with the mark of a gritty violent reality, Haneke's turn to digital video here also introduces indistinction between the subjectivized, diegeticized video surveillance gaze and the narrative and visual verisimilitude of the cinematic image. It is not of neutral interest that this apparently "aesthetic" (or simply common-sense) choice is made when not only are narrative films increasingly composed of digital production and postproduction, but when surveillance is increasingly composed of a relation between visual and informational technologies. (Catherine Wheatley, "Secrets, Lies, & Videotape," in *Sight and Sound* vol. 16 no. 2 [Fall 2006]: 32–36.)

44. Interestingly, the high resolution video we were watching is now shown to be a VHS tape, which is a bit incongruous here.

45. Osterweil, "*Caché* (Review)," 36.

46. Ibid.

47. Wheatley, "Secrets, Lies," 35.

48. In the essay noted above, Thomas Levin makes a compelling critique that *Caché* in fact does the exact opposite of what I am arguing by increasingly identifying the film's spectator with the surveillant narration, which ultimately abandons the question of "Who is watching here?" in favor of the investigatory question of "What is going on here?" While I agree that the film has a degree of complicity with the surveillant forms it examines, I think that ultimately the spectator is actually left floating in between those two questions, showing that in fact the two questions are completely inseparable—one cannot be answered (or even asked) without reference to the other, and thus the space in between those questions becomes an interesting trap for both the film and its viewers ("Five Tapes," 88).

49. Clive Norris and Gary Armstrong, *The Maximum Surveillance Society: The Rise of CCTV* (Oxford and New York: Berg, 1999), 59.

50. Ibid, 91.

51. Osterweil, "*Caché* (Review)," 38.

52. Brian Price and John David Rhodes, from their introduction to their edited volume, *On Michael Haneke* (Detroit, MI: Wayne State University Press, 2010): 6.

53. Frantz Fanon, *Black Skin, White Masks*, trans. Charles Lam Markmann (New York: Grove Press, 1967), 140.

CHAPTER 2. COMMODIFIED SURVEILLANCE

1. Guy Debord, *The Society of the Spectacle* (Detroit: Black and Red Press, 1983), chapter 1, section 24.
2. Mark Zuckerberg, "Improving Your Ability to Share and Connect," on *Facebook Blog* (4 March 2009), available at https://www.facebook.com/blog/blog.php?post=57822962130 (accessed 4/6/2013).
3. This incorporation of consumers into surveillance structures will be discussed in terms of its more explicitly militarized and political forms in the following chapter.
4. Haggerty and Ericson, *The New Politics of Surveillance and Visibility*, 21.
5. Thomas Mathieson, "The Viewer Society: Michel Foucault's 'Panopticon' Revisited," in *Theoretical Criminology* vol. 1 no. 2 (May 1997): 215–234.
6. Lyon, "9/11, Synopticon," 36.
7 Hille Koskela, "'The Other Side of Surveillance': Webcams, Power and Agency," in *Theorizing Surveillance*, ed. Lyon, 163–181.
8. Debord, *The Society of the Spectacle*, chapter 1, section 3.
9. Notable critical work on reality television includes the anthology *Reality TV: Remaking Television Culture*, ed. Susan Murray and Laurie Ouellette, 2nd edition (New York: NYU Press, 2008), and Mark Andrejevic's *Reality TV: The Work of Being Watched* (New York: Rowman & Littlefield, 2003).
10. Debord, *The Society of the Spectacle*, chapter 1, section 23.
11. The earliest example of a feature film dominated by first-person camera is the film noir *Lady in the Lake* (Robert Montgomery, 1947), and faux-found-footage horror (narrative that claims that what you are seeing is actual caught reality) emerged in 1980 with *Cannibal Holocaust* (Ruggero Deodato). However, until the full incorporation of video cameras into the feature format, this pseudo-genre did not become popularized. *The Last Broadcast* (Stefan Avalos and Lance Weiler, 1998), similar in both form and content to *Blair Witch*, was released a year earlier, but did not have the same success.
12. Because the amateur or home video aesthetic of these films allow for filmmaking on an extremely limited budget, one can find a sizable number of first-person-camera films in the straight-to-home-viewing market.
13. There are also some faux-reality-TV films that occasionally overlap, though in a somewhat different form, with first-person-camera films. *My Little Eye* (Marc Evans, 2002) and *Series 7: The Contenders* (Daniel Minahan, 2001) are examples that both do and don't belong in the same subgenre as the other films I mentioned, a fact with a significance that I will discuss at the end of this chapter.
14. The "compulsive documentation" films and the first-person-camera films often coincide with what have been examined as "mockumentaries." Though I will not be referring to them as such nor addressing those discussions, I do not intend to

imply that such a generic description of them is inaccurate or not worthwhile as a framing device for understanding their cultural significance; I will simply be focusing on more specific technological and stylistic aspects that position them in relation to consumer electronics, surveillance, and social media, and position some "mockumentaries" as often more closely related in formal and narrative structure to other first-person-camera films that would not fall into that category. For further discussion of the fake-documentary aspects of some of these films, see *F Is for Phony: Fake Documentary and Truth's Undoing*, ed. Alexandra Juhasz and Jesse Lerner (Minneapolis: University of Minnesota Press, 2006); *Faking It: Mock-Documentary and the Subversion of Factuality*, by Craig Hight and Jane Roscoe (Manchester, UK: Manchester University Press, 2002); and *Too Bold for the Box Office: The Mockumentary from Big Screen to Small*, ed. Cynthia J. Miller (Lanham, MD: Scarecrow Press, 2012), among others.

15. Turner, "Collapsing the Interior/Exterior Distinction."

16. Fuchs borrows the term from Alvin Toffler's initial celebratory usage of the term to provide a critical political economy approach to the intersection of labor and surveillance on the internet. See Christian Fuchs, "Web 2.0, Prosumption, and Surveillance," in *Surveillance and Society* vol. 8 no. 3 (2011): 288–309 (particularly page 296 for the definition and history of the term "prosumer").

17. Ibid.

18. Mark Andrejevic, *iSpy: Surveillance and Power in the Interactive Era* (Lawrence: University of Kansas Press, 2007), 2.

19. In the *Wall Street Journal*'s study of which popular websites trigger the most tracking files that send information about your online activity to multiple companies, Dictionary.com ranked highest by a wide margin. This couldn't make it more evident that even the use of the internet for its most seemingly neutral informational purposes positions the user as consumer above all else. See "What They Know," n.d., in *Wall Street Journal*, available at http://blogs.wsj.com/wtk/ (accessed 4/17/2013).

20. In some ways, I am here substituting "surveillance" for "information" to demonstrate that the "information economy" has developed in such a way that exchange of information on the web is increasingly surveillant in both form and function.

21. Though it is a matter of some interest why digital surveillance has not lent itself to narrative in any particularly successful forms, I will leave that for another discussion.

22. To borrow Levin's phrase.

23. Comolli, "Machines of the Visible."

24. David Antin, "Video: The Distinctive Features of the Medium," in *Video Culture: A Critical Investigation*, ed. John Hanhardt (Rochester, NY: Visual Studies Workshop Press, 1987), 147–166.

25. Ibid., 153.

26. Rosalind Krauss, "The Aesthetic of Narcissism," in *Video Culture*, ed. Hanhardt, 179–191.

27. Evangelos Tziallas, "Of Doppelgängers and Alter Egos: Surveillance Footage as Cinematic Double," in *Écranosphère* no. 1 (Winter 2014), available at http://www.ecranosphere.ca/article.php?id=21 (accessed 7/21/2014).

28. Krauss, "The Aesthetic of Narcissism," 179.

29. Ibid., 183.

30. Ibid., 182.

31. Another notable example of isolated and fragmented bodies as represented by video is Bill Viola's *The Sleepers* (1992).

32. This is the title of the first chapter of Debord's book.

33. Debord, *The Society of the Spectacle*, chapter 1, section 5.

34. This is true even when the film's vision switches occasionally to black-and-white 16mm film.

35. This is by no means to say that the positioning of the cinematic spectator within narrative film is "simple," and of course the positioning of the cinematic spectator cannot be summed up either stylistically or theoretically by any one account.

36. Within Metz's framework of spectatorial identification, there are two possibilities, although they don't always function exclusively: primary identification is identification with the apparatus, the pure act of looking (here I mean the camera), and secondary identification is identification with a character within the film. When a viewer is presented with a character point-of-view shot, we lose the distinction between primary and secondary identification: we are given to understand that to look through the camera's eye is to also look through the eye of the character. See Christian Metz, *The Imaginary Signifier: Psychoanalysis and the Cinema*, trans. Celia Britton, Annwyl Williams, Ben Brewster, and Alfred Guzzetti (Bloomington and Indianapolis: Indiana University Press, 1982), part I, section 3: "Identification, Mirror."

37. At times, the perspective shifts to that of the 16mm camera, also incorporated diegetically, which the characters are also using to shoot their film. In some ways the 16mm film camera functions just like the video (as handheld and a character's perspective), but in other ways it signifies an aesthetic distancing, as it is this camera that is shooting the more formal "film" within the film that is being produced. The use of 16mm here as explicitly representational highlights the degree to which video is posited less as representational and more as representative—in this case of an embodied character perspective.

38. Vivian Sobchack, *The Address of the Eye: A Phenomenology of Film Experience* (Princeton, NJ: Princeton University Press, 1992), 5.

39. The degree to which video technology has come to signify death in horror films exceeds the bounds of the first-person-camera film. The number of films that incorporate video technology as an element of horror is quite remarkable. The insistence on this characterization of video as deadly is perhaps best represented by the Japanese film *Ringu* (Hideo Nakatu, 1998), remade in the U.S. by Gore Verbinski with great success in 2002. In this film the formulation is simple: the videotape around which the narrative circles represents the death of its maker,

who is dead, and watching it results in the death of the person watching it. The only way to avoid death is to make a copy and give it to someone, who will then die unless they reproduce it, and so on.

40. Of course, the self-protective filtering of reality that the camera-eye provides the film's characters is that which ostensibly provides a more *direct* engagement for the film's spectators, and thus the distinction between representation and reality is harder to understand and ultimately reversible.

41. Alice E. Marwick, "The Public Domain: Social Surveillance in Everyday Life," in *Surveillance and Society* vol. 9 no. 4 (2012): 378–393.

42. Target markets will be discussed in more depth as a surveillance concept in the following chapter.

43. Nicole S. Cohen, "The Valorization of Surveillance: Toward a Political Economy of Facebook," in *Democratic Communiqué* vol. 22 no. 1 (Spring 2008): 5–22; 7.

44. Ibid., 12.

45. Ibid.

46. Turkle, *Life on the Screen: Identity in the Age of the Internet* (New York: Simon and Schuster, 1997), 14.

47. Judith Donath, in *Communities in Cyberspace*, ed. Peter Kollock and Marc Smith (London: Routledge, 1998), 29.

48. Andrejevic, *iSpy*, 133.

49. Rich Juzwiak, "*Truth or Dare*: How Madonna's Documentary Changed the Next 20 Years," on *Gawker*, 3 April 2012, available at http://gawker.com/5898823/truth-or-dare-how-madonnas-documentary-changed-the-next-20-years (accessed 4/22/2013).

50. Much has been made about how digital surveillance models require alternative models of subject formation to the disciplinary panoptic model, and surveillance theorists have turned in large part to Deleuzian notions of the "assemblage," which serves well to look at the types of composite silhouettes that emerge from patterns of data and become identities. Cf. Haggerty and Ericson, "The Surveillant Assemblage." Given the connection I would like to make here between the first-person-camera films, self-documentation, and digital surveillance, it is also useful to examine the phenomenological work of Mark B. N. Hansen in *Bodies in Code: Interfaces with Digital Media* (New York: Routledge, 2006), which highlights the centrality of the perceptual body in digital culture.

51. J. P. Telotte, "*The Blair Witch Project* Project: Film and the Internet," in *Film Quarterly* vol. 54 no. 3 (Spring 2001): 32–39; 34.

52. Ibid., 35.

53. Ibid., 38.

54. Daniel North, "Evidence of Things Not Quite Seen: *Cloverfield*'s Obstructed Spectacle," in *Film and History* vol. 40 no. 1 (Spring 2010): 75–92.

55. Ibid., 76.

56. Ibid., 77.

57. Andrejevic, *iSpy*, 29.

58. North, "Evidence of Things," 80.

59. See, in particular, Henry Jenkins, *Convergence Culture: Where Old and New Media Collide* (New York: NYU Press, 2008).

60. Andrejevic, *iSpy*, 49.

61. Ibid., 124.

62. See the seminal essay "Film Bodies: Gender, Genre, and Excess," by Linda Williams, who has been tremendously influential in formulating how the genres of horror, pornography, and melodrama are specifically designed to elicit bodily responses from spectators.

63. North, "Evidence of Things," 84.

64. The irony of my use of the term "brand hijack" here is that it was originally popularized by so-called subversive marketer Alex Wipperfurth to describe the manner in which consumers were appropriating brands and defining their meaning for themselves, producing what he thinks of as "marketing without marketing." Wipperfurth's analysis of the marketing of *The Blair Witch Project*, among other things, wanted to describe how consumers drove the evolution of the brand, which we can see from the marketing campaigns is only marginally true, and certainly does not mean that consumers share in any of the profit derived from their participation in brand redefinition. But certainly marketing companies benefiting from the consumer labor would like those consumers to believe in their own power, and it is thus not surprising that Wipperfurth cast both himself and consumers as resistant to traditional marketing even as he is harnessing possibly subversive acts by consumers, once again for the benefit of marketers and their clients. In this case, and in keeping with what is currently driving marketing styles, I would suggest that the very notion of the empowered consumer has been hijacked and reappropriated as both labor and commodity, as I am here arguing that mediation is being rebranded as experience. (Alex Wipperfurth, *Brand Hijack: Marketing without Marketing* [New York: Viking Press, 2005].)

65. Emanuelle Wessels, "'Where Were You When the Monster Hit?': Media Convergence, Branded Security Citizenship, and the Trans-Media Phenomenon of *Cloverfield*," in *Convergence: The International Journal of Research into New Media Technologies* vol. 17 no. 1 (2011): 69–83. See also Andrejevic, *iSpy*, Chapter 5, for his discussion of labor and consumption in relation to television.

66. Wessels, "'Where Were You,'" 72.

67. Ibid., 79.

68. The statement released by the *Project X* studio in response to the often destructive copycat parties (which led to not just enormous damage of property but reportedly a death in one instance) seemed to of necessity attempt to undo the entire premise of their film, describing it as a "fictional movie . . . with conduct portrayed by actors in a controlled environment." This form of defense ends up simply bolstering the degree to which it is the structural elements of the film that were so tempting to reproduce. Quoted in Valerie Wigglesworth, "'Project X'

Movie Spurring Copycat Parties," *Dallas Morning News*, 23 March 2012, available at http://www.dallasnews.com/news/crime/headlines/20120323-project-x-movie-spurring-copycat-parties.ece (accessed 5/3/2013).

69. Cohen, "The Valorization of Surveillance," 17.

70. Wessels, "'Where Were You,'" 79.

71. The way consumer desire and action are being accessed through the term "demand" can also be seen in cable television's "On Demand" offerings to indicate programming that can be accessed at the viewer's convenience. Such terminology hails the consumer explicitly as part of an economic structure ("supply and demand"), and interestingly, despite the corresponding effort to convince the consumer of their particularity, encourages viewers to identify with their generalized structural position as a desirable one.

72. These videos and stills of the audience were shot with a night-vision camera, which is itself identifiable as a surveillant aesthetic and has been used as such in multiple films.

73. Quoted in Andrew Hampp, "How 'Paranormal Activity' Hit It Big," in *Advertising Age*, 12 October 2009, available at http://adage.com/article/madisonvine-news/low-budget-movie-marketing-paranormal-activity/139588/ (accessed 4/2/2013).

74. The phrase refers to an internet meme, discussed in some detail in relation to social networking by Cynara Geissler: "Pix or It Didn't Happen: Social Networking, Digital Memory, and the Future of Biography," in *The Book of MPub: New Perspectives on Technology and Publishing*, ed. Vanessa Chan et al. (Vancouver: CSSP Press, 2010), 135–141. For Bazin's discussions of realism, particularly indexicality, see "The Ontology of the Photographic Image," in *What is Cinema? Vol. 1.*

75. B. Ruby Rich's account of the converging conditions that resulted in the emergence of the New Queer Cinema highlights the import of consumer video (along with AIDS, Reagan, and low rent) to what became a cinematic revolution. *New Queer Cinema: The Director's Cut* (Durham, NC, and London: Duke University Press, 2013), xvi.

CHAPTER 3. THE GLOBAL EYE

1. Toby Miller, Nitin Govil, John McMurria, Richard Maxwell, and Ting Wang, *Global Hollywood 2* (London: British Film Institute, 2005), 51.

2. Fredric Jameson, *The Geopolitical Aesthetic: Cinema and Space in the World System* (Bloomington: Indiana University Press, 1992), 4.

3. Ibid.

4. Ibid., 3.

5. Ibid., 2.

6. Caren Kaplan, "Precision Targets: GPS and the Militarization of U.S. Consumer Identity," in *American Quarterly* vol. 58 no. 3 (September 2006): 693–713; 695.

7. Lisa Parks, *Cultures in Orbit: Satellites and the Televisual* (Durham, NC: Duke University Press, 2005), 1.

8. Ibid., 2.

9. Chad Harris, "The Omniscient Eye: Satellite Imagery, 'Battlespace Awareness,' and the Structures of the Imperial Gaze," in *Surveillance and Society* vol. 4 no. 1/2 (2006): 101–122; 102.

10. Ibid., 105.

11. James Der Derian, *Virtuous War: Mapping the Military-Industrial-Media-Entertainment Network* (Boulder, CO: Westview Press, 2001).

12. Parks, *Cultures in Orbit*, 2.

13. Paul Virilio has shown aerial surveillance and representational mediation have been operationally significant since World War I. However, in terms of American military action, the Gulf War of 1991 is in many ways regarded as having defined itself through its being waged in large part remotely, and televisually communicated in similar form. The war as tele-waged and televised media event was the topic of much critical work, with, for instance, Baudrillard's short series of essays "The Gulf War Did Not Take Place" positing it as the first "virtual war." But it has also been a focus for tacticians, since, as Chad Harris has noted, "it was considered a testing ground for the integration and interoperation of national imagery intelligence with command and control systems and was thus highly studied afterwards by military systems analysts" (Harris, "The Omniscient Eye," 103). With surveillance, targeting, and killing now increasingly being carried out by unmanned aerial vehicles (drones), there is an additional level of remove, even as the UAV surveillance might be said to mark a return to an earlier era of pre-satellite aerial imaging characteristic of World Wars I and II.

14. The narrative interchangeability of an animated rendering versus a photography-based image suggests that the cinematic use of satellite technologies is predicated more on function than on form, which is intriguing in relation to the history of surveillance in which objective status was afforded to images based on photographic realism.

15. GPS systems function through the "triangulation" of multiple satellite signals picked up by a GPS receiver; the differences in distance from the receiver to each of those satellites is calculated such that the position of the receiver can be established in three dimensions. Thus the basic functionality of GPS, even when rendered as a simple two-dimensional image, is dependent upon relational technologies serving to connect a single location to a multinodal system.

16. These elaborate chase scenes are the contemporary incarnation of the chase scenes of early cinema, discussed in the introductory chapter, which showed the degree to which narrative form developed in connection to surveillance. A surprisingly similar version of this structure appears in George Lucas's 1971 feature film (his first), *THX 1138*, a dystopic science fiction tale in which surveillance figures centrally. Much of the final portion of this film is comprised of a lengthy chase scene in which the titular character is pursued by android police—the chase is monitored and directed through video surveillance, and the film cuts to the centralized surveillance operation during this sequence

repeatedly. *THX 1138* adds a layer to this monitoring by including the state's budget for this police action as part of the surveillant gaze, with both audio and visual cues letting the audience and the authorities know that this chase is costing the state money. In an amusingly metatextual gesture, the chase (and the film) ends when the budget has been exceeded. As we will see later in this chapter, this reference to the economic structures underlying such cinematic representation is itself a prescient perspective on what will undergird the future developments of this narrative form.

17. *The Bourne Legacy* (Tony Gilroy), released in 2012, introduces a new cycle with a new protagonist, and a new franchise vehicle for A-list-aspiring actor Jeremy Renner, who picks up where Matt Damon left off.

18. Klaus Dodds, "Gender, Geopolitics, and Geosurveillance in *The Bourne Ultimatum*," in *Geographical Review* vol. 101 no. 1 (January 2011): 88–105; 102.

19. The operations office of the CIA that is tracking Bourne is almost a caricature of the surveillance aesthetic. At any given point, there are three to four projections that switch at high pace between satellite maps, GPS renderings, close-ups of evidence, CCTV images, pictures of the subjects under surveillance—and always a team of technicians working at frenetic pace at their computers managing information and consolidating everything we see before us at breakneck speed. This scene has now become familiar, and could easily describe any number of "operations centers" in films presenting large-scale surveillance operations.

20. I refer here to Jean-Louis Comolli's famous pronouncement in "Machines of the Visible" that "the photograph stands as at once the triumph and the grave of the eye" (123).

21. Harris, "The Omniscient Eye," 114.

22. Specifically, Harris discusses air reconnaissance practices, technologies, and analytics (ibid., 116).

23. Paul Virilio, *War and Cinema: The Logistics of Perception*, trans. Patrick Camiller (London and New York: Verso Press, 1989), 6.

24. Caren Kaplan's essay "Mobility and War: The Cosmic View of U.S. Air Power" traces these connections back to the European Enlightenment period, pointing to the use of hot-air balloons in the seventeenth century for the same intersecting purposes as contemporary satellites: scientific, surveillant, and military. (In *Environment and Planning A* vol. 38 [2006]: 395–407; 401.)

25. Virilio, *War and Cinema*, 20. Harris's essay includes multiple historical and contemporary implementations showing how consistently the camera/weaponry structure has been a part of aerial warfare since the time Virilio points to. An example from the 1991 Gulf War highlights the place of weapon-mounted cameras and shows how surveillance slips between tactic, strategy, and even outcome: "Aircraft videotape recordings (AVTR's), sometimes called armament delivery recordings (ADR's), were created by attaching videotape recorders to gun cameras and radar targeting systems built into the aircraft. These videotapes were collected during pilot debriefings after each mission and used to construct

mission reports (misreps) that would be fed back into the targeting cycle" (Harris, "The Omniscient Eye," 115).

26. Though this film is much more known for its satellite imaging and tracking, it is also very much an information technology narrative. It is ultimately digital information that defines the system and in this way it is similar to the earlier and much less successful *The Net* (Irwin Winkler, 1995). Both films invoke identity theft as part of the narrative possibilities of surveillance in the digital era, and in this way also highlight how the very idea and function of information as a system is intimately connected to an individual at the level of identity, or in this case the lack thereof.

27. Dodds, "Gender, Geopolitics," 102.

28. There have been critiques of the discourses of privacy and the construction of neoliberal hegemony in numerous contemporary contexts. See, for instance, Lisa Duggan's analysis of the rhetoric of privacy in gay rights activism in *The Twilight of Equality: Neoliberalism, Cultural Politics and the Attack on Democracy* (Boston: Beacon Press, 2004) or Christian Fuchs's analysis of the political economy of Facebook's privacy policies in "An Alternative View of Privacy on Facebook," in *information* vol. 2 no. 1 (February 2011): 140–165.

29. It is worth noting in this context that Virilio sees the rise of the star system in early Hollywood (and thus the rise of the cinematically defined celebrity) as emerging from the "same instability of dimensions" produced by the (representationally defined) war (*War and Cinema*, 25).

30. Corber, "Resisting History," 147.

31. Barbara Biesecker, "No Time for Mourning: The Rhetorical Production of the Melancholic Citizen-Subject in the War on Terror," in *Philosophy and Rhetoric* vol. 40 no. 1 (2007): 147–169; 156–157.

32. Michael J. Shapiro, *Cinematic Geopolitics* (New York: Routledge, 2008), 25.

33. In this light, Shapiro's description connects to the biopolitical formations discussed in relation to the torture films of Chapter One. This expansive "spatialization" of terrorist bodies in counterterrorist rhetoric and practice could be said to produce those bodies as their own zones of indistinction, reflexively serving to define such bodies as "bare life," life that may be killed. In this case, the indistinction serves to blur the line between the body and the space that defines and is occupied by that body.

34. The irony of this technological advancement is that the "next-generation disks" in the film are Minidiscs, introduced by Sony in 1992 and now defunct. Minidiscs represent a relative failure on the part of the Japanese tech industry to find a market overseas.

35. In some ways, the manipulability of digital imagery is now branded *as* digital: to say that a photograph is "photoshopped" is to claim that the image has been doctored and does not reflect reality, but the term specifically references the currently dominant digital photography editing software, Photoshop. Thus while

certainly images have been manipulated since the origin of photography, it is digitization that has come to represent manipulability.

36. Interestingly in this context, Graham Sewell notes (in reference to his own earlier case study with Barry Wilkinson) that in a U.K. subsidiary of a Japanese parent company, despite their initial presumptions, "none of the sophisticated electronic quality monitoring systems to be found in the U.K. appeared to be in operation in Japan" (15). The study suggests that "the impact of peer group pressure within the Japanese workplace . . . is a powerful instrument of normalization. The implication here is that in the Japanese plant overt disciplinary mechanisms of surveillance are deemed unnecessary as other more subtle and effective processes are in operation" (21). Thus, while certainly some of the representations of collectivist imperative offered in *Rising Sun* might fit with sociological studies of Japanese labor practice, the use of surveillance within that model might be more easily seen as the American fantasy of what collectivism entails, rather than its reality. (Graham Sewell, "A Japanese 'Cure' to a British 'Disease'? Cultural Dimensions to the Development of Workplace Surveillance Technologies," in *Information Technology and People* vol. 9 no. 3 [1996]: 12–29.)

37. Even if just coincidence or simply the circularity of the current American film genre that has been reformatting 1980s narratives for a contemporary, digitally enhanced market, it is not insignificant to my discussion that the 2010 remake/ franchise renewal of *The Karate Kid* starred Jaden Smith, son of Will Smith (discussed earlier in terms of his casting in *Enemy of the State*). Other updates in the new version are also worth mentioning: the original film was a Los Angeles–based tale of a local teen mentored in karate by a Japanese immigrant in order to defend himself against a group of (also white) bullies who have been taught karate by a sadistic white coach ("Sweep the leg!"); the 2010 film sends its African American "karate kid" abroad to China with his mother, who takes a corporate job there. The shifting of the economic influence from Japan to China is clear, but the influence is also restructured (from excorporative to incorporative). However, even the fact that the later film is actually about kung fu does not stop it from directly referencing the 1980s version in both its title and the orientalized cultural economy.

38. In "Mobility and War," Kaplan traces the orientalist discourse of the current U.S.-led "war on terror" back to the characterization of the Japanese forces by the U.S. in the World War II era (403). It is in fact clear in *Rising Sun* (especially given the film's title and emphasis on nationalist Japanese imagery) that the economic and cultural threat of Japan to the U.S. in the 1980s is cast in the mold of the military threat posed in World War II. This cycling back and forth between economic and military threats is characteristic of the geopolitical thriller genre as well.

39. This mastery of "exotic" urban spaces is certainly not confined to recent action films and is perhaps most notable in the James Bond franchise and Indiana Jones series.

40. Kaplan, "Mobility and War," 396.

41. At times the desert space becomes a threat to the protagonist by virtue of his alternately or additionally being targeted by his own forces (identified by the satellite gaze) alongside the people he now finds himself among, as is the case in *Syriana*—this is part of what often signals the desert space as a space of abandonment to Otherness. Instead of the orientalized desert being the source of the threat, it is now the protagonist's association with that desert that produces him as threatened by the West. In either case, the upshot is the same, and throughout all the generic variations of the films under discussion, the desert never appears as a space subject to the masterful maneuverings of a Western action hero.

42. Given the other orientalist connections provided in these films between East Asia and the area broadly designated as the "Middle East," it's notable that *Mission: Impossible III* (J. J. Abrams, 2006) offers its urban chase scene in Shanghai, China, in which Cruise also must challenge a very tall building. The next film clearly required a taller one.

43. These impossibly realistic masks have been a centerpiece of the series' style since the first scene of the first *Mission: Impossible* film released in 1996 (directed by frequent surveillance cinema figure Brian De Palma); in fact, this was our introduction to Cruise's character, Ethan Hunt, whom we see initially as an unknown Russian as viewed on surveillance video by American agents. He enters the room with the surveillance operators and pulls off his mask, revealing himself as the hero/star of the film. This is yet another surveillance cinema instance of video's narrative use as a misrepresentation, or space for ambiguity or reversal.

44. Chad Harris also emphasizes the distancing effect in satellite-based surveillance and warfare, but not just in relation to the distant perspective of the satellite gaze: the account Harris offers of the interoperability of surveillance, targeting, and assault shows the flipside of the interoperation as a "conglomeration of systems and processes that has no physical center and is disaggregated." The same principles that produce multiple functions of war as seamless and fused also produce a "system that is physically and operationally isolated from the actual violence it is designed to perpetrate, creating layers of distance between operators in the targeting centers and human targets on the ground" ("The Omniscient Eye," 108).

45. Biesecker, "No Time for Mourning," 161. I discuss Biesecker's nuanced analysis in greater detail in the next chapter.

46. Ibid., 158.

47. Homay King, *Lost in Translation: Orientalism, Cinema, and the Enigmatic Signifier* (Durham, NC: Duke University Press, 2010).

48. Ibid., 4.

49. The phrase appears in several of Virilio's texts and is the title of one of his major works. While distance is a part of this aesthetic, it is a phrase in no way reducible to my use of it here, and instead refers to the centrality of speed to an

understanding of contemporary forms of power. See *The Aesthetics of Disappearance*, translated by Philip Beitchman (New York: Semiotext(e), 1991).

50. Virilio, *War and Cinema*, 24.

51. Biesecker, "No Time for Mourning," 157.

52. Information about "civilian casualties" in drone strikes or the military actions in Iraq, Afghanistan, Pakistan, and other fronts of the ambiguously defined "war on terror" is naturally hard to come by in a largely covert war that is also predicated on ill-defined terms ("terrorist," "enemy combatant") for who might constitute a legitimate target. There is, however, enough research to suggest that the more mediated the war becomes, the greater the number of civilians who become subject to death, exemplified in the use of drones. See the 2012 report "Counting Drone Strike Deaths," by the Columbia Law School Human Rights Clinic, available at http://web.law.columbia.edu/sites/default/files/microsites/human-rights-institute/COLUMBIACountingDronesFinalNotEmbargo.pdf (accessed 7/15/2013).

53. It is perhaps not coincidence that as satellites emerge at every level of the plot, the agents themselves are put "under erasure": the aesthetics of disappearance (or dematerialization, as Biesecker offers) are here referenced in the film's very title. The agents in the film function in the ambiguous mode of the "ghost protocol," disavowed by their government, and thus characterized as spectral—in this case the war without bodies is presented as agents without an agency.

54. Similarly, the series *24*, one of the most representative instances on television of the geopolitical surveillance thriller, returned in 2014, with drones now defining both the plot and the surveillance aesthetic.

55. Kaplan, "Precision Targets," 696.

56. Ibid., 698.

57. "Psyops" refers to "psychological operations," the military term for operations in which a unified message accompanies U.S. operations, both military and diplomatic, following the general principle of "information dominance." See David Miller, "The Propaganda Machine," in *Tell Me Lies: Propaganda and Media Distortion in the Attack on Iraq*, ed. David Miller (New York: Pluto Press, 2003), for an in-depth account of psyops in the Iraq war.

58. Kaplan, "Precision Targets," 697.

59. Levin's essay "Rhetoric of the Temporal Index" points to the joint military/political/market agendas of the satellite-based multinational surveillance project ECHELON (579).

60. Kaplan, "Precision Targets," 708. For detailed technical information on the gradual immersion of satellites and GPS into the civilian market, see Mark Monmonier, *Spying with Maps: Surveillance Technologies and the Future of Privacy* (Chicago and London: University of Chicago Press, 2002).

61. The film's account of the difficulty in gaining access to the data needed to "ping" a prepaid cell phone is inaccurate. There is no technological problem or currently any legal problem in gaining access to this data. See Matthew J. Schwartz, "Lose

the Burners: Court Okays Prepaid Phone Tracking," in *Information Week*, 15 August 2012, available at http://www.informationweek.com/security/mobile/ lose-the-burners-court-okays-prepaid-pho/240005614 (accessed 4/19/2013). What is more difficult with a prepaid phone than locating it is connecting it to any specific user.

62. Stephen Graham, *Cities under Siege: The New Military Urbanism* (London: Verso Press, 2010), 62.

63. Ibid.

64. Also apt here is Michael Shapiro's notion of "violent cartographies," which he defines as "the 'historically developed, socially embedded interpretations of identity and space' that constitute the frames within which enmities give rise to war-as-policy. Violent cartographies are thus constituted as an articulation of geographic imaginaries and antagonisms based on models of identity-difference" (*Cinematic Geopolitics*, 18).

65. Dodds, "Gender, Geopolitics," 92.

66. Ibid., 94.

67. Allen Scott, "Hollywood and the World: The Geography of Motion-Picture Distribution and Marketing," in *Review of International Political Economy* vol. 11 no. 1 (February 2004): 33–61; 53.

68. Ibid.

69. Ibid., 54.

70. See Miller et al., *Global Hollywood 2*, for an in-depth account of the growth of U.S. dominance in the global market and the manner in which state and corporate interests have intertwined to further that end.

71. Scott Olson, "The Globalization of Hollywood," in *International Journal on World Peace* vol. XVII no. 4 (December 2000): 3–17; 4.

72. Miller et al., *Global Hollywood 2*, 7. The self-identification attending media consumption addressed here is in some ways just a more abstracted version of the self-identified media consumers I discuss in the preceding chapter in relation to first-person-camera films. Though it might appear to be, the relay of looks and identification produced in the geosurveillance thriller is in no way more of an identification with a system than the identification produced in the single, individualized look of the first-person-camera film; they are really just different modes of identification with the self-as-mediated. And, as may be suggested by the historical coincidence of the increasing emphasis on their respective surveillant structures in both generic formations, each version reinforces the other: the hyperindividualized body as rendered by a point-of-view shot is merely a shift in perspective from the body as pinpointed and targeted by the gaze of a surveillant system.

73. Revenue data from *Box Office Mojo*, available at www.boxofficemojo.com (accessed 11/1/2011).

74. Scott, "Hollywood and the World," 55.

75. Ibid., 56–57.

76. See also in this regard King's analysis of *Blade Runner* and its "notion of the Orient itself as simulacrum" (*Lost in Translation*, 100).

CHAPTER 4. TEMPORALITY AND SURVEILLANCE I

1. Levin, "Rhetoric of the Temporal Index."
2. Ibid., 582, 592.
3. Ibid., 590.
4. Ibid.
5. Gary Genosko and Scott Thompson, "Tense Theory: The Temporalities of Surveillance," in *Theorizing Surveillance: The Panopticon and Beyond*, ed. David Lyon (Devon, UK, and Portland, OR: Willan Publishing: 2006), 123–138.
6. Ibid., 130.
7. Greg Elmer and Andy Opel, "Pre-empting Panoptic Surveillance: Surviving the Inevitable War on Terror," in *Theorizing Surveillance*, ed. Lyon, 139–159. Genosko and Thompson, "Tense Theory," 130.
8. Joseba Zulaika, "The Self-Fulfilling Prophecies of Counterterrorism," in *Radical History Review* 85 (2003): 191–199; 192–193.
9. See also "Technonostalgia: Making the Future Past Perfect," in which Pat Gill makes an interesting and related argument about cinematic temporality and disavowal in the science fiction films of the 1980s and early 1990s. (In *Camera Obscura* 40/41 [vol. 14 nos. 1–2] [May 1997]: 161–179.)
10. Biesecker, "No Time for Mourning," 152.
11. Ibid., 153.
12. Ibid.
13. Ibid.
14. Ibid., 154.
15. Cf. Gill, "Technonostalgia," 164.
16. Wendy Brown, "Resisting Left Melancholy," in *Boundary 2* vol. 6 no. 2 (1999): 19–27; 20.
17. It is of course worth mentioning in this context that Brown, following Benjamin, is actually discussing leftist politics in this account of political melancholy, rather than the right-wing Bush era security practices I am referencing. Without going into the full details of Brown's account, it is of interest that her account of the left's romantic attachments maps so easily onto the right, suggesting that it is, among many other things, a melancholically inclined political view that is producing the left and the right as mirror images of each other in contemporary politics.
18. Biesecker, "No Time for Mourning," 149.
19. I am referencing here Kevin Haggerty and Richard Ericson's notion of "the convergence of once discrete surveillance systems." The result, what they call the "surveillant assemblage" (building on the thinking of Deleuze and Guattari), "operates by abstracting human bodies from their territorial settings, and separating them into discrete flows" ("The Surveillant Assemblage," 606). Though they are referring primarily to the production of "data doubles" through

information surveillance, the manner in which the narrative of this film is similarly constructed out of a series of individual perspectives into an identifiable conspiracy follows a similar logic of assemblage in surveillance.

20. McNamara, Mary. "TV Review: 'Person of Interest,'" in *Los Angeles Times*, 22 September 2011, available at http://www.latimes.com/entertainment/news/tv/la-et-person-interest-20110922,0,4850976.story (accessed 2/13/2012).

21. The new season with which *24* reemerged in 2014 was aptly titled "Live Another Day."

22. Richard Grusin, "Premediation," in *Criticism* vol. 46 no. 1 (Winter 2004): 17–39; 19.

23. Ibid., 23.

24. As Achille Mbembe states in his essay "Necropolitics," "To exercise sovereignty is to exercise control over mortality and to define life as the deployment and manifestation of power" (12). He goes on to state (in his interpretation of Hegel): "Politics is . . . death that lives a human life" (15). (In *Public Culture* vol. 15 no. 1 [Winter 2003]: 11–40; 12.)

CHAPTER 5. TEMPORALITY AND SURVEILLANCE II

1. Levin, "Rhetoric of the Temporal Index." His points are discussed in greater detail in the preceding chapter and in the introduction.

2. The question serves as the title for the two volumes of Bazin's collected essays, the first essay of which, "The Ontology of the Photographic Image," suggests the answer is for Bazin grounded in the indexicality of the photographic process. It is in part out of this "ontology" that Bazin's influential and idealistic theories of cinematic realism grew. See *What Is Cinema? Vol. 1.*

3. Bolter and Grusin, *Remediation*, 5.

4. Grusin, "Premediation."

5. For further discussion of *Zero Dark Thirty*, see this book's epilogue and also my review essay on the film in the context of Bigelow's early work, "Zero Point Breaky," on *Avidly*, 7 February 2013, available at http://www.avidly.org/2013/02/07/zero-point-breaky/ (accessed 7/21/2013).

6. Bolter and Grusin, *Remediation*, 231.

7. Haggerty and Ericson, *The New Politics of Surveillance and Visibility*, 14.

8. Mark Berrettini, "Can 'We All' Get Along? Social Difference, The Future, and *Strange Days*," in *Camera Obscura* 50 [vol. 17 no. 2] (2002): 155–188; 159.

9. The "snuff film" premise, hinging upon a recording that represents actual torture or murder, is also central to a number of the horror films discussed in Chapter One. The premise is an important one within surveillance cinema since it goes directly to the question of whether one is looking at evidence of a crime or simply a representation. Narratives such as *8mm* (Joel Schumacher, 1999) hinge upon making this determination. In *8mm* an investigator is given a box of 8mm films depicting torture and murder and asked to determine whether they are evidence of a crime or a fiction—thus the mystery narrative becomes an ontological quest focused on the status of the image. What distinguishes the narrative use of the

premise in *Strange Days* is that there is no question that the death is real—apparently a SQUID recording cannot be faked, which is another way that the technology appears antithetical to the discourse around digital technology and situates it closer to the realist status afforded the "indexical," analog forms of photography and cinema championed by Bazin.

10. In this respect, Mace's character can be considered within a long history of liberal or "race message" narratives producing black characters as sites of purity and redemption. For a more recent account, see Matthew Hughey's "White Redemption and Black Stereotypes in 'Magical Negro' Films," in *Social Problems* vol. 56 no. 3 (August 2009): 543–577.

11. Not surprisingly, given her role in the film, Mace's own (otherwise inexplicable) attachment to Lenny is presented through the more traditional cinematic flashback—presented here as "authentic" memory—that emerges and fades into the narrative in distinction from the punctuating insistence of the SQUID clips.

12. Berrettini, "Can 'We All' Get Along?" 184.

13. See Brian Carr, "*Strange Days* and the Subject of Mobility," in *Camera Obscura* 50 [vol. 17 no. 2] (2002): 191–217. His critique is in some ways related to that of Caren Kaplan in her essay "Mobility and War: The Cosmic View of U.S. Air Power," cited in Chapter Three in reference to the mobility of the global subjects in contemporary action-thrillers.

14. Omi and Winant, *Racial Formation*, 56.

15. This decree from Juan Gonzalez in a 2012 editorial also includes a characterization of the video's dissemination as "viral," which retroactively attributes the spread of media (and the spread of consumer surveillance) characteristic of the internet to this preinternet instance. (Juan Gonzalez, "George Holliday, the Man with the Camera Who Shot Rodney King While Police Beat Him, Got Burned, Too," in *New York Daily News*, 19 June 2012, available at http://www.nydailynews.com/news/national/george-holliday-man-camera-shot-rodney-king-police-beat-burned-article-1.1098931 [accessed 7/21/13].)

16. Berrettini, "Can 'We All' Get Along?" 179.

17. Despina Kakoudaki notes about Mace's character in this context that "[h]er allegiance is 'American' in the abstract, raceless aspect of treating the disk as the truth that should not be repressed. It is also specifically 'African-American' in the way that she treats the incident with a demand that it become meaningful in terms of race, even at some cost" (125). (Despina Kakoudaki, "Spectacles of History: Race Relations, Melodrama, and the Science Fiction/Disaster Film," in *Camera Obscura* 50 [vol. 17 no. 2] (2002): 109–153.) I discuss the ideological aspects of the SQUID disc as "truth" more below.

18. The presentation of the black female body as the marker of visible racial suffering clearly demands further consideration in this context, though I cannot fully address it here. It is clear that, as noted above, the use of Mace as a path to Lenny's redemption situates the film within a tradition of narratives of race that undermines some of the more interesting aspects of her characterization.

19. As Kimberlé Crenshaw and Gary Peller have pointed out in their discussion of the videotape and the legal handling of it, "Within the initial national outrage at the King videotape were many who saw the brutality depicted in the videotape as awful but exceptional, as part of another era which reared its ugly head only occasionally and happened to be caught on videotape" (65). (Kimberlé Crenshaw and Gary Peller, "Reel Time/Real Justice," in *Reading Rodney King/Reading Urban Uprising*, ed. Robert Gooding-Williams [New York and London: Routledge, 1993].)

20. The presentation of SQUID clips as a kind of pornography further ties the technology to the historical uses of video, since the introduction of video revolutionized both the production and distribution of porn film.

21. Interestingly, while the use of the SQUID in *Strange Days* is fictional, SQUIDs are real-world superconducting technologies used for both biomedical and military surveillance functions, among other uses. The actual functions of the SQUID thus in several ways parallel the fictional use of the technology in the film.

22. Bolter and Grusin, *Remediation*, 3–4.

23. Richard Grusin revisits *Strange Days* in his follow up work on "Premediation," which I discuss in the preceding chapter, arguing that the film "was already participating in a logic of premediation insofar as it was pre-mediating the United States (particularly Los Angeles) nearly five years into the future" and that it "anticipated the logic of premediation in imagining future media technologies as remediations of current ones" ("Premediation," 18).

24. Berrettini, "Can 'We All' Get Along?" 183.

25. Carr, "*Strange Days*," 211.

26. *Vertigo*, already mentioned in regard to *Déjà vu* in Chapter Three, is once again instructive: in that film, the spectator becomes so aligned with Scotty's subjectivity and melancholic desire that even though his efforts to recreate "Judy" as his lost "Madeline" are presented as sadistic and pathological, the moment of successful reproduction is presented as climactically satisfying.

27. Crenshaw and Peller, "Reel Time," 60.

28. Kakoudaki's central point in the essay, that "[b]y staging an insistent replay of exactly the events of the Rodney King landscape, disaster films of the nineties mark the rupture of meaning and national understanding, use the disaster as an organizational force, and propose a fantasy/utopian alternative to complex political conditions," is an apt one for my present argument, primarily in terms of a discussion of *Strange Days*' concluding scenes. But as Kakoudaki also notes, "*Strange Days* clearly privileges the race/gender axis that other texts of the decade work to obscure" through what appears in those other films as a "'postracist,' integrationist terrain" ("Spectacles of History," 126). Thus, what might be seen as a utopian note itself becomes a commentary on "postracist" representational strategies.

29. David Eng and David Kazanjian, eds., *Loss: The Politics of Mourning* (Berkeley: University of California Press, 2003), 4.

30. Mary Ann Doane, *Femmes Fatales* (New York: Routledge, 1991), 21.

31. Gilles Deleuze, *Cinema 2: The Time-Image* (Minneapolis: University of Minnesota Press, 1989).

32. Deleuze, *Cinema 2*, 130.

33. Gilles Deleuze, *Cinema 1: The Movement-Image* (Minneapolis: University of Minnesota Press, 1986).

34. Deleuze, *Cinema 2*, 78.

35. Ibid., 79.

36. Ibid.

37. Ibid., 69.

38. *Born in Flames* is also notable in the context of this book for its anticipation of several other historical events and cinematic narratives. While focused in large part on American race, gender, and class politics through the rhetoric of revolution, the film also includes frequent reference to terrorism and, remarkably, concludes with one of its characters placing a bomb on the roof of one of the World Trade Center towers and blowing them up. The actress and film-maker playing that character, Sheila McLaughlin, has recounted that they filmed her placement of the bomb on location at the World Trade Center, where she simply went unimpeded with a camera crew to the roof and deposited a leather suitcase containing the faux bomb. The 1983 film ends with a shot of the Twin Towers in flames: imagery that though never included serves as the structuring absence of virtually all the contemporary counterterrorism surveillance narratives discussed in the preceding chapter. That this film anticipates and even creates the future imagery that those later films fantasize traveling back in time to undo shows a circular temporality not just within individual surveillance narratives, but in the constitution of the broader history of surveillant narrative structure.

39. Turner, "Collapsing the Interior/Exterior Distinction," 94.

40. Deleuze, *Cinema 2*, 133.

41. Ibid., 150.

CONCLUSION

1. An early version of the chapter, "Surveillance and Social Memory: *Strange Days* Indeed," originally appeared in *Discourse* vol. 32 no. 3 (Fall 2010): 302–320.

2. I discuss this film in greater depth in the short essay "Zero Point Breaky."

3. Seasons 6 and 7 in particular seem deeply invested in presenting Muslims as scapegoats and victims. While this may function as a disavowal given the larger implications of the show's popularity in the post-9/11 era, sometimes the thought does actually count. That liberal critics have condemned 24 while *Homeland* has been valorized suggests that a show's visible politics matter less to a bourgeois audience than the perception of quality and gravitas.

4. This is not intended as an evaluation of the performances of Claire Danes or Jessica Chastain, who play these characters. For better or for worse my

scholarship has little investment in the quality of acting, and I feel ill qualified to judge on that basis. Nevertheless, the performance of Claire Danes in particular becomes of some interest in this context. Danes's character on *Homeland*, Carrie Mathison, was interpreted with such extreme pathos that it gave rise to the "Claire Danes Cry Face Project," a brilliantly hilarious blog-cum–viral internet phenomenon that visually reprocessed the actress's entire body of work through the frame of her ubiquitous quivering frown. It is thus not without basis to suggest that the *Homeland* phenomenon has included not just critical success but an implicit recognition that its lead character/actress has been defined by and come to define absurd emotional excess.

5. Der Derian, *Virtuous War*.

6. From the "Our Story" section on the Satellite Sentinel Project website, which also features the ambiguously constructed slogan, "The World Is Watching Because You Are Watching." Available at http://www.satsentinel.org/our-story/george-clooney (accessed 8/1/2013).

7. Paul Harris, "George Clooney's Satellite Sentinel Reveal Secrets of Sudan's Bloody Army," in *Guardian*, 24 March 2012, available at http://www.theguardian.com/world/2012/mar/24/george-clooney-spies-secrets-sudan (accessed 8/1/2013).

8. Taryn Ryder, "George Clooney Spends His Nespresso Paycheck on a Satellite . . . Find Out Why!" on *Yahoo omg!* 31 July 2013, available at http://omg.yahoo.com/blogs/celeb-news/george-clooney-spends-nespresso-paycheck-satellite-why-184530124.html (accessed 8/1/2013).

9. As mentioned, *Syriana*, but also *The Peacemaker* (Mimi Leder, 1997) and the Steven Soderbergh–directed Ocean's Eleven series (primarily the first and second films from 2001 and 2004, respectively).

10. John R. Parkinson, "NSA: 'Over 50' Terror Plots Foiled by Data Dragnets," on *ABC News*, 18 June 2013, available at http://abcnews.go.com/Politics/nsa-director-50-potential-terrorist-attacks-thwarted-controversial/story?id=19428148 (accessed 6/29/2013).

11. Matt Taibbi, "As Bradley Manning Trial Begins, Press Predictably Misses the Point," in *Rolling Stone* (web edition), 6 June 2013, available at http://www.rollingstone.com/politics/blogs/taibblog/as-bradley-manning-trial-begins-press-predictably-misses-the-point-20130605 (accessed 6/26/2013).

12. Among many, many others: "Snowden: A Very Modern Spy Thriller," in *France 24*, 27 June 2013, available at http://www.france24.com/en/20130627-snowden-very-modern-spy-thriller (accessed 7/27/2013); Jonathan DeHart, "Edward Snowden: The Real Jason Bourne?" in *Diplomat*, 2 July 2013, available at http://thediplomat.com/asia-life/2013/07/edward-snowden-the-real-jason-bourne/ (accessed 7/27/2013); and Katie von Syckle, "The Man behind the Bourne Movies is Obsessed with Edward Snowden," in *New York*, 13 June 2013, available at http://nymag.com/daily/intelligencer/2013/06/tony-gilroy-bourne-obsessed-edward-snowden.html (accessed 7/27/2013).

13. See, again among many others: Lily Rothman, "*Terminal* Errors: What Snowden Comparisons are Missing," in *Time*, 3 July 2013, available at http://entertainment. time.com/2013/07/03/terminal-error-what-snowden-comparisons-are-missing/ (accessed 7/27/2013), or Mark Silva, "Snowden: The Terminal, Two," on *Bloomberg News*, 25 June 2013, available at http://go.bloomberg.com/political-capital/2013–06–25/snowden-the-terminal-two/ (accessed 7/27/2013).

BIBLIOGRAPHY

Agamben, Giorgio. *Homo Sacer: Sovereign Power and Bare Life.* Translated by Daniel Heller-Roazen. Stanford, CA: Stanford University Press, 1998.

———. *Means without Ends: Notes on Politics.* Translated by Cesare Casarino and Vincenzo Binetti. Minneapolis: University of Minnesota Press, 2000.

———. *State of Exception.* Translated by Kevin Attell. Chicago: University of Chicago Press, 2005.

Altman, Rick. "The Evolution of Sound Technology." *Film Sound: Theory and Practice.* Edited by Elisabeth Weis and John Belton. New York: Columbia University Press, 1985: 44–53.

Anderson, Carolyn. "*The Conversation* as Exemplar and Critique of Sound Technology." *Post Script* 6, no. 3 (Spring/Summer 1987): 13–30.

Andrejevic, Mark. *iSpy: Surveillance and Power in the Interactive Era.* Lawrence: University of Kansas Press, 2007.

———. *Reality TV: The Work of Being Watched.* New York: Rowman & Littlefield, 2003.

Antin, David. "Video: The Distinctive Features of the Medium." *Video Culture: A Critical Investigation.* Edited by John Hanhardt. Rochester, NY: Visual Studies Workshop Press, 1987: 147–166.

Baudrillard, Jean. *The Gulf War Did Not Take Place.* Bloomington: University of Indiana Press, 1991.

Baudry, Jean-Louis. "Ideological Effects of the Basic Cinematographic Apparatus." *Narrative, Apparatus, Ideology: A Film Theory Reader.* Edited by Philip Rosen. New York: Columbia University Press, 1986: 286–298.

Bazin, André. "The Ontology of the Photographic Image." *What Is Cinema? Volume 1.* Translated by Hugh Gray. Berkeley and Los Angeles: University of California Press, 1968.

Becker, Jo, and Scott Shane. "Secret 'Kill List' Proves a Test of Obama's Principles and Will." *New York Times* (29 May 2012), http://www.nytimes.com/2012/05/29/world/obamas-leadership-in-war-on-al-qaeda.html.

Berrettini, Mark. "Can 'We All' Get Along? Social Difference, The Future, and *Strange Days.*" *Camera Obscura* 50 [vol. 17, no. 2] (2002): 155–188.

Biesecker, Barbara. "No Time for Mourning: The Rhetorical Production of the Melancholic Citizen-Subject in the War on Terror." *Philosophy and Rhetoric* 40, no. 1 (2007): 147–169.

Bigo, Didier. "Security, Exception, Ban and Surveillance." *Theorizing Surveillance: The Panopticon and Beyond*. Edited by David Lyon. Devon, UK, and Portland, OR: Willan Publishing, 2006: 46–68.

Bogard, William. "Surveillance Assemblages and Lines of Flight." *Theorizing Surveillance: The Panopticon and Beyond*. Edited by David Lyon. Devon, UK, and Portland, OR: Willan Publishing, 2006: 97–122.

Bolter, Jay David, and Richard Grusin. *Remediation: Understanding New Media*. Cambridge, MA: MIT Press, 1999.

Brodesser, Claude. "Why 'Torture Porn' Is the Hottest (and Most Hated) Thing in Hollywood." *Advertising Age* 78, no. 21 (21 May 2007): 3.

Brown, Wendy. "Resisting Left Melancholy." *Boundary 2* 6, no. 2 (1999): 19–27.

Burch, Noël. *Life to Those Shadows*. Berkeley and Los Angeles: University of California Press, 1990.

Butler, Judith. *Frames of War: When Is Life Grievable?* London: Verso, 2009.

Carr, Brian. "*Strange Days* and the Subject of Mobility." *Camera Obscura* 50 [vol. 17, no. 2] (2002): 191–217.

Cartwright, Lisa. *Screening the Body: Tracing Medicine's Visual Culture*. Minneapolis and London: Minnesota University Press, 1995.

Cohen, Nicole S. "The Valorization of Surveillance: Toward a Political Economy of Facebook." *Democratic Communiqué* 22, no. 1 (Spring 2008): 5–22.

Columbia Law School Human Rights Clinic. "Counting Drone Strike Deaths." Report. 2012. http://web.law.columbia.edu/sites/default/files/microsites/human-rights-institute/COLUMBIACountingDronesFinalNotEmbargo.pdf.

Comolli, Jean-Louis. "Machines of the Visible." *The Cinematic Apparatus*. Edited by Teresa de Lauretis and Stephen Heath. New York: St. Martin's Press, 1980: 121–142.

———. "Technique and Ideology: Camera, Perspective, Depth of Field." *Narrative, Apparatus, Ideology: A Film Theory Reader*. Edited by Philip Rosen. New York: Columbia University Press, 1986: 421–443.

Corber, Robert J. "Resisting History: Rear Window and the Limits of the Postwar Settlement." *Boundary 2* 19, no. 1 (Spring 1992): 121–148.

Crenshaw, Kimberlé, and Gary Peller. "Reel Time/Real Justice." *Reading Rodney King/Reading Urban Uprising*. New York and London: Routledge, 1993.

Courtney, Susan. *Hollywood Fantasies of Miscegenation: Spectacular Narratives of Gender and Race, 1903–1967*. Princeton, NJ: Princeton University Press, 2005.

Debord, Guy. *The Society of the Spectacle*. Detroit: Black and Red Press, 1983.

DeHart, Jonathan. "Edward Snowden: The Real Jason Bourne?" *Diplomat* (2 July 2013), http://thediplomat.com/asia-life/2013/07/edward-snowden-the-real-jason-bourne.

Deleuze, Gilles. *Cinema 1: The Movement-Image*. Translated by Hugh Tomlinson and Robert Galeta. Minneapolis: University of Minnesota Press, 1986.

———. *Cinema 2: The Time-Image*. Translated by Hugh Tomlinson and Robert Galeta. Minneapolis: University of Minnesota Press, 1989.

Denby, David. "Stolen Privacy: Coppola's *The Conversation*." *Sight and Sound* 43, no. 3 (Summer 1974): 131–133.

Denzin, Norman. *The Cinematic Society: The Voyeur's Gaze*. London: SAGE Publications, 1995.

Der Derian, James. *Virtuous War: Mapping the Military-Industrial-Media-Entertainment Network*. Boulder, CO: Westview Press, 2001.

Diken, Bülent, and Carsten Bagge Laustsen. "Zones of Indistinction: Security, Terror, and Bare Life." *Space and Culture* 5, no. 3 (August 2002): 290–307.

Dixon, Wheeler Winston. *It Looks at You: The Returned Gaze of the Cinema*. Albany: State University of New York Press, 1995.

Doane, Mary Ann. *Femmes Fatales: Feminism, Film Theory, Psychoanalysis*. New York: Routledge, 1991.

———. "Ideology and the Practice of Sound Editing." *Film Sound: Theory and Practice*. Edited by Elisabeth Weis and John Belton. New York: Columbia University Press, 1985: 54–63.

Dodds, Klaus. "Gender, Geopolitics, and Geosurveillance in *The Bourne Ultimatum*." *Geographical Review* 101, no. 1 (January 2011): 88–105.

Donath, J. S. "Identity and Deception in the Virtual Community." *Communities in Cyberspace*. Edited by Peter Kollock and Marc Smith. London: Routledge, 1998: 29–59.

Douglas, Jeremy. "Disappearing Citizenship: Surveillance and the State of Exception." *Surveillance and Society* 6, no. 1 (2009): 32–42.

Downey, Anthony. "Zones of Indistinction: Giorgio Agamben's 'Bare Life' and the Politics of Aesthetics." *Third Text* 23, no. 2 (March 2009): 109–125.

Duggan, Lisa. *The Twilight of Equality: Neoliberalism, Cultural Politics and the Attack on Democracy*. Boston: Beacon Press, 2004.

Eco, Umberto. *The Role of the Reader: Explorations in the Semiotics of Texts*. Bloomington and Indianapolis: Indiana University Press, 1984.

Edelstein, David. "Now Playing at Your Local Multiplex: Torture Porn." *New York* (6 February 2006), http://nymag.com/movies/features/15622/.

Elmer, Greg, and Andy Opel. "Pre-empting Panoptic Surveillance: Surviving the Inevitable War on Terror." *Theorizing Surveillance: The Panopticon and Beyond*. Edited by David Lyon. Devon, UK, and Portland, OR: Willan Publishing, 2006: 139–159.

Eng, David, and David Kazanjian, eds. *Loss: The Politics of Mourning*. Berkeley: University of California Press, 2003.

Fanon, Frantz. *Black Skin, White Masks*. Translated by Charles Lam Markmann. New York: Grove Press, 1967.

Fuchs, Christian. "An Alternative View of Privacy on Facebook." *information* 2, no. 1 (February 2011): 140–165.

———. "Web 2.0, Prosumption, and Surveillance." *Surveillance and Society* 8, no. 3 (2011): 288–309.

Geissler, Cynara. "Pix or It Didn't Happen: Social Networking, Digital Memory, and the Future of Biography." *The Book of MPub: New Perspectives on Technology and Publishing*. Edited by Vanessa Chan et al. Vancouver: CCSP Press, 2010: 135–141.

Genosko, Gary, and Scott Thompson. "Tense Theory: The Temporalities of Surveil-lance." *Theorizing Surveillance: The Panopticon and Beyond.* Edited by David Lyon. Devon, UK, and Portland, OR: Willan Publishing, 2006: 123–159.

Gonzalez, Juan. "George Holliday, The Man with the Camera Who Shot Rodney King While Police Beat Him, Got Burned, Too." *New York Daily News* (19 June 2012), http://www.nydailynews.com/news/national/george-holliday-man-camera-shot-rodney-king-police-beat-burned-article-1.1098931.

Graham, Stephen. *Cities under Siege: The New Military Urbanism.* London: Verso Press, 2010.

Gray, W. Russel. "Tuning in to *The Conversation*: Twenty-Five Years Later." *Journal of Popular Culture* 33, no. 2 (Fall 1999): 123–130.

Gregory, Derek. *The Colonial Present: Afghanistan, Palestine, Iraq.* Malden, MA, and Oxford: Blackwell Publishing, 2004.

Grossvogel, D. I. "Haneke: The Coercing of Vision." *Film Quarterly* 60, no. 4 (Summer 2007): 36–43.

Grusin, Richard. "Premediation." *Criticism* 46, no. 1 (Winter 2004): 17–39.

Gunning, Tom. "Tracing the Individual Body: Photography, Detectives, and Early Cin-ema." *Cinema and the Invention of Modern Life.* Edited by Leo Charney and Vanessa R. Schwartz. Berkeley and Los Angeles: University of California Press, 1995: 15–45.

Haggerty, Kevin D., and Richard V. Ericson, eds. *The New Politics of Surveillance and Visibility.* Toronto: University of Toronto Press, 2006.

———. "The Surveillant Assemblage." *British Journal of Sociology* 51 (2000): 605–622.

Hampp, Andrew. "How 'Paranormal Activity' Hit It Big." *Advertis-ing Age* (12 October 2009), http://adage.com/article/madisonvine-news/low-budget-movie-marketing-paranormal-activity/139588/.

Hansen, Mark B. N. *Bodies in Code: Interfaces with Digital Media.* New York: Rout-ledge, 2006.

Harris, Chad. "The Omniscient Eye: Satellite Imagery, 'Battlespace Awareness,' and the Structures of the Imperial Gaze." *Surveillance and Society* 4, no. 1/2 (2006): 101–122.

Harris, Paul. "George Clooney's Satellite Spies Reveal Secrets of Sudan's Bloody Army." *Guardian* (24 March 2012), http://www.theguardian.com/world/2012/mar/24/george-clooney-spies-secrets-sudan.

Hier, Sean. "Risky Spaces and Dangerous Faces: Urban Surveillance, Social Disorder, and CCTV." *Social Legal Studies* 13, no. 4 (2004): 541–554.

Hight, Craig, and Jane Roscoe. *Faking It: Mock-Documentary and the Subversion of Factuality.* Manchester, UK: Manchester University Press, 2002.

Howe, Lawrence. "Through the Looking Glass: Reflexivity, Reciprocality, and Defenes-tration in Hitchcock's *Rear Window*." *College Literature* 35, no. 2 (Winter 2008): 16–37.

Hughey, Matthew. "White Redemption and Black Stereotypes in 'Magical Negro' Films." *Social Problems* 56, no. 3 (August 2009): 543–577.

Jameson, Fredric. *The Geopolitical Aesthetic: Cinema and Space in the World System.* Bloomington and Indianapolis: Indiana University Press, 1992.

Jenkins, Henry. *Convergence Culture: Where Old and New Media Collide.* New York: NYU Press, 2008.

Juhasz, Alexandra, and Jesse Lerner, eds. *F Is for Phony: Fake Documentary and Truth's Undoing.* Minneapolis: University of Minnesota Press, 2006.

Kakoudaki, Despina. "Spectacles of History: Race Relations, Melodrama, and the Science Fiction/Disaster Film." *Camera Obscura* 50 [vol. 17, no. 2] (2002): 109–153.

Kammerer, Dietmar. "Video Surveillance in Hollywood Movies." *Surveillance and Society* 2, no. 2/3 (2004): 464–473.

Kaplan, Caren. "Mobility and War: The Cosmic View of U.S. Air Power." *Environment and Planning A* 38, no. 2 (2006): 395–407.

———. "Precision Targets: GPS and the Militarization of U.S. Consumer Identity." *American Quarterly* 58, no. 3 (September 2006): 693–713.

King, Homay. *Lost in Translation: Orientalism, Cinema, and the Enigmatic Signifier.* Durham, NC: Duke University Press, 2010.

Koskela, Hille. "'The Other Side of Surveillance': Webcams, Power and Agency." *Theorizing Surveillance: The Panopticon and Beyond.* Edited by David Lyon. Devon, UK, and Portland, OR: Willan Publishing, 2006: 163–181.

Krauss, Rosalind. "The Aesthetic of Narcissism." *Video Culture: A Critical Investigation.* Edited by John Hanhardt. Rochester, NY: Visual Studies Workshop Press, 1987: 179–191.

Lalvani, Suren. *Photography, Vision, and the Production of Modern Bodies.* Albany: State University of New York Press, 1996.

Lefait, Sébastien. *Surveillance on Screen: Monitoring Contemporary Films and Television.* Lanham, MD: Scarecrow Press, 2012.

Levin, Thomas Y. "Five Tapes, Four Halls, Two Dreams: Vicissitudes of Surveillant Narration in Michael Haneke's *Caché*." *A Companion to Michael Haneke.* Edited by Roy Grundmann. West Sussex, UK: Wiley-Blackwell, 2010: 75–90.

———. "Rhetoric of the Temporal Index: Surveillant Narration ad the Cinema of 'Real Time.'" *CTRL[SPACE]: Rhetorics of Surveillance from Bentham to Big Brother.* Edited by Thomas Levin, Ursula Frohne, and Peter Weibel. Cambridge, MA: MIT Press, 2002: 578–593.

Lockwood, Dean. "All Stripped Down: The Spectacle of Torture Porn." *Popular Communication* no. 7 (January 2009): 40–48.

Lyon, David. "9/11, Synopticon, and Scopophilia." *The New Politics of Surveillance and Visibility.* Edited by Kevin D. Haggerty and Richard V. Ericson. Toronto: University of Toronto Press, 2006: 35–54.

———. "The Search for Surveillance Theories." *Theorizing Surveillance: The Panopticon and Beyond.* Edited by David Lyon. Devon, UK, and Portland, OR: Willan Publishing, 2006: 3–20.

Marwick, Alice E. "The Public Domain: Social Surveillance in Everyday Life." *Surveillance and Society* 9, no. 4 (2012): 378–393.

Mathieson, Thomas. "The Viewer Society: Michel Foucault's 'Panopticon' Revisited." *Theoretical Criminology* 1, no. 2 (May 1997): 215–234.

Mbembe, Achille. "Necropolitics." *Public Culture* 15, no. 1 (Winter 2003): 11–40.

McNamara, Mary. "TV Review: 'Person of Interest.'" *Los Angeles Times* (22 September 2011), http://www.latimes.com/entertainment/news/tv/la-et-person-interest-20110922,0,4850976.story.

Merleau-Ponty, Maurice. *Phenomenology of Perception*. Translated by Colin Smith. London: Routledge, 1962.

Metz, Christian. *The Imaginary Signifier: Psychoanalysis and the Cinema*. Translated by Celia Britton, Annwyl Williams, Ben Brewster, and Alfred Guzzetti. Bloomington and Indianapolis: Indiana University Press, 1982.

Miller, Cynthia J., ed. *Too Bold for the Box Office: The Mockumentary from Big Screen to Small*. New York: Scarecrow Press, 2012.

Miller, David, ed. *Tell Me Lies: Propaganda and Media Distortion in the Attack on Iraq*. New York: Pluto Press, 2003.

Miller, Toby, Nitin Govil, John McMurria, Richard Maxwell, and Ting Wang, eds. *Global Hollywood 2*. London: British Film Institute, 2005.

Mills, Catherine. *The Philosophy of Agamben*. Stocksfield, UK: Acumen Publishing, 2008.

Modleski, Tania. "The Master's Dollhouse." *The Women Who Knew Too Much: Hitchcock and Feminist Theory*. Second Edition. Edited by Tania Modleski. New York: Routledge, 2005: 69–88.

Monmonier, Mark. *Spying with Maps: Surveillance Technologies and the Future of Privacy*. Chicago and London: University of Chicago Press, 2002.

Murray, Susan, and Laurie Ouellette, eds. *Reality TV: Remaking Television Culture*. Second Edition. New York: NYU Press, 2008.

Norris, Clive, and Gary Armstrong. *The Maximum Surveillance Society: The Rise of CCTV*. Oxford and New York: Berg, 1999.

North, Daniel. "Evidence of Things Not Quite Seen: *Cloverfield*'s Obstructed Spectacle." *Film and History* 40, no. 1 (Spring 2010): 75–92.

Noys, Benjamin. *The Culture of Death*. Oxford and New York: Berg, 2005.

Olson, Scott. "The Globalization of Hollywood." *International Journal on World Peace* XVII, no. 4 (December 2000): 3–17.

Omi, Michael, and Howard Winant. *Racial Formation in the United States: From the 1960s to the 1990s*. New York: Routledge, 1994.

Osterweil, Ara. "*Caché* (Review)." *Film Quarterly* 59, no. 4 (Summer 2006): 35–39.

Palmer, Daniel, and Jessica Whyte. "'No Credible Photographic Interest': Photography Restrictions and Surveillance in a Time of Terror." *Philosophy of Photography* 1, no. 2 (2010): 177–195.

Palmer, R. Barton. "The Metafictional Hitchcock: The Experience of Viewing and the Viewing of Experience in *Rear Window* and *Psycho*." *Cinema Journal* 25, no. 2 (Winter 1986): 4–19.

Parenti, Christian. *The Soft Cage: Surveillance in America from Slavery to the War on Terror*. New York: Basic Books, 2003.

Parkinson, John R. "NSA: 'Over 50' Terror Plots Foiled by Data Dragnets." *ABC News* (18 June 2013), http://abcnews.go.com/Politics/nsa-director-50-potential-terrorist-attacks-thwarted-controversial/story?id=19428148.

Parks, Lisa. *Cultures in Orbit: Satellites and the Televisual*. Durham, NC: Duke University Press, 2005.

Price, Brian, and John David Rhodes, eds. *On Michael Haneke*. Detroit, MI: Wayne State University Press, 2010.

Puar, Jasbir K. "On Torture: Abu Ghraib." *Radical History Review* 93 (Fall 2005): 13–38.

Rich, B. Ruby. *New Queer Cinema: The Director's Cut*. Durham, NC, and London: Duke University Press, 2013.

Rothman, Lily. "Terminal Errors: What Snowden Comparisons Are Missing." *Time* (3 July 2013), http://entertainment.time.com/2013/07/03/terminal-error-what-snowden-comparisons-are-missing.

Ryder, Taryn. "George Clooney Spends His Nespresso Paycheck on a Satellite . . . Find Out Why!" *Yahoo* (31 July 2013), http://omg.yahoo.com/blogs/celeb-news/george-clooney-spends-nespresso-paycheck-satellite-why-184530124.html.

Sarris, Andrew. *Politics and Cinema*. New York: Columbia University Press, 1978.

Scarry, Elaine. *The Body in Pain: The Making and Unmaking of the World*. New York and Oxford: Oxford University Press, 1985.

Scott, Allen. "Hollywood and the World: The Geography of Motion-Picture Distribution and Marketing." *Review of International Political Economy* 11, no. 1 (February 2004): 33–61.

Sekula, Alan. "The Body and the Archive." *October* 39 (Winter 1986): 3–64.

Sewell, Graham. "A Japanese 'Cure' to a British 'Disease'? Cultural Dimensions to the Development of Workplace Surveillance Technologies." *Information Technology and People* 9, no. 3 (1996): 12–29.

Shaffer, Lawrence. "The Conversation." *Film Quarterly* 28, no. 1 (Autumn 1974): 54–60.

Shapiro, Michael J. *Cinematic Geopolitics*. New York: Routledge, 2008.

Silva, Mark. "Snowden: The Terminal, Two." *Bloomberg News* (25 June 2013), http://go.bloomberg.com/political-capital/2013-06-25/snowden-the-terminal-two.

Sobchack, Vivian. *The Address of the Eye: A Phenomenology of Film Experience*. Princeton, NJ: Princeton University Press, 1992.

Stam, Robert. *Reflexivity in Film and Literature: From Don Quixote to Jean-Luc Godard*. New York: Columbia University Press, 1995.

Stewart, Jacqueline Najuma. *Migrating to the Movies: Cinema and Black Urban Modernity*. Berkeley: University of California Press, 2005.

Tagg, John. *The Burden of Representation: Essays on Photographies and Histories*. Minneapolis and London: University of Minnesota Press, 1993.

Taibbi, Matt. "As Bradley Manning Trial Begins, Press Predictably Misses the Point." *Rolling Stone* (6 June 2013), http://www.rollingstone.com/politics/blogs/taibblog/as-bradley-manning-trial-begins-press-predictably-misses-the-point-20130605.

Telotte, J. P. "*The Blair Witch Project* Project: Film and the Internet." *Film Quarterly* 54, no. 3 (Spring 2001): 32–39.

Turkle, Sherry. *Life on the Screen: Identity in the Age of the Internet.* New York: Simon & Schuster, 1997.

Turner, Dennis. "The Subject of The Conversation." *Cinema Journal* 24, no. 4 (Summer 1985): 4–22.

Turner, John S. "Collapsing the Interior/Exterior Distinction: Surveillance, Spectacle, and Suspense in Popular Cinema." *Wide Angle* 20, no. 4 (October 1998): 93–123.

Tziallas, Evangelos. "Of Doppelgängers and Alter Egos: Surveillance Footage as Cinematic Double." *Écranosphère* no. 1 (Winter 2014), http://www.ecranosphere.ca/article.php?id=21.

———. "Torture Porn and Surveillance Culture." *Jump Cut: A Review of Contemporary Media* no. 52 (Summer 2010), http://www.ejumpcut.org/archive/jc52.2010/evangelosTorturePorn/text.html.

Virilio, Paul. *The Aesthetics of Disappearance.* Translated by Philip Beitchman. New York: Semiotext(e), 1991.

———. *War and Cinema: The Logistics of Perception.* Translated by Patrick Camiller. London and New York: Verso Press, 1989.

Von Syckle, Katie. "The Man Behind the Bourne Movies Is Obsessed with Edward Snowden." *New York* (13 June 2013), http://nymag.com/daily/intelligencer/2013/06/tony-gilroy-bourne-obsessed-edward-snowden.html.

Wessels, Emanuelle. "'Where Were You When the Monster Hit?': Media Convergence, Branded Security Citizenship, and the Trans-Media Phenomenon of *Cloverfield.*" *Convergence: The International Journal of Research into New Media Technologies* 17, no. 1 (2011): 69–83.

Wheatley, Catherine. "Secrets, Lies, & Videotape." *Sight and Sound* 16, no. 2 (Fall 2006): 32–36.

White, Armond. "Eternal Vigilance in *Rear Window.*" *Hitchcock's Rear Window.* Edited by John Belton. Cambridge, UK: Cambridge University Press, 1999: 118–140.

Wigglesworth, Valerie. "'Project X' Movie Spurring Copycat Parties." *Dallas Morning News* (23 March 2012), http://www.dallasnews.com/news/crime/headlines/20120323-project-x-movie-spurring-copycat-parties.ece.

Williams, Linda. "Film Bodies: Gender, Genre, and Excess." *Film Quarterly* 44, no. 4 (Summer 1991): 2–13.

———. *Hard Core: Power, Pleasure, and the "Frenzy of the Visible."* Berkeley and Los Angeles: University of California Press, 1989.

Wipperfurth, Alex. *Brand Hijack: Marketing without Marketing.* New York: Viking Press, 2005.

Zbikowski, Dorté. "The Listening Ear: Phenomena of Acoustic Surveillance." *CTRL[SPACE]: Rhetorics of Surveillance from Bentham to Big Brother.* Edited by Thomas Levin, Ursula Frohne, and Peter Weibel. Cambridge, MA: MIT Press, 2002: 33–41.

Zimmer, Catherine. "The Eye of Horror: *Peeping Tom* and Technological Perversion." *Horror Film: Creating and Marketing Film.* Edited by Steffen Hantke. Jackson: University of Mississippi Press, 2004.

——. "Surveillance and Social Memory: *Strange Days* Indeed." *Discourse* 32, no. 3 (Fall 2010): 302–320.

——. "Zero Point Breaky." *Avidly* (7 February 2013), http://www.avidly.org/2013/02/07/zero-point-breaky/.

Zulaika, Joseba. "The Self-Fulfilling Prophecies of Counterterrorism." *Radical History Review* 85 (2003): 191–199.

INDEX

Abu Ghraib, 34, 44–45, 57

Acconci, Vito, 85

activism, 115, 181, 204, 214–215, 219, 238n28

affect, 201, 226n5, 227n13; in *Caché*, 59–62; CCTV and, 56; in *Déjà vu*, 164; in first-person-camera films, 106–110, 114; in *Homeland*, 248n4; in horror films, 104; in *Red Road*, 70; in *Source Code*, 174–175; in *Strange Days*, 195–201

Afghanistan war, 175, 209, 241n52

Agamben, Giorgio, 23, 25, 33, 40–43, 46, 51–57, 227n12, 227n13. *See also* bare life; biopolitics; states of exception; zones of indistinction

aircraft videotape recordings (AVTR's), 237n25

Algeria, 58, 62

All the President's Men, 116–117

American Mutoscope and Biograph Company, 6

American Pie, 79

America's Funniest Home Videos, 90

analog technologies, 81, 182, 186, 245n9; transition away from, 181; video as, 83, 88

Anderson, Carolyn, 19

Andrejevic, Mark, 26, 74–75, 80, 102–103, 108, 114

Antin, David, 84–85

Armstrong, Gary, 64

Arnold, Andrea: *Red Road*, 33, 69–70

As Seen through a Telescope, 7

assemblage theory, 17, 112, 162, 216, 233n50; surveillance assemblage, 170, 203–204, 243n19

audiences, 82, 89, 144, 154, 223n25, 232n36; of Abu Ghraib photographs, 45; of *Benny's Video*, 68; of *The Blair Witch Project*, 94, 99, 109; of *Caché*, 59, 62, 229n48; of *Cloverfield*, 109; of *Déjà vu*, 160–161, 177; of *Funny Games*, 65; of *Homeland*, 247n3; of *The Karate Kid*, 138; of *My Little Eye*, 50; of *The Nigger in the Woodpile*, 11–12; On Demand offerings and, 235n71; of *Paranormal Activity*, 109–110, 111, 235n72; of *Saw*, 36, 38; of *Saw II*, 52; of *Strange Days*, 187, 191–192, 195–199; of *THX 1138*, 237n16; viewer society, 74, 76. *See also* spectatorship audio surveillance

Audition, 226n3

The Bad Boys' Joke on the Nurse, 10–11

bare life, 25, 41–44, 53–57, 147, 227n12, 238n33. *See also* biopolitics; states of exception; zones of indistinction

Baudrillard, Jean, 236n13

Baudry, Jean-Louis, 5

The Bay, 77, 111–112

Bazin, André, 112–113, 181, 244n2, 245n9

Benny's Video, 25, 33, 58, 66–68, 67

Berrettini, Mark, 185–186, 188–191, 197

Bertillonage, 4

Beverly Hills Cop, 137

Biesecker, Barbara, 133, 143–145, 163–164, 167, 240n45, 241n53

Big Brother, 49

ABOUT THE AUTHOR

Catherine Zimmer is Director of Film and Screen Studies and Associate Professor of English at Pace University in New York City. Her articles on the politics of cinema have appeared in journals ranging from *Camera Obscura*, *Framework*, and *Discourse* to *Surveillance and Society* and *GLQ*.

CPSIA information can be obtained
at www.ICGtesting.com
Printed in the USA
LVHW110156040423
743413LV00003B/92